STREETWISE®

SELLING YOUR BUSINESS

STREETWISE®

SELLING
YOUR
BUSINESS

How to Attract Buyers
and Achieve the
Maximum Value for
Your Business

by Russell Robb

Adams Media Corporation
Avon, Massachusetts

A Streetwise® Publication.
Streetwise® is a registered trademark of Adams Media Corporation.

Published by Adams Media Corporation
57 Littlefield Street, Avon, MA 02322 U.S.A.
www.adamsmedia.com

ISBN: 1-58062-602-5

Printed in the United States of America.

J I H G F E D C B A

**Library of Congress Cataloging-in-Publication Data
is available upon request from the publisher.**

This publication is designed to provide accurate and authoritative information with regard to the subject matter covered. It is sold with the understanding that the publisher is not engaged in rendering legal, accounting, or other professional advice. If legal advice or other expert assistance is required, the services of a competent professional person should be sought.
    —From a *Declaration of Principles* jointly adopted by a Committee of the American Bar Association and a Committee of Publishers and Associations

Cover illustration by Eric Mueller.

*This book is available at quantity discounts for bulk purchases.
For information, call 1-800-872-5627.*

Visit our exciting small business Web site: www.businesstown.com

CONTENTS

PART IV: PRICING YOUR BUSINESS

PART V: NEGOTIATING THE DEAL

PART VI: ALTERNATIVES TO OUTRIGHT SALE

CONTENTS

PART VII: CLOSING

PART VIII: CONCLUSION

APPENDICES

Acknowledgments

Six years ago I wrote my first book, *Buying Your Own Business*, the companion to this book, *Streetwise® Selling Your Own Business*. These complementary projects would not have happened without help from some significant people.

Since 1992, I have worked with a wonderful partner, Tom West, to produce our industry newsletter, *M&A Today*, which is distributed nationally to those involved in mergers and acquisitions. It is from *M&A Today* that much of the material in this book is derived. Contributions from numerous experts and industry professionals have greatly enriched the text of both this book and the newsletter.

Writing a book and a monthly newsletter while maintaining a job as an investment banker required heavy-duty support from family and friends. I am blessed to have an understanding wife, Leslee; an experienced literary partner, Tom West; and a fantastic assistant who produces my work, Liza Cormier.

This second book is the product of some persistent arm-twisting. A former classmate of mine, Bill Marshall of Acton, Massachusetts, kept prodding me to write "another" book. If it were not for his unrelenting encouragement, I would not have persisted. Family and friends have been my most important supporters.

Completing a manuscript of some 100,000 words is like running a marathon; there were times when I just hit the wall and felt I would not finish, but my editor kept urging me forward. Thank you to Jill Alexander, Acquisitions Editor at Adams Media Corporation, for her confidence in me. Let's hope we sell a million copies.

INTRODUCTION

This book was written for those who want to sell a business, particularly a business in the middle market, which typically includes companies with annual sales between $2 million and $100 million.

Having sold three small businesses of my own, and having been an intermediary for buyers and sellers since 1985, I have firsthand knowledge of this subject. This book is an attempt to share that knowledge and to educate company owners so that they will have a better chance of successfully selling a business.

Unlike the real estate market, which is highly efficient in bringing buyers and sellers together, the buying and selling of middle-market businesses is somewhat inefficient. Why? Because of the need to keep most transactions confidential. Strict adherence to confidentiality prevents information from being easily obtainable or widely known. The secretiveness of selling a business often prompts owners to retain a business broker, an intermediary, or an investment banker to be their representative in order to exercise the utmost in confidentiality.

Another difficult aspect of selling a business is the valuation of the company—particularly small or middle-market companies. For example, let's assume the owner of a company plans to leave the business as soon as it is sold. However, the owner, founder, and chief executive officer *is* the business in terms of attracting new customers, maintaining key relationships, and innovating new products or services. How much do you think the buyer will discount the price of the business because the company is virtually a "one-man band?" There is no standard answer—it is subjective. The point is that there are so many elements in the valuation of a company aside from the multiple of earnings that determining the price for a middle-market company is difficult indeed.

After confidentiality and pricing have been discussed, there are other critical elements in successfully selling a company. Timing the sale at a period when the economy, the company's industry, and the company itself are doing well is also important. For example, if the owner of a business is fifty-nine years old and he or she intends to sell at age sixty-five in order to retire, then perhaps the owner should sell earlier than originally planned in order to maximize the sale price. If an owner has to sell because of his or her advanced age, then he or she has given up important negotiating leverage. From a negotiating perspective, the best time to sell is when one does not *have* to sell.

Planning is yet another critical aspect. Selling a company from beginning to end often takes six to twelve months; if there are one or two aborted transactions, the selling process could take longer. Why does planning take so long? Because it is relatively easy to sell a company at "any old" price if the owner just wants to unload the business. On the other hand, obtaining the best price and terms from a reputable acquirer requires careful preparation. There are many things an owner must do to plan for the selling of his or her business. This book will address not only the proper preparation for selling a business but will also address the actual steps to be taken in the process.

Long-Term Considerations

Ideally, the seller will start planning a full year in advance of a sale because numerous elements will take considerable time and expense to execute. Most small private companies, for example, have their financial documents "reviewed" or "compiled" but rarely audited. Auditing statements involves conducting an actual physical inventory, with each accounts receivable and other financial details verified in the process. While audited statements are mandatory for public companies, many private companies opt not to pay the extra cost of auditing, which can range from $10,000 to $40,000. However, an audited statement, which is a verification of the reported numbers in the financials, will often result in a 20-percent higher offer by the buyer.

Other items to be addressed in preparation for selling a company include cleaning up the balance sheet of old debts and writing off uncollectable accounts receivable and old inventory. This ensures that the buyer is not deterred by anything less than a pristine financial statement. Settle outstanding lawsuits and engage top management in non-competitive and stay agreements. Further, make sure the plant is in excellent physical shape; spruce it up if need be. Believe me, if the facility does not show well, it will turn off buyers very quickly.

Short-Term Considerations

In addition to the long-term issues that we've discussed, certain elements need to be considered in the short term. Prior to going to market with the sale of a company, you need to allocate about two to four months for purposes of organization. A critical element in organizing your sale is to assemble a team of advisors, including a representative from an investment bank or a mergers and acquisition (M&A) intermediary. This representative will be your partner during the entire selling process and will probably be in contact with you almost daily for the next six to twelve months. The investment firm will orchestrate the process and act as "quarterback" for the team of advisors. A transaction attorney, your accountant, and most likely a tax attorney who will be knowledgeable about your personal affairs should also be by your side.

Next, it is advisable to have a valuation of your business that not only determines your "anchor" price but also supports your reasoning in the negotiating process. Along with the business appraisal, consider obtaining a machinery/equipment appraisal and a real estate appraisal. The buyer will need these separate appraisals to know what will be required in order to finance some of the hard assets.

Finally, the preparation of the selling memorandum by the investment bank is the major selling tool in the entire process. This document of twenty to thirty pages describes in detail the industry, the company, the financials, and investment considerations. For many investment banks, the selling memorandum is the foundation of their practice. Along with this, one has to set up a "war room" of various documents pertaining to the business: lease agreements, bank agreements, a sales representative agreement, and corporate minutes. The war room would be the single place where all of the necessary secured files are kept. These files contain all the pertinent facts of the company, which the buyer will want to review as part of their due diligence process.

Steps in the Selling Process

Having briefly discussed the necessary preparation for selling a business, the following overview lays out the sales cycle. The methodology for selling a business is a sequence of events described in the following six separate steps, which will help prepare you for the forthcoming chapters.

Step One: Identify Potential Buyers and Prepare Selling Memorandum

There are basically four different types of buyers: strategic, financial, competitors, and management buyouts. Normally, the strategic buyer will offer the highest price while the other types are apt to pay less (in descending order). There are, of course, exceptions to the rule and other factors at play. For example, a seller might take a lower price from a management buyout in order to continue the owner's legacy rather than sell to a financial buyer whose intention may be to resell the company in seven years or to a competitor who will shut down the plant and move the business.

The objective of step one is to find buyers who are likely to place the highest value on the business—the strategic buyer—as well as buyers to whom you might sell the company. To clarify the meaning of strategic, let me offer the following example. Suppose a manufacturer of crackers that sells only through food service channels (restaurants or hotels) was to sell their business to a cookie manufacturer that only deals with supermarkets. By merging the two companies, the benefits of cross-selling are enormous. However, if the two companies both produce a graham or a saltine cracker, then they are considered competitors.

In most cases identifying potential buyers can be an extensive project taking two to four months of thorough research. It is at this stage that the potential buyers are contacted to determine whether they have an interest in pursuing your company even though you will not present them with the actual name or location of the business. In this way, one can rate buyers by placing them into different groups of desirability. But be careful not to proceed to step two until step one is completed.

While potential buyers are being identified, the crucial selling memorandum is being prepared over the next two to four months.

Step Two: Qualify and Screen Buyers

At this point, your investment bank or M&A intermediary may have contacted 500 potential buyers of which 100 may respond favorably. After talking with them on the telephone, you may be left with seventy-five companies that have sufficient interest and financial resources to proceed in the winnowing process. The investment banker may then send out confidentiality agreements to the interested parties to sign and return.

Step Three: Present Opportunity to Qualified Prospects

Upon receipt of the signed confidentiality agreement and the approval of the seller, a selling memorandum is released to the potential buyer. At this stage, perhaps thirty potential buyers have sufficient interest to proceed with the prospect of buying your company, and the remaining parties return the selling memorandum. Depending on the investment banker, it is often customary that the buyer is asked to submit a proposal letter or a range of value that they assign to the company for sale.

Step Four: Receive Bids from Buyers

Based on this hypothetical example, perhaps only fifteen buyers are willing to present their proposal letter or range of value. The investment banker may decide that only five initial offers are worthy of pursuing and eliminates all other prospects. At this point, the five prospects visit the seller and commence their initial due diligence.

Step Five: Enter Negotiations

With five remaining prospects, the seller wants to create an atmosphere of competitive bidding in order to establish the most favorable price, terms, and conditions for the seller. Without letting the time period drag, the seller should select one of the final prospects as the ultimate buyer, enter into a letter of intent, and take the company "off the market" until the deal either closes or is aborted.

Step Six: Prepare for Closing

At the final stage, it is customary for the buyer to take several months to complete the final due diligence and receive the Purchase and Sale Agreement from the buyer's attorney. Maximum effort should be made at this point to complete the transaction without delay. According to some experts, deals that drag don't close.

With the sale of a business, you will bear much responsibility, have a lot of uncertainty, and rely greatly on intuition. Often sellers have only one chance in their lifetime to sell a company while buyers are accustomed to acquiring numerous different businesses. This phenomenon usually means that buyers having more experience in transactions than sellers. Therefore, this book will give you a better chance to complete a successful transaction.

How to Use This Book

One of the difficult points in the process of selling a business is when the high anticipation of closing quickly meets up with the realization that the closing of a transaction seems to take forever. Hopefully, *Selling Your Business* will help those who are either contemplating the sale of their business or for whom the process is already underway.

Because the mergers and acquisitions business may have terminology foreign to many readers, it is advisable to review the Glossary section early on. The jargon of mergers and acquisitions includes such terms and acronyms as I-bankers, which stands for investment bankers (brokers or agents), and EBIT, which is short for Earnings Before Interest and Taxes.

INTRODUCTION

The outline of the book is sequential:

Why people sell their business;
When you should sell;
The seller's disadvantage.

Then I move into the macro issues of selling:
The important points in selling a business;
The different ways to sell a business;
The key steps in selling a business.

Moving forward, I address certain concerns such as:
Sellers' most common mistakes;
Selling troubled companies;
Valuation techniques.

My hope is for *Selling Your Business* to be easy to read, informative, enjoyable, and of ongoing reference value. It should be noted that throughout the book I refer to and quote from many authorities in the mergers and acquisitions business. These additional viewpoints make *Selling Your Business* even more comprehensive.

Good luck on your journey.

Russell Robb
June 2002

The Big Picture

Summary of Part I

- **Common reasons why people sell their businesses**
- **How to overcome the seller's disadvantage**
- **A look at common myths in selling a business**

Chapter 1

Why People Sell Their Businesses

In this chapter, you'll learn:

- The most common reasons people sell their businesses
- Options when there is competitive pressure
- How to handle an unsolicited offer

For some owners, selling their business can be an emotional and dramatic experience, especially if it is a family business that the owner has spent many years developing. People become creatures of habit and so accustomed to working—especially if it is their own company—that they learn to truly enjoy their vocation. In fact, it is not uncommon for business owners to have "seller's remorse" and to end up reneging on the sale of the company at the last moment.

Privately owned companies, both small and large, are sold for a number of different reasons. The following are just a few of those reasons.

The Batteries Run Low

Considered the major reason for selling a company, boredom or burn-out from the day-to-day drudgery frequently afflicts business owners. For example, owners of pizza parlors and dry cleaning establishments have a particularly high turnover due largely to excessively long hours and the repetitive nature of the work.

In my earlier days, I manufactured, distributed, and sold canoes. During our peak years, we produced 3,000 canoes annually and distributed another 2,000. It got to the point that I could not stand attending another boat show. My wife too became bored as she witnessed me doing the same thing day in and day out. Finally she said to me (rather sarcastically I might add): "What color canoes did you produce today . . . red, blue, yellow, or green?" Needless to say, I was glad to sell the business and move on to something more intellectually challenging.

The following case involves an owner of a company who became bored with his business and sold out. Paul Farrow founded Walden Paddlers in Concord, Massachusetts, in 1992. Like many entrepreneurs, Paul started on little more than the proverbial shoestring. He felt that he could capitalize on a flawed kayak market that primarily appealed to the whitewater and ocean market rather than the family recreational market. Paul's original goal was to rapidly grow the business and then sell it in five years and go on to another venture. He grew the business to $2 million in annual revenues and sold the business at a profit in 1999, two years later than his original target.

> Considered the major reason for selling a company, boredom or burn-out from the day-to-day drudgery frequently afflicts business owners.

His motivation for selling was an integral part of his original plan: to only be involved with the business for a relatively short time.

There Is No Heir Apparent

Owners of companies frequently are in self-denial and do not want to face the future. Either they do not properly cultivate someone within the family to take over the management of the company or they do not mentor a younger person to be in a position to become president at the proper time. As a result, the business often fails to remain competitive with its peers, as the owner ages and runs the company until he can no longer do so.

Selling a company at this point—when the boss is often a "one-man band" acting as chief executive officer, chief financial officer, and chief operating officer—the owner is less likely to receive the full market price of a similar company with management responsibilities in place with different people. If planned properly, the owner could retire or partially retire and have the business continue under a management team that has been groomed accordingly. The alternative is to sell the business.

> Owners of companies frequently are in self-denial and do not want to face the future.

Insufficient Capital

Often a company exists in spite of itself. Perhaps the owner takes out most of the profits and does not reinvest in new equipment, or the company does not generate enough cash flow to increase working capital to support the growth of the business.

A number of years ago, Amesbury Machine Manufacturing Company produced large plastic molding machines principally for the "Big Three" automobile companies in Detroit. These molding machines sold for $200,000 to $400,000 each. Unlike other customers, Ford, General Motors, and Chrysler would not make partial payments during the four to six months' production time necessary to complete the order. Since Amesbury was marginally profitable and had exhausted its bank loans, the company had insufficient capital to finance the new orders, which started to pile up. Unable to finance Amesbury's growth, the owner had to sell out.

Divorce or Illness in the Family

A sudden and dramatic change in one's life, such as divorce or illness, can trigger the sale of a business. A friend of mine had been diagnosed with cancer. While it was premature to sell his business, he wanted to get his financial affairs in order. The prospect of being incapacitated to the point where his spouse would have to deal with selling the business was reason enough for the owner to sell the company right away.

Liquidity Is Running Low

> Many owners of small private companies have most of their assets tied up in their businesses.

Many owners of small private companies have most of their assets tied up in their businesses. It is analogous to having most of a person's money in the stock market invested in one stock. The rationale of some business owners is that they have built the company over the past ten to forty years; this is their life's work, their family nest egg, and now is the time to cash out, before the business, the industry, and/or the stock market collapses. The choices for an owner could be to sell out and leave the company, to sell out and stay on, or to sell the majority of the company and retain the balance to hopefully participate in the future upside of the business.

The following case involves a family business in which most of the owners' assets were tied up in the company. Dave Logan was a professional hockey player for the Chicago Blackhawks and Vancouver Canucks from 1974 to 1983. Upon his retirement from the National Hockey League, Logan joined his father-in-law's company, Baker School Specialty Co., Inc., in Orange, Massachusetts, which manufactured a wide array of bulletin boards sold to schools and office product superstores. In 1997 he became president. During Logan's fourteen-year tenure, sales grew from $2 million to $20 million. Most of the family assets were tied up in the business, which caused considerable concern because more than 50 percent of the sales were with one customer—Staples. The loss of that one customer would have been devastating.

In an effort to diversify its product line, Baker School Specialty Co. conducted a search to acquire another company in the school supply business. That effort was unsuccessful, so the owners felt that their only solution was to sell the business to a larger company within the same industry for which the sales to Staples might only amount to 10 to 20 percent of its total revenues. Baker was sold and the family was able to preserve their net worth in spite of competitive pressures in the industry.

Competitive Pressure Is Building

In today's business world, competitive pressure is so great that for most businesses, standing still is not an option. A number of years ago Chrysler's leader Lee Iaccoca popularized the slogan: "Lead, follow, or get out of the way." Then Jack Welch of General Electric Company said: "Buy, sell, or merge." The implication of these quotes is that as all industries are consolidating, the tough and unsentimental business world will put enormous pressure on the small independent companies. For many businesses, the best option may be to sell before it is too late.

The following case involves a company in a very competitive industry. A plumbing supply distributor in New Hampshire with sales of $13 million showed a modest cash flow profit before interest and depreciation charges. Stockholders' equity, however, had been declining over the last few years, especially since there were substantial inventory write-offs the year before. The plumbing supply business was highly competitive because there were four other distributors in the same city all vying for the same customers. To top it off, the company was run by the son of the founder who apparently did not have the business toughness or friendly customer relations skills of his father. The business needed to maintain large inventories and to extend credit to most of their customers who were contractors.

The company had three alternatives: hire a turnaround expert to stabilize the declining business; liquidate inventory and assets; or try to

When the Tank Comes Up Empty

Burnout is the most common reason businesses are put up for sale, according to merger and acquisition experts. Often in as few as five years, business owners are worn out from living and breathing their corporate creations. Boredom and frustration also take their toll, leaving owners disinterested or resentful of the business routine. At a certain point, walking away from something they started appears the lesser of two evils, and is often an act of survival.

sell the company. The owners first tried to sell the business for book value, which would amount to assumption of all assets and all liabilities. After three months of an exhaustive search, no buyer came forward. The owners then hired a turnaround specialist, but after a year he could not "stop the bleeding." Finally, the owners ended up selling the assets at a loss to one of their competitors located twenty miles away.

Adversity Is Too Hard to Overcome

Many small businesses may be highly successful, but often they are vulnerable. They may be dependent on others for a particular component to their business, such as a retail store with a long-term lease in the busiest part of town, or they may be a small manufacturer with 50 percent of its business with a *Fortune* 500 company. In each case, if the lease is not renewed or the contract with the *Fortune* 500 company is cancelled, the business faces such adversity that the best choice is to sell.

Some years ago, Frank Wyman owned Bailey's of Boston, a successful ice cream parlor, restaurant, and candy store chain with nine outlets. While Bailey's of Boston was doing very well when Wyman sold it eighteen years ago, many of the leases in key locations in downtown Boston were up for renewal and at much higher rates. This adverse condition was an important reason he chose to sell Bailey's at that time.

> Many small businesses may be highly successful, but often they are vulnerable.

Outside Investors Become Factors

For companies that have outside investors–friends, family, venture capital–there is often a time at which the investor has the option to "put" the stock back into the company at a previously arranged buyout formula, such as multiple of cash flow or book value. Under the circumstances, if the majority owners cannot afford or choose not to buy out the minority investor, often the terms of the investment contract is to sell the company in order to have a so-called liquidity event. It may be a friendly or forced sale, but the contract is usually legally binding.

An Unsolicited Offer Is Placed on the Table

In this age of mega merger and acquisition deals, many large companies make unreported acquisitions of companies with model sales—$10 to $50 million. Large companies such as General Electric are so compelled to obtain potential products before one of their competitors that they offer the owner of the company a huge price for the business. The owner is in a position in which the offer is too good to refuse, so the company is sold.

Why people are selling their business is usually one of the first questions asked by a buyer. As attorney Gabor Garai, managing partner of Boston-based Epstein Becker & Green, states, "Buyers will want to know why owners are choosing to sell, and it is up to the owners to fashion a story that maximizes their company's perceived value. For instance, two partners who can never agree will not want to emphasize their disharmony as the reason for a sale. Stories should stress growth and opportunities for market leadership. Buyers, for instance, will be excited about the possible value of a business run by two partners who say that they have taken it as far as their capabilities allow, and who seek an acquirer to move it to the next level."

Conclusion

There are plenty of reasons why businesses change hands, some unexpected, others that can be foreseen. Given how often it happens, however, it is surprising how unprepared business owners can be. Based on a survey of business owners of small private companies conducted by a leading CPA firm, 85 percent of the owners have no exit strategy. I therefore conclude that many companies are acquired serendipitously—by buyers who happen to be in the right place at the right time. Hopefully, this book will prepare the seller properly for undertaking the seemingly difficult task of selling his or her business. The next chapter will explore the hurdles that sellers most commonly face.

Does This Sound Familiar?

While burnout is the most likely reason why an owner would give up a business, the following are other common reasons cited by merger and acquisition experts:

- Business has grown too big to handle alone
- A desire to relocate
- Retirement
- Partnership dispute
- Death of one of the partners
- Employee problems
- Customer or supplier problems
- The need for estate planning

For more information on this topic, visit our Web site at www.businesstown.com

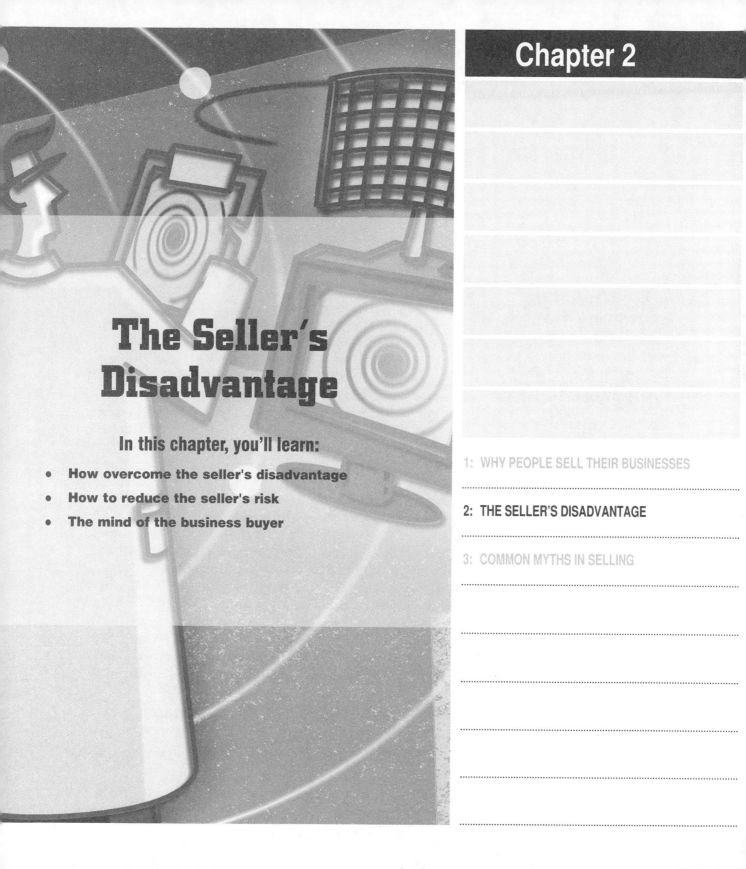

The Seller's Disadvantage

In this chapter, you'll learn:

- How overcome the seller's disadvantage
- How to reduce the seller's risk
- The mind of the business buyer

Most individual sellers sell only one company in their lifetime. Often, that company is their life's work. Therefore, the process of selling a company is usually a new experience. If it is a corporate buyer who is interested in the company, an experienced and savvy buyer sits on the other side of the negotiating table. The amateur versus the professional—without proper coaching and advice, the seller can be at a decided disadvantage.

The seller is behind the eight ball for a number of other reasons. Selling a business is unlike selling real estate; the asking price is usually not disclosed and confidentiality is tightly maintained so that employees, customers, and vendors will not be disturbed. Through all this, the owner must not let the sales process distract management personnel from their day-to-day responsibilities.

Usually, a seller of middle-market companies is committed to divest when he or she places the business on the market, especially if it is done through a mergers and acquisition intermediary that is often paid a retainer fee ranging from $5,000 to $100,000. Of course, the seller can withdraw if he or she does not receive the anticipated price or acceptable terms. But the seller is usually more committed to consummating a transaction than a buyer who can more easily walk away from the deal. Therefore, sellers must know whether the purchaser has the creditworthiness and commitment to complete the deal.

John T. Byrnes captured what is at stake when he wrote the following for *M&A Today*: "For the seller of a business, nothing is worse than a deal that falls apart because the buyer is unable or unwilling to close. An aborted acquisition has an adverse impact on employees, vendors, and customers, as well as other potential buyers who will question why the deal fell through. Thus, a false start could diminish the value of the business—and, in some cases, result in missing the market 'window' for the sale. In a tight credit environment, it is especially important to examine the buyer's financial resources, as well as his personal and professional qualities, to assure that he can—and will—close the deal."

Overcoming the Seller's Disadvantage: Reversing Due Diligence

Businesses up for sale are generally subjected to extensive due diligence; it is examined by accountants, appraisers, lawyers, and other

The Mind of the Business Buyer

Who is looking to buy a business? Some people have personal reasons such as wanting to be in charge, to be their own boss. Others may be seeking to make a career change or simply searching for an activity to help them feel productive. The business you want to sell may be involved in an area that matches their leisure activities and interests. Good business sense motivates other potential purchasers. Perhaps your business complements one they already own, or they need a good investment.

professionals. The buyer should undergo a comparable level of scrutiny. Does he have the resources, both in equity and borrowing capacity, to complete the transaction? Does he have a reputation for negotiating a fair purchase agreement, without making unreasonable demands, coming up with last-minute surprises, or taking forever to get the paperwork done? Has he kept his commitments to management and employees of his previously acquired companies? Finally, if he has future obligations to the seller, such as payments under a consulting agreement, what is his track record for observing similar obligations in the past?

Tracking Down the Cash

All buyers, no matter how large or small, must adequately convey to the seller that they have the financial resources to pay for the business. To verify the buyer's financial strength, detailed financial statements should be obtained. The seller's accountants should examine these statements, with particular emphasis on the availability of liquid assets. If possible, credit reports should also be obtained. If the buyer owns other companies, the financial statements and credit reports of those companies should be requested, both to get a sense of the buyer's track record and to verify what other demands exist on the buyer's financial worth. A potential purchaser who has the means and savvy to complete an acquisition will make no claims of privacy.

> To verify the buyer's financial strength, detailed financial statements should be obtained.

Checking the References

The seller should also seek "soft" information about the buyer. He should ask for a list of the buyer's senior, mezzanine, and equity financing contacts, and should talk to each of them concerning the specifics of the buyer's prior transactions, including the amount of each loan, the speed with which the transactions were completed, and the current status of the lending relationship. He should also ask for a list of potential lenders for the proposed acquisition and confirm that those lenders are indeed interested in the transaction. A specific list of questions should be developed for each lender with the assistance of the seller's advisors. Again, the seller should not hesitate to ask pointed and detailed questions.

Contacting Prior Sellers

Many prospective buyers seek to establish their credibility by touting their track record of prior acquisitions. These claims offer an excellent opportunity for the seller; by contacting the previous owners of the businesses acquired by the buyer, the seller can learn valuable information. How did the buyer and his advisors behave during the negotiation of the purchase agreement? Have there been any claims against the other sellers for breach of the legal documents? Has the buyer honored his obligations under consulting and non-competition agreements, or under any promissory notes? What are the prior sellers' perceptions of their company's post-acquisition performance? Did the buyer retain the company's management and employees as promised? How have vendors and customers been treated?

What Do Managers Say?

If the buyer has bought other companies, the managers of those companies can be a fertile source of information. Specific questions concerning the buyer's management style or his track record of employee relations would be relevant, especially if the seller has deep loyalties to his company's management and employees or if he intends to maintain a continuing relationship with the company.

Checking the Buyer's Character

Above all else, the seller must feel comfortable with the integrity and approach of the buyer. These qualities not only pertain to the buyer's ability to close the transaction but also to the relationship that will be established between the seller and the buyer during and after the acquisition. Through a clear understanding of the buyer's financial and personal characteristics, the seller can maximize the likelihood of a successful sale.

Deferred Pleasure: Reducing the Seller's Risk

Even though a seller knows his business better than the buyer, the seller may be at a disadvantage because most small businesses are

> If the buyer has bought other companies, the managers of those companies can be a fertile source of information.

sold with some form of deferred payment. David M. Bishop, a CPA and practicing attorney with the law firm of Bishop & Kelly in Charlotte, North Carolina, wrote the following in *M&A Today*:

"If you are fortunate enough to sell your business for all cash, then you need not concern yourself with protecting yourself after the sale. But very few transfers are consummated today without some form of deferred payout. The deferral usually comes in the form of an interest-bearing installment note that is payable to the seller over a five- to ten-year period. Other forms of deferred payment include non-compete agreements, consulting arrangements, royalty fees, and non-qualified supplemental retirement plans. Whatever the deferral mechanisms, they all create a risk to the seller that the promised and expected funds may not be collected."

The business owner nearing retirement wants security, not risk. Apprehension about receiving payments in the future may be the number one reason owners fail to plan for transferring the business to the next generation or for selling to an outsider. Conveying ownership rights to the next generation may be psychologically good for the heirs, the family, and the business itself, but the owner leaves himself dependent on someone else for his future income, and most owners don't like that feeling. The apprehension is even greater when selling to a third party since outsiders usually are not trusted as much as family.

The best protection the seller can have is to select a qualified buyer. Finding someone who can afford the business is important, but not enough. A qualified buyer should also be able to run the business. Of course, selling the business for a reasonable price with reasonable terms increases the seller's chance of finding the right buyer.

Even with a qualified buyer, it is important to insist on security devices and triggers to legally ensure that payment will not be interrupted. Often this calls for a balancing act: if the measures are too restrictive, the buyer may not be able to obtain needed working capital. In those cases, the protective devices handicap the buyer, increasing the likelihood of a default.

> Apprehension about receiving payments in the future may be the number one reason owners fail to plan for transferring the business to the next generation or for selling to an outsider.

Guarantees, Caps, and Dividend Limitations

If the buyer is a corporation that is newly formed or without significant assets, the individual shareholder or shareholders should personally guarantee any obligations. Generally, if a buyer in this situation is not willing to personally guarantee the obligation, then he is not ready to own a business.

To keep sufficient working capital in the corporation, it may be necessary to set compensation levels or restrict dividend payments during the deferral period.

Collateralization and Restrictions on Additional Financing

Creditors of a company sometimes have different priorities on corporate assets in the event the company fails to pay its debts. As the holder of an installment note, the seller is a creditor who stands in line with other creditors in the event of a default. Creditors who secure their obligations with collateral, such as corporate assets, are in a more senior position to collect money owed than a general creditor. Consequently, it is extremely important that an installment note given to a seller be secured by corporate assets.

If the business' pre-existing lines of credit or other banking arrangements require that the seller be subordinated to a junior position, then the seller should insist that lines of credit not be expanded without his consent and that there be no additional indebtedness that further subordinates the seller. Another good security device is a cross-default provision whereby a default on any obligation throws all obligations into default.

If the seller still has personal guarantees on any corporate indebtedness, they should be removed before, or at the same time, ownership is transferred. If the guarantees cannot be removed, the seller should insist that the buyer indemnify the seller from any loss incurred by the seller by virtue of his guarantee. Of course, if the buyer is unable to pay the underlying debt the indemnification may also be worthless.

Cash Flow and Balance Sheet Requirements

Provisions that require the business to meet certain cash flow levels or to maintain certain financial ratios may give the seller early

Selling a Business, By the Numbers

Each year, more than four million small businesses are placed on the market in the United States, and more than two million businesses in the country change hands. The vast majority of these sellers are first-timers.

Those going it alone without professional help typically receive considerably less than fair market value for their businesses, according to corporate observers. And more than half of all small- and medium-sized business sales arranged by sellers without professional help result in buyer dissatisfaction or default, according to Corporate Investment International.

warning that the business is not faring as well as expected. These triggering devices enable a seller to re-acquire the business before the new owner has run it into the ground.

Financial Review by Third Party

An outside accounting firm or third party should review interim monthly and annual statements. Have a third party hold stock certificates in escrow.

Other Safeguards

Restrictions on asset sales, acquisitions, and expansions can help ensure that the former owners receive the entire payout. The buyer should satisfy obligations to the seller before embarking on any expansion or acquisition program. Life and disability insurance on the new owner is another important safeguard. The proceeds should be collaterally assigned to the seller so that the seller can be assured of collecting any amounts due in the event the buyer dies or becomes disabled.

Many other security devices are available to a seller and new safeguards are devised daily. With some creativity, it is possible to custom design safeguards for each situation.

> The buyer should satisfy obligations to the seller before embarking on any expansion or acquisition program.

Conclusion

Selling a business is usually a once-in-a-lifetime event, a fact that the prospective buyer knows all too well. The seller is also a lot more anxious to sell his business than the potential buyer is to purchase it. But this uneven power relationship should not cloud the seller's judgment. The best protection for the seller is to identify and select a qualified buyer, and that can be done using many of the pointers discussed in this chapter.

> **For more information on this topic, visit our Web site at www.businesstown.com**

Common Myths in Selling

In this chapter, you'll learn:

- What to tell employees about a potential sale
- Who should contact potential buyers
- How to handle confidentiality issues

A s a seller of a business, it is easy to become paranoid over the thought of having others hear that your company is for sale, especially if those people are employees, customers, vendors, or competitors. I believe sellers are generally overly concerned about the breach of confidentiality, which if it occurs is apt to happen at the end of the selling process, too late in the game to cause serious damage.

Facing Reality

If you want to sell your company by attracting the strongest potential buyers—those who will offer you the best deal in terms of price and structure—then you should consider the following:

> Contact, on a confidential basis, most of the industry players, including some competitors.

- Confide in a few of your top managers, especially the chief financial officer.
- Contact, on a confidential basis, most of the industry players, including some competitors.
- Release an offering memorandum to potential buyers, after a confidentiality agreement has been signed, that will disclose a substantial amount of confidential material on your company.
- Allow some potential buyers to walk through your premises and operations during working hours.
- Similarly, provide access to some of your more important customers and vendors as part of the due diligence process prior to the final signing of the purchase and sale agreement.

Confide in Your Managers

Assuming you have a company with several million dollars in sales, you should confide in your financial officer because it will be difficult to pull all the financials together without enlisting the confidence of a few key people in the company. One way to enlist their faith and loyalty is to confidentially tell them your plans, tell them of your need to secure their cooperation, and offer to reward them with three or more months of additional salary if they stay with you through the closing. Alternatively, you could offer them phantom stock in the company so they would participate in the equity.

Another approach is to tell your key people that you are planning to recapitalize the company by selling some of the equity so that the company has the necessary capital to aggressively grow the business.

Contact Industry Players

Contacting industry players who are potential buyers should be done by a third party, such as an investment banker, so the identity of your company is not identified until a confidentiality statement is signed by the buyer and approval is granted by you, the seller.

Release an Offering Memorandum

Buyers need to have enough information on the company in the form of documentation to determine whether they want to proceed and to be able to present a price range prior to a visit with management. The point of the process is to boil down the best candidates to just a few. The seller may choose not to show this memorandum to some of the closest competitors. The critical part for the seller is to enforce a strict timeline on the process so that the shorter time period the memoranda are "out and about" the better. Therefore, sellers should request a price range by interested buyers within a month with the expectation that the Letter of Intent, Purchase and Sale Agreement, and final due diligence should take no more than three more months until closing.

Give Potential Buyers a Tour

When it comes to walking prospects through the company facilities, buyers want to see a "going concern" and not a flashlight tour at night. It is probable that over the years a company has given tours to numerous customers, insurance agents, and bankers and therefore has a good sense of how to conduct one for a potential buyer.

Provide Access to Important Customers

The final consideration—of whether or not to allow the buyer access to some of your key customers and vendors—should only be done at the last possible moment prior to closing, and on a case-by-case basis. Alternatively, if the principals of the acquirer are

> The critical part for the seller is to enforce a strict timeline on the process so that the shorter time period the memoranda are "out and about" the better.

forbidden to speak to the key relationships to ensure the business will remain intact with the new entity, then due diligence firms are often retained to conduct interviews. Specifically, the due diligence firm will call under the aegis of conducting a marketing survey to measure the satisfaction of "their client" which, of course, is the undisclosed potential buyer. While the seller may abhor letting the buyer exercise these privileges, sometimes there is no choice. In other words, if the buyer absolutely insists on conducting this type of due diligence, particularly if you, the seller, has a certain degree of concentrated customer concentration, then you must concede or find another buyer.

A Case of Paranoia

A number of years ago, I was retained to sell a print-on-demand printing company with annual profitable sales of $7 million. At the time, selling prices for printing companies were stable because there was a fair amount of consolidation occurring within the industry. The owners had decided to sell because they were burned out and wanted to excuse themselves from the company's debt for which they were personally liable. The owners had previously sold the company some years ago, but after the buyer reneged on the notes, the owners repossessed the company. Naturally, they had a distaste for the mergers and acquisitions process and viewed me, their new investment banker, with a certain amount of skepticism.

As I embarked on the selling process with the printing company, I could sense the nervousness and apprehension of my client. Initially, I could not call the principals at the office and we had to meet "off campus." It was not until later that they established my presence as the company's consultant. Ironically, in spite of my client's paranoia, they were in the process of selling their building to pay off their mortgage and had installed a huge sign on the premises: "Building for Sale."

While the printing industry is huge, with an estimated 37,000 printers nationwide, the obvious buyers for small printers, such as my former client, are those located in the immediate area. Reluctantly, and in hindsight foolishly, I allowed my client to exclude

Lowering the Cone of Confidentiality

A confidentiality agreement is a legally binding contract, enforceable in a court of law. It establishes "common ground" between you, the seller, who wants the agreement to be extensive; and the buyer, who wants as few restrictions as possible. It allows the seller to share confidential information with a prospective buyer or a business broker for evaluative purposes only. This means that the buyer or broker promises not to share the information with third parties. If a confidentiality agreement is broken, the injured party can claim a breach of contract and seek damages.

about two dozen other printers who were considered too close of a competitor for me as an investment banker to contact.

As the story unfolds, I mistakenly called the ABC Printing Company (not its real name), which was one of the companies excluded from the target list of potential buyers. Part of my problem was that ABC had changed its name and I had failed to make the connection. While I received a blind confidential agreement that was signed by ABC, the CEO of the company had guessed the name of my client. I flatly denied the identity.

I told my clients of the unfolding events and when he heard of my mistake, he was furious. He called his attorney, and I was immediately fired and the assignment was turned over to my partner. Still, at this point, the CEO of ABC did not know for sure that I represented the company he had guessed.

My partner wisely convinced ABC managers to swallow their pride and meet with the interested buyer. After numerous meetings and extensive negotiations, my former client sold the printing company to ABC. In fact, ABC was the only company that made an official offer.

From this experience of a paranoid seller, one can learn several lessons:

1. Do not be too restrictive of which buyers can be approached because by doing so, you could limit the possibility of a successful transaction.
2. Mistakes do happen on matters of confidentiality, so it is very important to keep one's cool.

A Breach of Confidentiality, and Its Happy Aftermath

Quite a few years ago, I was retained to sell an office supply manufacturer. The company, with $10 million in sales, was nicely profitable, but it had a customer concentration problem that scared numerous potential buyers.

After an extensive search for acquirers, I finally identified another office supply manufacturer with sales of $50 million that was

> Do not be too restrictive of which buyers can be approached because by doing so, you could limit the possibility of a successful transaction.

interested in my client. The buyer signed the traditional confidentiality agreement and before long it appeared that there might be a deal. For some unknown reason, the chief executive officer of the acquirer felt that it was a done deal even though there was no signed letter of intent, much less a signed purchase and sale agreement. At this point, this CEO started to talk to other people in the office supply industry about the pending acquisition, mentioning the acquisition by name.

When my client heard about this obtuse violation of confidentiality, he immediately withdrew the company from the market. My client was tempted to sue the former potential acquirer, but in this type of situation, the plaintiff has to prove damages such as loss of orders or loss of employees. To my knowledge, there were no losses.

More than one year later, our client was still withdrawn from the merger and acquisition market, but was resolicited by a $125 million competitor. By now, my client's sales had increased to $18 million. The end result? My client sold for about twice the price it was offered previously, and everyone had forgotten about the devastating breach of confidentiality some time before.

From such an experience, we can appreciate that even though confidentiality was breached, the game was not over. In this case, the selling company was extremely lucky, for it sold for considerably more money in spite of—and perhaps because of—the confidentiality breach.

> My client sold for about twice the price it was offered previously, and everyone had forgotten about the devastating breach of confidentiality some time before.

Success After Losing a Key Employee

One of the first companies I sold as an investment banker more than fifteen years ago was memorable because I was fortunate to overcome difficult circumstances. My client was a hydraulic press manufacturer producing reaction injection molding for plastic parts. Most of the orders were received from the three largest American automobile companies. Unfortunately, these customers refused to pay progress payments on the $250,000 machines, so as business increased, there was insufficient working capital to meet the delivery dates. As a result, the owners decided to sell the company.

I was retained to represent the seller. One of my first tasks was to draft an offering memorandum. In it, I developed an organizational chart of all the employees, on which I applied the actual names of the senior management team.

Later, I went into market and contacted other plastic machine manufacturers both in the United States and Germany. None of the companies was interested in making an offer, so I decided to contact other companies that used hydraulics as its core competency. Here I hit pay dirt, and identified and qualified a company that was interested in acquiring my client. However, negotiations broke off and months went by without further communication.

Not long after, the acquirer secretly hired my client's chief engineer and hydraulic expert whose name was specifically documented in the offering memorandum. The situation appeared gloomy indeed because not only were there no remaining buyers but the company's most important technical expert had been stolen by one of the potential buyers. Then, without warning, the previous buyer re-entered the picture with a satisfactory new offer and miraculously the company was successfully sold.

From this experience, we can appreciate that while there are often upsetting episodes and unpleasant bumps in the process of selling a company, eventually the situation may be remedied.

How to Deal with Your Confidentiality Jitters

Based on my years of experience, I believe owners are overly concerned with confidentiality and unnecessarily seized by the fear of losing customers and employees. That is not to say you should not be very careful regarding confidentiality. The concern should just be tempered. The following suggestions should be considered.

Keep a Short Timetable

Anyone selling a business must realize that there is a Catch-22 between keeping the selling process completely confidential and contacting numerous potential buyers in order to create a hotly contested bidding process. The more companies you contact, the greater the risk for a leak. The critical aspect for maintaining confidentiality

---

Setting the Rules for Sharing Secrets

The following are some of the questions that you as a seller can expect a confidentiality agreement to cover:

What type information can and cannot be disclosed?

Are the negotiations open or secret?

What is the time frame for which the agreement is binding? The seller should seek a permanently binding agreement.

What is the patent right protection in the event the buyer, for example, learns about inventions when checking out the operation?

Which state's law will apply to the agreement if the other party is based in a different state? Where will disputes be heard?

What recourse do you have if the agreement is breached?

is to keep to a fairly short timetable, moving forward to a closing as soon as possible after the offering memorandum has been released (perhaps four months in total). Do not allow the process of selling a company to drag on. There is always a chance the news that the company is for sale will leak; in such a case, your best hope is for the deal to be completed before there is serious damage.

An alternative to this scenario is to approach only one or two buyers to reduce the risk of a leak, but that also reduces the chances of obtaining the best price.

Get Your Script Straight

Create a reasonable story that you can tell the employees as to why there will be unknown people walking through the facilities from time to time. For example, you could say that you are recapitalizing or refinancing the company in order to grow it more aggressively, such as adding new product lines through an acquisition. If you decide not to use this explanation as a smokescreen, then at least be prepared to have an answer if an employee confronts you with the question: "Are you selling the company?" If in doubt, you could always respond by saying that if you were approached by a company such as General Electric, you would have to consider your options.

Seek a Safe Buffer

Retain a third-party intermediary such as an investment banker to act as a buffer to channel all information between the buyer and you, thus reducing the potential of a confidential breach.

Use Diversionary Tactics

Get employees used to having unknown people (potential buyers of the company) walk through the facility by having other unrelated people, such as customers, vendors, or bankers walk through the facility as well.

Keep the Information Flow Open

The investment banker will need to communicate with you on an almost daily basis, particularly when potential buyers need to

> Create a reasonable story that you can tell the employees as to why there will be unknown people walking through the facilities from time to time.

have numerous questions answered. Therefore, you must not encumber the selling process by restricting the free flow of information via telephone, e-mail, or fax. If you are concerned about security, limit telephone communication to cell phone conversations or direct faxes to your private machine.

When using e-mail, be aware that a slight mistake by the sender can send the message into a general company mailbox, where it might be picked up by the MIS or IT manager. For example, if the e-mail address is rrobb@atlantic.com and the sender uses robb@atlantic.com, it will go into the general mailbox only to be seen by the wrong person.

Be a Nag

Constantly remind buyers of the importance of confidentiality. Signing the confidentiality agreement is essential, but verbal reminders are also important.

Become a Neat Freak

Finally, get organized! You will have a lot of paperwork, documents, and memoranda passing over your desk and through your office. Place them in three-ring binders and lock them up or lock your office door.

Conclusion

Concerns about confidentiality are understandable, but a seller of a business must learn to accept that a process cannot be so tightly controlled as to guarantee that word will not leak out. There is also a cost to being too restrictive on which buyers can be approached; by doing so, you could limit the possibility of a successful transaction. Mistakes do happen on matters of confidentiality, so it is very important to keep one's cool.

> You will have a lot of paperwork, documents, and memoranda passing over your desk and through your office.

For more information on this topic, visit our Web site at www.businesstown.com

Preparing the Ground

Summary of Part II

- How to run your business when contemplating a sale
- Important decisions to make prior to selling your business
- How to find potential buyers
- What steps to take when you find a potential buyer
- How to prepare a selling memorandum
- The best ways to time your sale

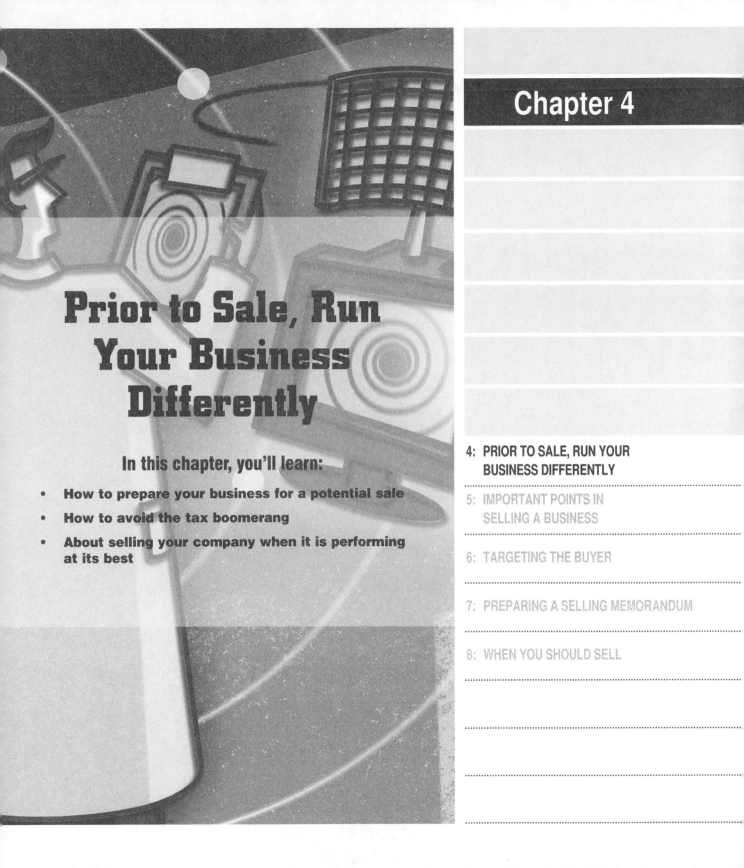

Prior to Sale, Run Your Business Differently

In this chapter, you'll learn:

- How to prepare your business for a potential sale
- How to avoid the tax boomerang
- About selling your company when it is performing at its best

A while ago I visited some company owners who were contemplating the sale of their privately held family business with sales of approximately $25 million. As an investment banker, I was being asked for my advice and whether or not my firm could be hired for this assignment.

As a specialty food producer, the company was at a crossroads in its life cycle. In order to continue growing it had to make some serious decisions; it was at a major disadvantage in many respects compared to its competitors who were larger companies. The company operated in an inefficient and antiquated plant with multiple floors, and its large warehouse was half a mile away. Its infrastructure, such as its computer and information systems, desperately needed to be updated. On the one hand, the company wanted to invest money to improve the plant and infrastructure, but on the other hand, the family was seriously considering the sale of their business.

The owners asked me the following question: "Should we spend the money now on the necessary upgrades prior to selling the business?" My answer was an emphatic "No." I emphasized that prior to selling a company, you drive the bottom line by running the company to show maximum profits. It was a particularly obvious and necessary strategy in this case, because the strengths of this company were its strong brand identity, wide distribution, and proprietary products. The company's shortcomings were its inefficient plant and lack of significant capital. I further pointed out that if a strategic or competitive buyer acquired the company, its managers may very well move the operation and use their own computer and information systems, so that most of the selling company's improvements would be "down the drain."

Let's use a simple case in which a company's EBITDA (earnings before interest, taxes, depreciation of capital equipment, and amortization on intangible assets) is $1 million, and the valuation multiple is five times EBITDA, making for a $5 million valuation. Now, let's say the owners withhold certain capital expenditures and bonuses the year prior to selling; the EBITDA is then $1.2 million and all of sudden the valuation is $6 million (using the five multiple), or $1 million dollars more!

Theoretically, that is the way it works in the mergers and acquisitions business. You should be aware, however, that some buyers,

> Should we spend the money now on the necessary upgrades prior to selling the business?

particularly financial buyers, incorporate a different valuation formula, because they usually look at such an acquisition as a stand-alone operation. In such a case, they may impose a valuation formula that is EBITDA-CAPX, which refers to "earnings before interest, taxes, depreciation, amortization, minus capital expenditures."

Therefore, if a financial buyer is unable to bring an existing plant and information system to the acquired target company, then it may determine that the upgrades, in this case, are worth $1 million dollars. A financial buyer, therefore, may analyze the valuation to be EBITDA of $1 million times a multiple of five or $5 million, less $1 million of necessary capital expenditures, or $4 million net valuation.

Notwithstanding the above analysis, it is much better to defer capital expenditures if you are selling the company in order to show the best possible bottom line results—namely *profits*.

Timing the Sale of the Business

There are a number of businesses such as capital equipment manufacturers that are cyclical and that should be sold at the peak of their industry cycle in order to capitalize on the company's peak earning power. Other cyclical businesses, such as commodity businesses like oil, pulp and paper, and steel, should be sold at their industry peak.

Aside from cyclical businesses, there are also seasonal businesses, such as boat and ski companies, that should be sold at the end of their peak selling months, showing their strongest earnings and lowest inventory—theoretically at a point at which their balance sheet is the healthiest. Traditionally, retail stores generate one-third of their entire annual business over the Christmas shopping season, so by January the retailer is in its best position to sell because of its strongest financial position.

Finally, and most importantly, sell the business when both the company and the economy are performing at their best. In hindsight, for those of us who own Cisco Systems, we should have sold the stock when its price hit $82 per share because eighteen months later, the stock was $14 per share. Look at your company the same way; time the sale at its peak performance.

EBITDA a Career Killer?

EBITDA—earnings before interest, taxes, depreciation of capital equipment, and amortization on intangible assets—is used to represent a company's cash flow by focusing on operating expenses while excluding the cost of taxes, credit, and non-cash expenses. In other words, it shows how much money a business would have if those pesky things, such as interest, taxes, depreciation, and amortization did not exist.

But this method ignores the fact that companies must repay debts and profitable companies must pay tax. EBITDA does not accommodate new capital expenditure or intangible assets such as patents.

Many in the financial community now see EBITDA as a way of dressing up an unprofitable or marginally profitable company. In fact, the September 2001 issue of *Strategic Finance* featured an article by Alfred M. King entitled, "Warning: Use of EBITDA May Be Dangerous to Your Career."

Sell Off Non-Producing Assets

Prior to the sale of the company, sell off non-producing assets such as unused machinery and equipment or very slow-moving inventory. A buyer's due diligence team will identify these nearly worthless assets anyway, so you might as well clean up the balance sheet ahead of time and turn unproductive assets into cash.

There are a number of ways a buyer can acquire your business. If he acquires the "stock" of the company, he assumes all assets and liabilities. Nowadays, however, the buyer's attorney will have extensive protective clauses such as representation and warranties, escrow accounts, and hold backs that will protect the buyer from assuming non-producing assets. As a seller, you might as well realize that your chance of unloading undesirable assets without the buyer taking exception is highly unlikely.

Handling Excess Cash and Debt

One of the traditional ways to value a company is to apply a multiple of earnings to EBIT or EBITDA and then to subtract interest-bearing debt. Let's assume your company's EBIT is $1 million and we use a five multiple or $5 million valuation before interest-bearing debt (bank debt). Let's also assume your company has $2 million of bank debt. Normally, the buyer will pay you $5 million "debt free," which means you pay off the debt and net $3 million for the business, or the buyer merely pays $3 million and he keeps the $2 million debt in a stock transaction. Either way, the buyer pays $5 million total and you net $3 million.

A seller could be cute prior to selling by running out the accounts payable from the normal thirty days to ninety days in order to use the incoming cash from accounts receivable to pay off part of the bank debt, thus reducing the $2 million of notes to $1.5 million. Using the same formula of EBIT of $1 million times a five multiple equals a $5 million valuation, minus only $1.5 of bank debt, makes for a $3.5 valuation. As the seller, you just increased your valuation by $500,000.

While the above financial engineering is perfectly legal, a sharp buyer will catch this maneuvering and place a value on the business that will increase or decrease on a predetermined working capital and book value numbers.

How to Avoid the Tax Boomerang

Give yourself lots of time—years, in fact—to show your business at its most marketable. If you are like most people, you have been trying to minimize taxes, which means your account books minimize the value of your business.

By recasting your balance sheet to make your business more appealing, you may be open to paying back-taxes and penalties. Instead, if you plan ahead you will have time enough to change your accounting practices and show maximum profits.

Another item to be considered prior to selling the business is whether the company has excess cash. Most S corporations (unaffiliated corporations owned by seventy-five or fewer individuals in which profits flow to the individual without corporate level tax being imposed) pay out the company's earnings to stockholders, but C corporations (in which taxes are paid by the corporation and on earnings distributed to shareholders) often let earnings build up excess cash because if they paid it out in dividends, there would be a double tax hit. So now you may have the circumstance whereby you have built up $3 million of cash on the balance sheet, or $2 million more than necessary to run the business on a day-to-day basis.

Based on the above case, you should consult your accountant or financial advisor to determine how to distribute the excess cash with the least amount of tax impact.

You Cannot Have It Both Ways

There are some sellers who believe they can run a cash business without reporting all the income, yet expect the buyer to recognize the unreported income. No way!

And, there are some sellers who run their business in such a way as to show minimal profits, but document an extraordinary amount of "perks" (some carefully hidden) and expect the buyer to pay for the phantom earnings. Also, no way!

Additionally, if the seller cheats the government by avoiding taxes, then the buyer will surmise that the seller will somehow cheat him in the transaction, too.

> If the seller cheats the government by avoiding taxes, then the buyer will surmise that the seller will somehow cheat him in the transaction, too.

Conclusion

As a seller, run the business to the best of your ability to improve sales and profits, because the buyer will be scrutinizing the company as closely as possible.

For more information on this topic, visit our Web site at www.businesstown.com

Important Points in Selling a Business

In this chapter, you'll learn:

- How to decide who will be in charge
- Why you should hire professional advisors to assist in the sale
- How to locate buyers for your company
- How to compensate employees during a sale
- What to request from potential buyers

Chapter 5

T raditionally speaking, a seller should be rather coy and not too revealing of his or her ultimate intentions. Cary Reich, author of *The Life of Nelson Rockefeller*, offers a good example: "The modest unassuming and subservient John D. Rockefeller, Jr. was overly burdened with his father's obligations, but he surprised all as an astute negotiator. When the indomitable J.P. Morgan was seeking the Rockefeller's Mesabi iron ore properties to complete his assemblage of what was to become U.S. Steel, it was Junior who went head-to-head with the financier. 'Well, what's your price?' Morgan demanded, to which Junior coolly replied, 'I think there must be some mistake. I did not come here to sell. I understand you wished to buy.' Morgan ended up with the properties, but at a steep cost."

For a company to admit that it *has* to sell the business is akin to being the bleeding animal in a hunt—nothing short of devastating. Sellers should do everything possible to negotiate with more than one buyer in order to create a horse race. Psychologically, the seller should negotiate on his or her own turf and, realistically, the seller should not let the deal drag on.

Invariably, a good deal has to be "win-win" for both sides. You must first look after your own interests, but if the buyer is left with resentment and a sense of injustice, those ill feelings may be turned against you at a later date. Start with the following guidelines.

> Sellers should do everything possible to negotiate with more than one buyer in order to create a horse race.

Make a Firm Decision About Selling the Company

I remember my first potential sale as an investment banker in 1985—the largest Italian bakery in New England, which sold bread to supermarkets and restaurants. The company was equally owned by five Italian families, two of whom had sons working in senior positions.

This was a difficult business to sell because of the competitive industry and low profit margins. Nevertheless, after six months of hard work, I produced a Letter of Intent for what I thought would be an acceptable offer. Boy, was I wrong. The five families took the Letter of Intent and locked themselves in a conference room for further discussion. It wasn't long before the ranting and raving began, so I left the premises knowing they would never reach a consensus. The company was never sold and, to my knowledge, the second and third generation owners continue to struggle along, barely surviving and without hope for a liquidity event in the future.

Using hindsight is easy, but I learned to beware of selling a company when there are several owners from the same family. The chances are it will not happen. The moral of the story is to be sure that the owners are totally committed to selling at a reasonable price and willing to be flexible as to the structure of the deal. As an investment banker, I often test the seller's sincere intent by asking: "Are you sure you want to sell the company? Explain again why you want to sell."

The decision to sell is, of course, irreversible, but as I mentioned in the Introduction, there is considerable work to be done to properly prepare the company for sale. It is not uncommon to prepare one year in advance before going to market with your company. Once the decision has been made to sell, it is better not to waver from it, otherwise your team of advisors will lose faith in you and be less responsive in the future.

Selling a company is not only time consuming but also emotionally draining for the owner. The anticipation and anxiety of the selling process is not one that an owner usually enjoys, so when you decide to sell try to bring the matter to conclusion in less than a year's time.

Decide Up Front Who Is in Charge of the Sale

Even though there may be multiple owners, there should be only one point person who handles all the communication with the investment banker and attorneys.

I remember working with the chief executive officer of an office supply manufacturer who owned 20 percent of the company. The real decision-maker was the absentee chairman who owned 51 percent. Unfortunately, I never established a good rapport with the chairman and that ultimately handicapped my ability to complete a deal.

Usually, the president or owner is in charge of the sale, but often the investment banker has been given the authority to make

> Once the decision has been made to sell, it is better not to waver from it, otherwise your team of advisors will lose faith in you and be less responsive in the future.

the major decisions. In any event, if there is any ambiguity on the seller's part as to who is in charge, the potential buyer will lose confidence in completing a transaction.

One of the advantages of retaining an investment banker is that all communication should go through him, leaving the president or owner in a position to think about various offers before responding. There is also a protocol in the merger and acquisition business that if there is an investment banker on each side of the transaction, communication must be directed through them and they in turn will talk to their clients.

Present Pristine Financials

Audited financial statements will almost always produce a higher price and less onerous "reps and warranties," which implies that auditing the statements is well worth the extra cost. If the prospective buyer uncovers accounts receivable that cannot be collected and discovers outdated inventory during the due diligence, he will look dubiously at most other items on the balance sheet. The buyer may lose interest in the transaction and thus jeopardize the closing.

The seller's objective in cleaning up the balance sheet is to present a pristine financial report, which is neither inflated by such entries as "goodwill" nor burdened with questionable items such as "loans to the owner." Even if the book value is reduced in order to write off uncertain assets, it is better than trying to give false impressions. Buyers are elated to find a clean balance sheet and will be less suspicious in their due diligence process.

> Buyers are elated to find a clean balance sheet and will be less suspicious in their due diligence process.

Set Time Frames and Milestones

There is an expression in the merger and acquisition business that, "If the deal drags, it won't close." The following time schedule is the type of model that might be considered:

Four weeks: Completion of selling memorandum; compilation of target buyers

Twelve weeks: Contact all potential buyers

One week: Receive Letter of Intent

One week: Buyer receives required information

Two weeks: On-site due diligence

Two weeks: Buyer provides first draft of Purchase and Sale agreement

Two weeks: Buyer provides second draft of Purchase and Sale agreement

One week: Trial closing

One week: Final closing

The completion of sale from beginning to end should be approximately twenty-six weeks or six months (the time period could be twice as long if letters of intent are aborted or there are other unforeseen delays).

Time frames are benchmarks. It is not the end of the world if they are not precisely met, but if there is no discipline in the selling process, then the sense of urgency turns into a sense of malaise. If the selling process takes too long, the buyers' attention is distracted. Furthermore, there is always the fear that if the selling process takes too long, the company's growth rate slows and the company misses its projections. Buyers become apprehensive when the selling company "misses its numbers" during the negotiation stage. By setting time frames as target dates, there is less chance of losing momentum in the selling process.

> The completion of sale from beginning to end should be approximately twenty-six weeks or six months.

Partner with Professionals

The last place you want to cut corners financially in the sale of a business is in hiring transaction personnel—attorneys, accountants, appraisers, investment bankers—who are not topflight or experienced.

Ken Kames, formerly vice-president of New Business Development at the Gillette Company, often tells a "Bernie the Attorney story." Briefly, when Gillette was trying to negotiate a Purchase and Sale Agreement with a country lawyer who was unfamiliar with the deal process, Ken felt the deal was coming unglued. As the story goes, Ken pulled the owner aside and said: "We really like Bernie, but this deal is not going anywhere. May I suggest that if you engage one of the top law firms in Boston which we approve, Gillette will pay out-of-pocket up to $50,000 for their legal costs." Needless to say, the transaction closed successfully.

Part of the reason you need time to properly prepare for the sale of the business is to select your team of professional advisors. For example, if you have a family business with numerous shareholders, you may want to hire a special tax attorney in order to be able to structure the transaction to your benefit. You also need time to select the best investment banker for your particular company. Maybe you should select an investment banker who is a specialist in your industry. Beware of selecting professionals who charge considerably less than the norm for their type of services. When it comes to professional expertise, this is not the place to strike a bargain.

> Beware of selecting professionals who charge considerably less than the norm for their type of services.

Communicate with Your Bank

Often sellers will tell their attorney about selling the company but will not communicate with their bank. Bankers hate surprises. Aside from the credibility issue, the bank would probably like to keep the business and could therefore be an excellent source of financing for the new owner.

Bankers could also be helpful in advising you not only of potential professional advisors but also potential buyers. You may want to use your banker as a reference when the buyer is conducting due diligence. You may want to run out your trade payables from thirty to ninety days and pay down your bank note just prior to selling the company. A customary way to value a company is using a "multiple of earnings" times the cash flow minus the bank debt. Therefore, if you paid off your $1 million of bank debt by extending your payables instead, you could theoretically pick up another $1 million in a transaction.

My advice is to be friends with your banker; he or she may be helpful in selling your business.

Target Companies That Would Perceive Yours as Valuable

While this statement sounds obvious, there are some sellers who are so paranoid about a confidentiality leak that they will restrict some of the key industry players from the target list.

It takes time and intelligent analysis to determine which companies to target that would perceive your company to be the most valuable. Usually, it is a company with the best strategic fit, such as one that is on the edges of your industry and is eager to enter your business area now. On the other hand, it may be a European company that needs to utilize your distribution system in the United States in order to launch their products in this country. Perhaps your company has a special technology that a *Fortune* 500 company will literally overpay for in order to acquire your company because the window of opportunity for them is *now*. Or maybe your corner drugstore is unable to compete with CVS and Walgreens, but the real estate is so valuable for Dunkin Donuts that you close down the store and sell the property.

Openly Recognize Off-Balance-Sheet Items

The best policy is to be up-front early with a number of issues, most of which will be discovered in due diligence such as:

- Prepayment or deposits from customers
- Work-in-progress billing, frequently exercised by large capital goods manufacturers and/or companies with government contracts
- Contract obligations, such as predetermined pricing over the next several years
- Lease obligations, such as escalation clauses or contractual restriction from subleasing
- Legal threats by customers, vendors, or employees that have not yet materialized

Paint a Picture of What Can Be

Lying or misrepresenting your business is a serious no-no, but you can still draw up an income statement that reflects what profits might result after the sale was been completed.

For example, consider removing your salary and perks, and those of family members you don't expect to remain with the company. Remove expenses or income that would not be expected to continue after the sale, such as income or expenses associated with discontinued products or losses from the sale of business assets. And remove interest payments on any business loans.

The off-balance-sheet items are not obvious to the buyer, but if not disclosed by you up front it will shatter the buyer's confidence in you when, and if, they are disclosed in due diligence.

Many times off-balance-sheet items are innocently overlooked by the seller. About twenty years ago, I sold a sporting goods store that I owned. Not knowing whether or not the pending sale was to be consummated, I ran the business in a normal manner. To promote our new line of Fuji bicycles, I placed a discount coupon advertisement in the local newspaper. Over the next few weeks, I focused on the sale of the business and failed to inform the buyer of the discount coupons. The day after the sporting goods store was sold, customers started to redeem their coupons with the purchase of bicycles. This undisclosed liability amounted to only $5,000, which I did not hesitate to repay. The point of this story is to show that off-balance items can be overlooked unintentionally.

Negotiate Stay Agreements with Management

> Selling a company without key management's involvement is almost impossible.

Selling a company without key management's involvement is almost impossible. For a small company, key management might be just the chief executive officer and chief financial officer. It is imperative to have key management support the sale process because if they leave the company or if sales drop off, the results could be disastrous. Therefore, to contractually offer these people anywhere from two to six months extra monthly compensation is highly recommended.

It is quite possible that a small company, let's say with $5 million or less in annual sales, can be successfully sold with only the knowledge of the owner/CEO. For companies with more than $5 million in sales, however, the buyer is more apt to insist on interviewing the senior management team such as the chief financial officer, chief operating officer, or sales manager. It would be disconcerting if any of these people started to bail out of the company because of the impending sale, hence the need for stay agreements.

Furthermore, it is important for the top management team to participate in a two-hour or so presentation to the final prospective acquirers. Stay agreements for top management help ensure a cohesive team until the end.

Set Up a War Room

Sooner or later, buyers will want to see various documents pertaining to the business, probably most at the due diligence stage. It is advisable to plan ahead and locate all the documents in one file drawer, preferably at your attorney's office. This is known in the merger and acquisition business as the "war room."

Such documents would include:

- Lease agreement/real estate appraisal
- Machinery and equipment appraisal
- Corporate minutes
- Stock certificate book
- Sales representative agreements
- Banks agreements
- Customer, vendor, employee agreements

Your attorney, accountant, and investment banker will provide you with a checklist. If you do not have recent real estate and machinery/equipment appraisals, it is advisable to have them updated. The buyer's due diligence SWAT team will descend on the war room and expect to find all the required items in one place.

> The buyer's due diligence SWAT team will descend on the war room and expect to find all the required items in one place.

Tell the Buyer What You Would Like in the Letter of Intent

Listed below are some, but not all, of the items that should be addressed in a first draft of a Letter of Intent. Ultimately, these factors will be discussed in such a letter. If you feel that asking for a detailed Letter of Intent will intimidate the buyer, request a "term sheet" for openers. Term sheets might offer a price range and range of closing dates, among other things.

Ideally, the Letter of Intent will include such items as:

- The price
- The form of purchase—stock or asset sale (assumption of what the assets and liabilities are and exactly what is being purchased and what is not)
- The structure—cash, notes, stock, non-compete and/or consulting agreements, contingencies
- Management contracts—for whom, duration, incentives
- Closing costs and responsibilities of buyer and seller, such as environmental due diligence or title searches
- Brokerage fees—who pays and how much
- Timing for completion—drop-dead date for due diligence and financing, time frame before the exchange of money, final closing
- Statement that this is a non-binding agreement subject to satisfactory due diligence by both parties
- Stipulation of confidentiality of buyer (a breach could cause the seller to sue the buyer)—buyer promises not to disclose information of seller to outsiders and not to disclose that negotiations are underway

It is customary for the buyer to draft the Letter of Intent, but you would be wise to offer to draft this document. It is easier to negotiate off your document since your side has staged the points to be discussed.

Be Prepared to Ask and Answer Critical Questions

There are three crucial questions you need to ask yourself:

1. What is your bottom price based on net after-tax and net after-closing costs?
2. What are the most lenient terms you are willing to offer?
3. What will be the severance packages for key employees?

> It is customary for the buyer to draft the Letter of Intent, but you would be wise to offer to draft this document.

Once you have decided on these items, have a dress rehearsal with your advisors regarding negotiating strategy and tactics. Decide which one among you will be the lead negotiator, how you will plan to rationalize your higher price, and what items are not negotiable. Negotiations require various skills, including careful listening, knowing when to caucus separately with your team, knowing how to make concessions slowly, and when to counter with requests. Above all, you must predetermine your bottom price and your most lenient terms before the negotiations begin.

Let's reflect on history and remember when Senator Ted Kennedy ran for president of the United States. When Senator Kennedy was being interviewed on national television, David Frost, the commentator, asked: "Why do you want to become president of the United States?" Kennedy stuttered and stammered his way through the response in a very unconvincing way. His response was so lackluster that the campaign virtually ended there. The moral of this story is: Prepare yourself for obvious and critical questions, such as:

- Why do you want to sell the business?
- How would a new owner grow the business?
- What is the company's competitive advantage?

Selling a business is in many ways selling yourself. You can't be overly anxious, but you should be able to articulate how the buyer can grow the company. You should be able to paint a bright picture of the company's future, but in doing so, be careful not to dominate the conversation. Anticipate the questions you will be asked by the buyers, particularly the critical questions.

> Anticipate the questions you will be asked by the buyers, particularly the critical questions.

Recognize Deal Breakers

Most people in the merger and acquisition business recognize that when a seller reaches the Letter of Intent, the chance of closing is only about 50 percent. Recognizing the various deal breakers will help sellers anticipate hurdles to overcome. The following items are merely a few potential deal breakers.

Understand What Bugs a Buyer

In *12 Secrets to Cashing Out* (Prentice Hall), author Bob Bergeth states: "By understanding the buyers' needs, sellers stand a better chance to be prepared." Some of a buyer's concerns might be:

- Is the business totally dependent on one person?
- Is it a relationship business with sales concentration?
- Will the earnings continue?
- Are the add-backs justified?
- Is the capital equipment up-to-date?
- Is the pension fund fully funded?

The buyer's concerns are apt to be more prevalent when the acquirer is relatively inexperienced with acquisitions or the acquirer is from another industry. Furthermore, the natural tendency of the buyer is to be somewhat suspicious of you, the seller, and the buyer tries to uncover potential problems in the business. As the seller, you should be empathetic toward the buyer's concerns, because it is important to build trust between the two parties.

- Undisclosed material facts surfacing in due diligence, such as loss of a major account, customer concentration, product recall, environmental problems, missed sales/earnings projections
- Higher than anticipated taxes, which may be due to an asset sale for a C corporation
- Unacceptable details of Purchase and Sale Agreement for either the buyer or seller (collateralization of note, the insistence of escrow account, or the rigidity of the "reps and warranty" agreement)
- Lack of chemistry between the principals of the buyer and seller
- Undercapitalized buyer who cannot provide the necessary financing
- Remorseful seller who has second thoughts about selling
- A buyer or seller who becomes discouraged when the deal lags and walks away

Deal breakers can sometimes be short-circuited if most of the potential problems are addressed early on in the buyer-seller relationship and if both parties are willing to consider alternative solutions.

Part of the problem is not recognizing the deal breaker until it is too late to resolve. To overcome this pitfall, it is useful to have several people on each side during the various meetings to improve the overall communications. Another way to recognize deal breakers is to bluntly ask the buyer his or her concerns in the expectation that concerns can be addressed if uncovered, but if concerns do not surface, then it is unlikely they will be resolved.

I have seen numerous deals fail because of sellers' greed. Instead of accepting a slightly lower price from a well-financed buyer, some sellers will go with buyers who offer a slightly higher price, only to find they cannot finance the deal.

The way to close is to offer all cash at closings with few contingencies. Conversely, complicated deal structures with numerous contingencies have a less likely chance of closing.

Many deals are aborted because the actual financial results for the recent quarter are substantially lower than the projections. Consequently, the buyer gets cold feet and withdraws, often without a counteroffer. One of the most important factors for a seller is to not let up on increasing sales and earnings, as the buyer will be carefully scrutinizing each quarter, each month, and maybe each week to measure any weakness in the seller's performance.

Be Prepared to Deal with Due Diligence

Two transaction attorneys, Scott McDermott and David White, say that if they were representing a seller of a private company, they would initially sit down with their client and advise them accordingly:

"Mr./Ms. Jones, we would like to help you conclude a successful transaction as your advisor and transaction attorney. In doing so, it is exceptionally helpful for us to be proactive in anticipating the various due diligence requirements that a prospective buyer will inevitably expect us to satisfy. Due diligence can be a straightforward exercise—generally, the buyer's requirements are standard and predictable. However, despite having a good sense of what to expect, diligence often becomes a colossal headache for the seller who has not taken the time or dedicated the resources to preparing in advance of the term sheet. Lack of preparation can be a costly mistake for a seller, who instead of enhancing the favorable and positive perspective of the company held by the potential buyer, actually destroys goodwill by appearing disorganized, unprepared, and slow off the mark in providing documentation and information."

As McDermott and White point out, the seller must recognize that the buyer will seek full disclosure of all the material facts and will insist upon knowing about material adverse changes along the pathway to a final closing. Ultimately, since the pace of many deals can be so rapid, extensive due diligence is often still evolving as the definitive agreements are taking final shape. Often, as the unprepared seller is still trying to respond to follow-up due diligence requests, he faces a buyer insisting upon comprehensive representations and warranties in such areas as threatened litigation, environmental risks, tax matters, undisclosed liabilities, title to intellectual property, and the condition of assets.

> Diligence often becomes a colossal headache for the seller who has not taken the time or dedicated the resources to preparing in advance of the term sheet.

The buyer's counsel will frequently add more stringent language to these representations and warranties in the face of late disclosures or surprising, negative information about the seller's business. Worse, the indemnification associated with the representations is often made more perilous to a seller because of surprising disclosures made late in the deal-making process.

While it remains imperative to continue to run a company on all cylinders (sales, marketing, production, delivery) to avoid a downturn that will cause the potential buyer to hesitate and reconsider, the seller is burdened with the responsibility of pulling together all the documents required by the buyer. The accumulation of leases, contracts, purchase orders, employment agreements, employment benefit information, and other material documentation is so widespread that the office staff will wonder, or worse, will guess, what is really going on.

Therefore, to disguise the nature of this information gathering, it is suggested that your attorneys call for a legal audit and request that the seller send the entire collection of material over to their office. When the potential buyer needs to review this material, it will be set up in a data room at the attorney's off-campus site. Not only will this preserve confidentiality, it will imply that other buyers are also interested in acquiring the company.

Since experience tells us that the devil is in the details, certain seemingly immaterial matters—such as missing stock certificates, incomplete stock ledgers, inconsistencies in ownership rights of the intellectual property, unsigned agreements, and other corporate flaws—can turn out to have a major impact on the price and terms of the transaction. Often the seller's business is highly relationship-driven and the company's assets are found in commercial leases, OEM manufacturing agreements, or sales contracts. It is important to evaluate these contracts at an early date to see if the relationship assets are transferable; sometimes, the fundamental structure of the deal may have to be changed from an asset sale to a stock sale to provide for the buyer to be able to acquire the benefits of the relationships built by the seller.

Your counsel will pretest the potential "hot spots" that might arise when your company is to be sold; he will ask what matters

> It is suggested that your attorneys call for a legal audit and request that the seller send the entire collection of material over to their office. When the potential buyer needs to review this material, it will be set up in a data room at the attorney's off-campus site.

worry you and where you think the exposure exists. It is important to bring to the light of day, between attorney and client, any contingent liabilities, threatened claims, and potential litigation.

The preparation and professionalism projected by the seller's team may seem more like form than substance, but the indexing, packaging, and organization of the due diligence documentation will send important signals to buyers and their advisors. The time spent in gathering the material early and chronicling it in an orderly fashion will reflect a company that has properly committed to the selling process.

Conclusion

Since issues are identified and addressed, and often disclosed at an early stage, the seller should be able to avoid the renegotiation of a deal or terms based upon a material adverse change. A material adverse change covers a lot of ground—but the most avoidable example is a sales downturn caused by the fact that the chief rainmaker is the chief executive officer whose attention is focused on too many details in an attempt to close the deal.

Similarly, rosy forecasts are often not achieved because key employees must take their eyes off the prize to attend to issues that could have been addressed months earlier instead of in the face of an imminent closing. The seller must be made aware of the compression caused by trying to run a company, manage a transaction, and address the demands of the buyer.

A company that is properly prepared for sale will allow the seller to stay focused on the essentials of guiding the business to a smooth and bloodless closing.

> A company that is properly prepared for sale will allow the seller to stay focused on the essentials of guiding the business to a smooth and bloodless closing.

For more information on this topic, visit our Web site at www.businesstown.com

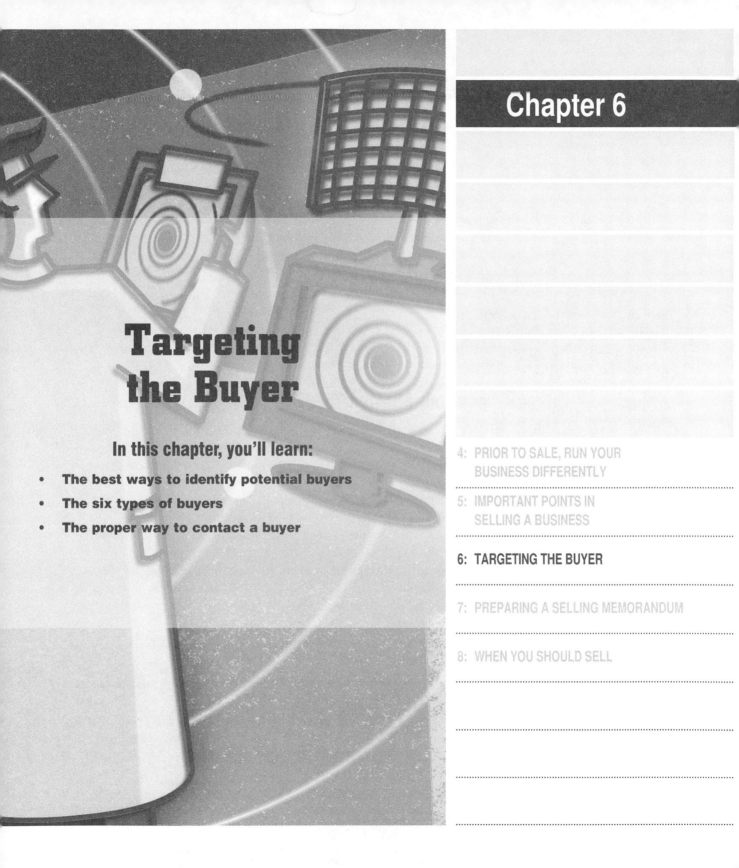

Targeting
the Buyer

In this chapter, you'll learn:

- The best ways to identify potential buyers
- The six types of buyers
- The proper way to contact a buyer

Chapter 6

In the preparation stage of selling your business, the two most important aspects are writing the offering memorandum and targeting the buyers. Assuming you retain an intermediary or investment banker as we recommend, there is no set way to target buyers. For example, if you own a small regional business with only $2 to $3 million in annual sales, the most likely acquirers could be qualified individuals in your community. If you own a company with huge customer concentration of, say, 70 percent of its sales to just one company, then you might limit your buyers to just a few large competitors.

These two examples are anomalies, and we will not focus on the exceptions. This chapter is an overview of how to identify as many qualified buyers as possible from different categories.

Your Mission Today

Let us assume you own an instrument company with very profitable sales of $10 million. Many of your technical products are patented, and you have cornered 10 percent of the $100 million market that exists for your products in the United States. Gross margins are 60 percent and EBITDA is 20 percent. There is a realistic opportunity to significantly raise sales to original equipment manufacturers.

Your objective is to identify a broad selection of qualified buyers—one hundred interested companies, called referrals, willing to sign a confidentiality agreement entitling them to receive an offering memorandum. The ultimate goal is to have the five best prospects in the final round of negotiations. Based on my experience, the process will probably unfold the following way:

> Overall referrals—100
>
> Referrals interested after reading the offering memorandum—60
>
> Referrals willing to submit to a term sheet—30
>
> Referrals in desired range—10
>
> Referrals considered best prospects—5

> Your objective is to identify a broad selection of qualified buyers—one hundred interested companies, called referrals, willing to sign a confidentiality agreement entitling them to receive an offering memorandum.

To do a thorough job, you will contact different types of buyers: strategic, competitors, financial, overseas, customers, or vendors (very select) and individuals (only those with industry background and third party equity financial backing). And you will contact a number of investment bankers who represent buyers not identified by you.

Fire Only When Ready

To use a military analogy, the battery of artillery guns will receive the command to fire when ready, but not before. In targeting buyers, you will need considerable time to uncover most of the prospects; identify the key contact person; qualify their interest and financial capacity; receive a signed confidentiality agreement from them; and send the offering memorandum. These steps could take three or four months.

Do not send out the offering memorandum to one prospect until you are ready to release them to all. In other words, fire only when ready. There are three reasons for adhering to the system of releasing the memoranda all at once.

1. You want to create a time schedule for the buyers with deadlines so it would be unfair to have one buyer take three months to review while another buyer only has one month.
2. You want to create excitement and momentum with the company for sale, because you are setting the stage for a bidding process.
3. The name of the selling company is not revealed until the memorandum is released. It is easier to preserve confidentiality if you limit the period of time the company's name has been "put in play."

How to Identify Buyers

There are about ten different ways to identify buyers; each has its advantages and disadvantages.

Search Your Web of Contacts

Sometimes a prospective buyer is right under your nose. He or she may be a relative or an employee or someone in a related business. Other times, you may have to go looking for a buyer. Printed advertisements in newspapers, magazines, and trade journals are a way of letting buyers know you have a business for sale; and with increasing frequency, people are turning to the Internet to advertise (and hunt) for a business.

But if there's no one knocking on your door you may want to turn to a professional. Business brokers will market your business to prospective buyers and buffer you from inquiries. They are also discreet about which particular firm they represent until definite interest has been shown. More about business brokers will be covered in Chapter 13.

Client: From the investment banker's point of view, there is certainly no better source of information regarding competitors than you, the client. You will probably exclude some competitors and rate the balance as to highest probability. As the client, you will also be able to suggest numerous likely strategic acquirers. In my experience, the client's ongoing suggestions are critical in the success of identifying the most likely buyers.

Standard Industry Code (SIC): All companies are categorized in one or several specific industries known in the jargon as SIC codes. Almost every state has business directories for manufacturers, and some states have business directories for service companies in which businesses are listed in numerous categories including SIC. Additionally, other services such as Dun & Bradstreet provide names of companies in certain SIC categories as well as companies in a certain sales range or geographic location.

Internet: The power of the Internet cannot be overstated. If you enter the words "silicon rubber" into a search engine, the Internet will produce a list of companies in that industry, particularly ones that may not appear in directories for one reason or another.

Trade publications: Underrated as a source of information to identify buyers, trade publications and the advertisements they publish are enormously helpful. As the expression goes, a picture is worth a thousand words.

Trade shows: Almost all the major players are present at these industry events. One can talk person to person with company representatives and often with senior management about their interest in acquisitions. Observing firsthand the potential buyers of the product line is also very helpful. If the trade show does not occur within the initial time frame of the selling process, however, then obviously this resource is of no use.

Investment bankers: Soon after I have pursued the first-cut of potential buyers, I contact other investment bankers who

> All companies are categorized in one or several specific industries known in the jargon as SIC codes.

may represent buyers that I have not identified. The fact that there are two transaction fees in the deal, one for the seller and one for the buyer, does not bother me; it is the best deal that counts.

Associations: Investment bankers representing sellers should leverage their own industry relationships. For example, if the investment banker belongs to the Association for Corporate Growth, the 5,500-member, premier organization for merger and acquisition professionals, there are approximately 850 I-bankers who are all accessible. Similar organizations include Corporate Finance Associates, International Mergers & Acquisitions Professionals, M&A International, and International Business Brokers Association.

I-Banker's Database of Buyers: Again, assuming you have retained an investment banker, they should have their own database of buyers, specifically private equity groups.

Networking: The investment banker who represents you will be able to access his own network either in a formal or informal way searching for buyers who may not be identified through the other sources.

Advertising: Perhaps a last resort but under certain circumstances, a carefully presented blind advertisement in an industry trade journal might be considered.

Getting to Know the Six Buying Types

There are at least six types of potential buyers of a business. They are known as: strategic, competitive, financial, overseas, customer/vendor, and individual. Let's take a closer look at each one.

The Strategic Buyer

A strategic buyer is one in a similar business but not the same business. Using the example of the liquid flow instrument company,

---

Look Deep into Their Crystal Ball

In addition to checking out the buyer's credit and management history, see what he or she plans for your company's future. This is especially important if you will be maintaining some involvement with the company as a consultant or employee, or if a portion of the purchase price will be deferred.

Even if you'll be making a clean break from the business, you should be reasonably confident that the buyer is capable of running the enterprise successfully. Otherwise, you run the risk of being sued for fraudulently misrepresenting the business's financial state, assets, or products if the new owner fails miserably.

a strategic buyer might be a manufacturer that measures the viscosity or temperature of liquids but not the flow of liquids. Or a strategic buyer might be one that is not necessarily an instrument company but a pump manufacturer that sells into similar markets.

Usually a strategic buyer will pay the highest price for a seller because it allows them to enter a related business less expensively and more rapidly than if they were to replicate it from scratch.

The Competitive Buyer

A competitive buyer offers many synergies and can provide reduced cost advantages, cross-selling, and increased market share. These are direct competitors that may use similar technology and sell into the same markets. For confidentiality reasons, you may decide not to approach them or at least not approach them unless they are the last resort.

The merger of Daimler-Chrysler is an example of two competitors—but not direct competitors—merging. The high-end Mercedes vehicles do not compete directly with Chrysler's low- to medium-price cars, trucks, SUVs, and Jeeps. Daimler and BMW, by contrast, are direct competitors.

The Financial Buyer

A financial buyer is a significant acquirer in the middle market. They may have portfolio companies in a similar industry as your business, thus indirectly making them a strategic or competitive buyer if the acquisition is an add-on. Assuming the latter is not the case, financial buyers bring no synergies to the deal, but rely on financial engineering to improve the profitability of the company after an acquisition. Such a standalone acquisition is called a platform company in which the financial owner will often change management and make other acquisitions in order to increase the company's value before reselling the business in five to seven years.

Financial buyers have different styles of management, namely either hands-on or hands-off, which means they are either active or not active in day-to-day operations. A few years ago, a $30-million specialty adhesive company decided to sell its operations and only approached financial buyers in order to safeguard potential

> A competitive buyer offers many synergies and can provide reduced cost advantages, cross-selling, and increased market share.

confidentiality leaks and to mitigate the possibility that the business would be moved, leaving employees without jobs.

Financial buyers are able to structure acquisitions such that either the selling company or current management will maintain 20 to 30 percent of the equity, giving them some potential upside in the years ahead. Industry buyers generally insist on buying 100 percent of the selling company.

The Overseas Buyer

An overseas buyer can be more difficult to access; however, many investment banks are members of industry associations that have counterparts or members overseas. For example, the Association for Corporate Growth has chapters in London, Paris, the Netherlands, and Mexico City. Overseas buyers are less likely to acquire small companies but often will pay a premium, particularly if you have excellent channels of distribution in the United States.

The Customer or Vendor Buyer

Customers or vendors are possible buyers, but seldom do sellers approach them because vertical integration is rarely utilized as a strategy nowadays (compared to years past when John D. Rockefeller successfully implemented this approach).

A few years ago, Walden Paddlers, a kayak company, sold to its major supplier, Hardigg Industries. Hardigg owned 40 percent of Walden Paddlers, but initially the plastic roto-molder of kayak hulls and decks did not want to own 100 percent of Walden or be involved with the distribution of the products. Walden hired an investment banker to find a new owner for 60 percent of the company, but after considerable effort the consultant failed to identify the right buyer. Faced with the possibility of the 60 percent stockholder selling to an undesirable buyer, Hardigg acquired the majority interest, thus giving them 100 percent ownership.

> Customers or vendors are possible buyers, but seldom do sellers approach them because vertical integration is rarely utilized as a strategy nowadays.

The Individual Buyer

An individual buyer should only be considered if the person is adequately qualified, is preferably a former chief executive officer, is experienced in your industry, and has substantial financial backing.

Some individuals are financed by private equity groups; the individual puts the deal together but the private equity group finances the majority of the equity and owns a majority of the company.

The Obstacles to Reaching a Buyer, and How to Get Around Them

Identifying which buyers to target is essential in reaching a successful sale of your company, but how to reach them is also very important. There are various obstacles to be considered, all of which must be overcome in order to generate interest in the buyer.

Obstacle 1—Finding the right person: You may contact the president of the company only to learn later that he is no longer there. Perhaps the president's secretary opens your letter and throws it away because it appears to be a form solicitation letter. Consider directing the inquiry to the director of corporate development if it is a large corporation. Do not assume that your message, whether it is written or verbal, will be referred to the correct person.

Obstacle 2—Hitting at the right time: You may approach the company when the person is on vacation and somehow your message is lost or misplaced. Maybe the buyer is completing another acquisition and at the time is not able to focus on your company. The CEO or director of corporate development could be distracted by something else at the time you approached him.

Obstacle 3—Employing the right method: You may not be properly describing your company so the prospect does not see the fit with the two companies. Maybe you failed to show what is proprietary with your company or to adequately explain the markets it serves. The difficulty, of course, is to be able to communicate enough information prior to a signed confidentiality agreement in order to interest the buyer.

There are basically four different ways to approach buyers, and even though it is redundant, I suggest you approach buyers in more than just one of them. The various approaches are as follows:

Letter. The most common way to communicate is to have an investment banker send a letter to prospective buyers with a blind description. This type of letter is usually just one

> Identifying which buyers to target is essential in reaching a successful sale of your company, but how to reach them is also very important.

page, commonly known as a teaser. It is somewhat impersonal and you may not know if it reached the correct decision-maker.

Fax/E-mail. As an investment banker, if I have not received a response from the buyer either from my solicitation letter or telephone call, then I follow up with a fax. Furthermore, I use a one-page fax as the preferred way to communicate with private equity groups and other investment bankers.

Telephone. As an investment banker, this is my preferred method of approaching buyers because of the directness, the ability to have a dialogue, and the immediate response from the buyer. Obviously, it is very time-consuming, but my willingness to spend the time pursuing the buyer in person is one of my competitive advantages as an investment banker.

Other I-Bankers. As an investment banker, I often approach other I-bankers because they may have an inside track with target companies that I have been unable to reach, or they may know of a target company that I have overlooked. I am not overly concerned that there may be two commissions in the deal. For example, on a $10 million transaction, I may make a 3 percent commission and the other I-banker also makes 3 percent, but I am more concerned about the remaining 94 percent of the deal.

Conclusion

It cannot be said often enough: targeting buyers is critical in the preparation stage. My advice is to take the necessary time to do a complete and thorough job of targeting the buyers before the offering memorandum is mailed out, even if it takes three or four months of preparation to do so.

> Targeting buyers is critical in the preparation stage.

For more information on this topic, visit our Web site at www.businesstown.com

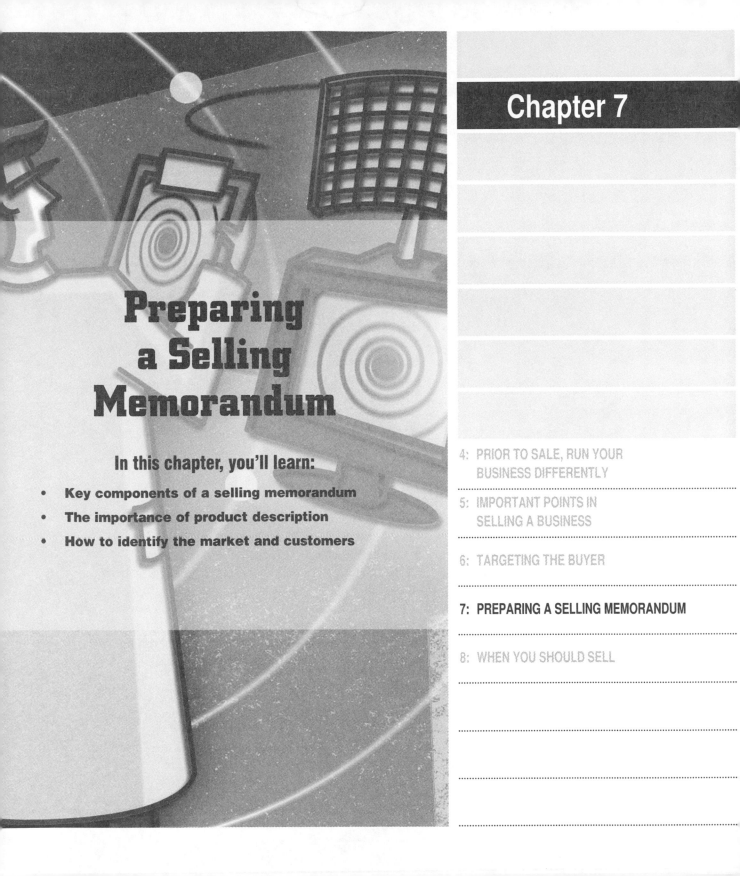

Chapter 7

Preparing a Selling Memorandum

In this chapter, you'll learn:

- **Key components of a selling memorandum**
- **The importance of product description**
- **How to identify the market and customers**

The process of selling middle-market companies starts with the preparation of the selling memorandum. The purpose of this written document is eloquently explained by Kimberly Wilson, who prepares business plans for her clients. According to Wilson, a selling memorandum does the following:

- It offers you as a seller the opportunity to present your company in a clear, compelling light.
- It allows face-to-face meetings to be productive. A good profile readies both the buyer and seller for negotiations and reduces the time wasted by asking questions that the document can effectively address.
- It speeds up the due diligence process. A good profile provides a point of departure for the buyer. After reading it, the buyer may immediately focus on the areas needing further research.
- It shows the buyer that the seller is serious. A good profile will position the seller favorably in negotiations, maximizing your opportunity to command the best price and terms.
- It allows the buyer to qualify him- or herself. A good profile will indicate the kind of management and financial resources the buyer needs to bring the company to transact the sale and become a successful owner.
- It enables the company to disclose weaknesses and address them, preventing them from becoming bargaining points later.
- It prepares management—through the process of focusing information for the document—so that they can present the company clearly and concisely in meetings with the buyer.

Kimberly Wilson also points out that a good selling memorandum addresses the functional areas of marketing, operations, and finance. It includes an analysis of the company's customer base, competition, marketplace, and industry. It describes its competitive advantage and position relative to key strategic influences. And it

> A good selling memorandum addresses the functional areas of marketing, operations, and finance.

includes an executive summary, financial statements, and financial projections.

As with any business plan, the best profile derives from a thoughtful, objective reflection of the company relative to its strategic environment and an intelligent plan for growth. Your challenge then is to draft a selling memorandum that translates into words and numbers the essence of your company. The chief purpose of a selling memorandum is to build credibility, increase the perception of potential, reduce the perception of risk, and create an inducement for the reader to take the next step. If you have never prepared a profile of your company, here are some tips.

How to Create a Selling Memorandum

Length

Fifteen to twenty concise pages of text should be just long enough to present a convincing story of your business while creating an appetite for more information. Financial statements, both historical and projected, should be indicated in a summary form with clear projections attached. If you believe you are omitting important information, include it in an appendix or prepare separate due diligence packages, making that information available to serious buyers only.

Form

Form goes hand-in-hand with content. Good form shows you take your business seriously. Neatly written, word-processed pages that have been carefully checked for grammar and spelling are critical to making a good impression. Include meaningful charts where appropriate and clear photographs of your facility or product line.

Content

What you choose to emphasize in the contents of the memorandum will vary according to the type of business you manage. In general, assume your buyer and their legal and financial

Take a Memo, Jack

There are several hallmarks of an effective selling memorandum. Consider the following when drafting your pitch:

- A solid memorandum gives the buyer a reason to take the next step. A strong overview or executive summary discloses information while generating interest and presenting value.
- It shows opportunities for growth. The presentation should clearly impart how and in what direction the business can grow.
- It demonstrates infrastructure. A buyer needs to know that when he assumes operations of the company, he can draw on a solid corporate infrastructure (including good reporting systems, management, and financial practices) to effect his own plans for the business.
- It includes "recast" financials along with unaltered financials. Historical statements and financial projections should add the soon-to-be-former owner's compensation and other pertinent expenses to the net income to indicate the financial potential for a new owner.

advisors do not know your industry. Avoid using specialized terminology or abbreviations unless you clearly define them. Here are other suggestions:

Use every opportunity to build credibility. If your company is not highly visible, then associate yourself with institutions that are. Capitalize on your relationships with recognized suppliers, customers, financial institutions, and legal and accounting firms.

Use every opportunity to create potential for growth. Paint the picture of a strong future for your buyer: untapped customer groups, emerging market segments, new sales strategies, products on the drawing board, service opportunities, creative management, pending laws and regulations. In the case of a troubled company, make every effort to show opportunity for a successful turnaround.

Provide an executive summary. A brief executive summary, no longer than two pages, should describe the company's legal form, financial position, and ownership. It should outline the company's key markets, customers, and competitors, as well as its products and services. Most important, it should make clear, powerful statements about the company's competitive strengths and the need, or niche, it addresses in the marketplace.

Include a description of the deal. List exactly what is being sold, including the rights to use the name of the business, patents, and real estate.

Describe products. Describe your products, services, and technology in relation to market need or demand. Key product benefits and competitive advantages are more important than detailed descriptions.

Articulate market strategy and plan. Be sure to indicate principal goals and objectives that define your market approach and how you currently implement those goals.

> If your company is not highly visible, then associate yourself with institutions that are.

Identify markets and customers. While it is important to define and quantify your markets and their current and potential demand, it is just as important to list key customers. At the same time, create confidence in the buyer that your business is not dependent on one or two customers.

Be honest with your sales figures. Be sure to give a clear picture of your sales strategy and infrastructure. Your buyer will be concerned if he or she believes your business's sales depend on your own energy and customer relationships.

Identify your competition. List your chief competitors, their locations, annual sales, and number of employees as well as their strengths and weaknesses. You will lose credibility if you omit significant competition.

Describe manufacturing processes. Describe your basic processes, capital equipment, and suppliers. Be sure to discuss capacity and efficiency issues. Your buyer will want to know whether you are dependent on any suppliers for critical raw materials or aspects of your service or product delivery.

List management personnel. Include resumes or summaries of your key managers. A buyer needs to know a solid team is in place to take over in your absence and to implement his or her own plans.

In short, the best selling memorandums are those that are short, easy to read, believable, professional, and show opportunity for growth.

> ### A Picture May Be Worth Big Bucks
>
> A selling memorandum is an opportunity to *sell* your business. It is a guidebook, a marketing tool, to be used to promote your business and persuade the buyer.
>
> In addition to the written content described in this chapter, such as your company profile and financials, you may want to include photographs of both the interior and exterior of the business. But remember, this information is private, and anyone who sees it must sign a confidentiality agreement beforehand.

A Sample Memorandum

While an entire selling memorandum will not be reproduced, the following information can be used as a guide, starting with a table of contents. For purposes of this book, the name of the hypothetical company for sale is Concord Cookie Company.

TABLE OF CONTENTS

I. CONDITIONS OF ACCEPTANCE

(Without replicating the exact words, this section is used as a disclaimer by the selling agents, and includes the following such sentences.)

This Memorandum contains certain statements, estimates, and projections provided by Concord Cookie Company with respect to its anticipated future performance. Such statements, estimates, and projections reflect assumptions by Concord Cookie Company concerning anticipated results, which assumptions may or may not prove to be correct. No representations are made as to the accuracy of such statements, estimates, or projections.

Further, this section also uses strong language regarding the importance of keeping all confidential material confidential, and if there is a selling agent involved, that all communications relating to these materials should be directed to that agent. Management at Concord Cookie Company should not be contacted under any circumstances.

II. THE PROPOSED TRANSACTION

Recipients of this Memorandum should determine their degree of interest in acquiring Concord Cookie Company. If upon review of this information, it is decided that there is no further interest, it is requested that the Memorandum be returned to (The Agent). Such parties are minded that they will continue to be bound by the Confidentiality Agreement.

Interested parties are asked to advise (The Agent) of their interest, including a preliminary range of value and a suggested timeframe for closing a transaction.

From those expressing interest, a small number will be invited to meet the management and tour the facility. Proposals will be invited from those making the tour, following which a buyer will be selected. Final negotiations will be conducted, followed by a Letter of Intent, Purchase and Sale Agreement, and a closing.

While price will be an important consideration, interested parties are advised that other conditions will also be important in selecting the successful bidder. Such conditions may include payment terms, timing, availability of necessary financing, etc.

Information Regarding This Offering

All questions or requests for additional information or discussions with Management are to be directed through the Agent at the address below:

(The Agent)(Agent's Address)

(Agent's Telephone)(Agent's Fax)(Agent's E-mail)

Under no circumstances should any employee, customer, or supplier of Concord Cookie Company be contacted directly about information contained in this Memorandum or regarding this contemplated transaction without prior approval of (The Agent).

III. EXECUTIVE SUMMARY/COMPANY PROFILE

Company: Concord Cookie Company
6 Elm Street
Concord, New Hampshire 00000

Ownership and Organization:

This private C corporation was re-established in 1990 by Gilbert Castle. Mr. Castle previously ran the business, which was established in 1950 in Lowell, Massachusetts. Under new Management and Ownership, the New Hampshire Venture Capital Fund owns 30 percent of the Company, the directors own 40 percent, and approximately twenty other stockholders own the balance.

Business:

A highly automated producer of branded specialty cookies, which are low in fat and sodium and with no cholesterol. Nearly 80 percent of the company's production is vanilla wafers targeted for the food service sector (90 percent).

Financial Highlights:

Concord Cookie Company is on target to deliver planned results for year-end 2000 (dollars rounded to thousands).

HISTORIC PERFORMANCE AND PROJECTIONS

Year	Sales	Sales Growth	Gross Profit	% of Sales	EBIT	% of Net Sales	EBIT Growth
1998	$5,224	22%	$2,316	44%	$604	12%	90%
1999	$6,684	28%	$2,962	44%	$848	13%	40%
2000	$9,000	35%	$4,474	50%	$1,448	16%	71%
2001	$11,250	25%	$6,082	54%	$2,246	20%	55%

Products:

There are two products and four SKUs: the Vanilla Wafer Cookie, which is packaged in an eight-ounce pack and a two-pound bag; and the Peanut Butter Cookie, which is packaged in a four-cookie pack and a three-pound bag. The cookies have a unique flavor and texture; the brand name "Concord Cookies" retains significance and is recognized by consumers.

Markets:

The preponderance of Concord's sales are through food service distributors who in turn sell to restaurants and institutions. The largest concentration of sales geographically is in New England.

Real Estate:

The Company leases 60,000 square feet with extended renewal options and the ability to expand its production space adjacent to its current operation in an industrial park in Concord, New Hampshire.

Summary Investment Considerations:

The Company is poised for dramatic growth of a projected compound rate in excess of 20 percent, with gross margins over 50 percent and EBIT margins over 20 percent through the year 2005. Concord has the manufacturing capacity now to increase sales by another $4 million to $14 million without significantly adding to their plant and equipment. The management team is mature and experienced and has proven its ability to grow the business profitably.

The Company is a very attractive acquisition candidate for strategic buyers or could be a platform company for a financial acquirer desirous of entering the specialty food business.

Reason for Sale:

The Board of Directors has unanimously voted to provide a liquidity event for outside ownership either through a recapitalization or outright sale of the business. Management is desirous of continuing under the new ownership.

Selling Memorandum—Final Thoughts

The balance of the selling memorandum should follow the table of contents as previously outlined. Bear in mind that the table of contents will vary somewhat depending on whether the company is a manufacturer, distributor, service company, or retail operation. Distributors should emphasize their broad product lines, quality customers, and operation efficiencies. Service companies should emphasize their superior employees and their repeat business with long-term customers. Retail companies should emphasize their niche, favorable leases, and customer demographics.

Conclusion

These may be the twenty most important pages you will ever write. The selling memorandum is your best vehicle to laying out the case for your company. Use every opportunity to build credibility and the opportunity for growth, and by doing so in convincing fashion you will speed up the sales process and command the highest price. Once you have a winning selling memorandum in the can, though, there is still the matter of deciding on the right timing, which is the subject of the next chapter.

> The selling memorandum is your best vehicle to laying out the case for your company.

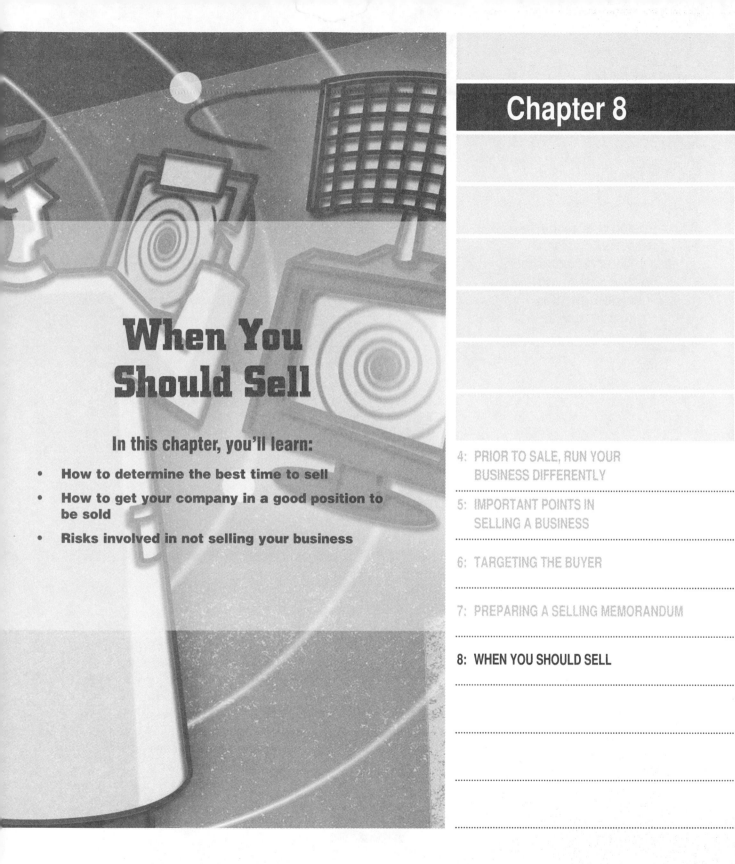

When You Should Sell

In this chapter, you'll learn:

- **How to determine the best time to sell**
- **How to get your company in a good position to be sold**
- **Risks involved in not selling your business**

Chapter 8

In today's business
environment with
continuing consolidation
and fierce competition,
standing still is
not an option.

In today's business environment with continuing consolidation and fierce competition, standing still is not an option. If you are not a buyer, then you should be a seller, and if you are a seller, it is just a matter of time before you do so.

To underscore the seemingly simple point of selling before it is too late, I offer you the case study of Wang Laboratories. In 1984, Wang had sales of $2 billion with earnings of $210 million. Five years later, sales were $3 billion with losses of $424 million. Between 1984 and 1992, the stock price went from $42 per share to less than $1 per share. By the fall of 1992, Wang was in Chapter 11 bankruptcy protection.

Those who have read any books about An Wang, such as *Lessons* or *Riding the Runaway Horse*, understand that this family business, whether public or private, would never be sold as long as there was a family heir apparent. What really was disappointing was that Wang Laboratories could have been sold to a company such as AT&T back in the mid to late 1980s, saving both employees and shareholder investment. But that did not happen. The overriding factor in Wang's demise was the disastrous choice of selecting An Wang's son, Fred, to succeed as chief executive officer instead of either moving the highly touted John Cunningham in as CEO or selling the business.

While Wang is an infamous example of how a family business can self-destruct, it is important to realize that there are probably thousands of small businesses and small family firms that fail for similar reasons, albeit on a different scale.

Here is another example of a small family business that waited too long to sell. Several years ago, the small three-store Massachusetts Home Center retail business, with sales of $8 million, was under severe pressure from its bank. The recession certainly was a major factor in the company's problems, but loose controls on accounts receivable and inventory were also major factors. Nevertheless, the owner waited until his banker demanded that the business be placed on the market for sale. However, it was too late to put the business up for sale, as most of the potential buyers were worried about Home Depot's strength in the market and its new fifteen-store expansion program in New England.

An intermediary was retained to sell the business and was given 90 to 120 days to find a qualified buyer who would enter into a Letter of Intent. A terrific selling memorandum was quickly prepared and the three-store chain was offered to a comprehensive group of potential buyers. But it was too late; the intermediary tried to sell the two satellite stores separately, tried to sell the real estate without the business, and tried a number of other combinations. At the end of 120 days, the bank forced the company to liquidate the inventory for two of the stores, and sometime thereafter to liquidate the third store.

In summary, the best time to sell is when the business is doing great and the economy is rising. Don't expect to sell the other fellow your problem—he is looking for a going business with a proven income stream and conservatively valued assets.

When an Owner Fails to See the Light

The third generation owner of a well-established, profitable retail/distributor of lighting fixtures and electrical supplies decided to sell the business. This was at a time when real estate in Massachusetts was booming and new construction, a major source of business, was at an all-time high. There was no question that the owner had selected exactly the right time to sell in order to maximize the business value.

There were numerous interested buyers and eventually one buyer in particular made an offer to acquire the business at a slight premium to book value. The seller had his mind set on selling at a capitalization rate of five times net before taxes, including the owner's assumption of seller's debt, a formula which the intermediary felt was excessive for this industry.

Negotiations eventually fell apart and the owner returned to operating his business. A number of years ago, a front-page article in the *Boston Globe* was headlined, "After 60 Years, A Family Business Goes Under." Apparently, the lighting business was devastated by the drop in new construction, bad debts, and high leverage, which resulted from expansion during the good times.

In this case, the owner was receiving advice from two different advisors. The merger and acquisition people encouraged selling at what they considered a reasonable price, while the other advisors recommended holding out for more money.

This Is No Time to Kid Yourself

In the above examples, either it was too late to sell the business or the business was overpriced when there was a short window of opportunity to get out. Here are some lessons we can take from these experiences:

1. Treat owning a business like owning stock; in spite of the compassion for employees and customers, the company is dispensable.
2. If the owner cannot properly train the heir apparent to succeed the founder at a normal retirement age (sixty-five), then he should seriously consider selling the business to a very responsible new owner or replacing the chief executive officer with the most competent choice he can select.
3. The time to sell a company is when the business is thriving . . . not when sales and profits start to deteriorate.

> The time to sell a company is when the business is thriving . . . not when sales and profits start to deteriorate.

There is an old cliché that "timing is everything." Whether it is investing in the stock market or fishing, timing can be the difference between success and failure. Selling a company at the right time is critical for maximizing a successful transaction. All too often owners decide to sell their company without pragmatically thinking through the selling process. When planning on selling your business, you should consider the timing in terms of your readiness to sell and the market's readiness to buy.

Remember that it could take one year to properly organize your business affairs before putting the company on the market, and that it could take another six to twelve months to actually sell the company. The company's financial trends—its sales and earnings, for example—should be on the upswing, and general business conditions, such as the stock market and employment numbers, should be fairly rosy.

Of course, your financial advisor should have given you proper advice that you will net-out a significant amount after taxes, debt repayment, and closing costs to justify the transaction price based on a professional corporate valuation.

Not too long ago an attorney called me to inquire whether I would be interested in selling a small manufacturing company with profitable sales of $5 million. The company was a "job shop" making products to order with an 80/20 customer base: 80 percent of the business came from only 20 percent of the customers.

Upon visiting the plant, I found the operation not only to be disorganized but a total mess. The owner's financial advisor was not accustomed to valuing companies of this type. The owner's price expectations were roughly one times sales, or eight times cash flow, and the owner wanted mostly cash at closing. The owner really did not want to stay on after the business was sold, and his management team was thin. To make matters worse, the financials were not audited and most of the earnings were "add-backs" such as automobile leases and expenses.

Needless to say, as a merger and acquisition intermediary, I walked away from this potential sell-side assignment because the owner was unwilling to accept my fifteen years of experience, and he was unrealistic. This was a case where the owner was not prepared to sell, particularly because he did not take the time or display the interest to understand the selling price.

All too often, sellers of businesses become caught up with the euphoria of selling their business at a high price, without taking the time to analyze what they will net after the sale: net of taxes, net of closing costs. In addition, this type of seller often assures the buyer that the key employees will remain until the completion of the sale, or that employees will not compete with the new owner.

The wise course of action is to begin with the end in mind. In other words, if you are the seller, investment banker, attorney, accountant, or advisor for merger and acquisition transactions, you owe it to yourself or your client to run the numbers to see what the owner will net after all deductions.

A Case Study

Let's suppose you and your 50 percent partner started an electronics company with virtually no capital invested because you were

Tick-Tock, Avoid a Shock

Buyers will be cautious about what may be motivating you to sell. The more vulnerable or desperate you appear to be, the more leverage the buyer has, meaning you may have to compromise on price or other terms of sale.

The best time to sell your business is when you're on top—either your industry is riding high or your business is flourishing and an even better year is around the corner. This is when you will get the most money for your business.

If retirement is motivating you to sell, start several years in advance of your anticipated retirement date. You don't want to find yourself pressured to accept a lowball offer or provide financing simply because the clock is ticking and the golf course is calling.

Avoid selling just before major leases or other key contracts are due to expire. Prospective purchasers will want to be able to predict what they'll need to spend for rent, labor, materials, supplies, and other big-ticket items. If you *must* sell right before a contract is scheduled to expire, try to renegotiate it early so that you will get a favorable rate locked in for your purchaser. At the same time, have your lawyer make sure the contract can be assumed by a new owner.

originally a consulting firm billing out consulting fees. Time progressed and you hired key employees who were responsible in helping you develop proprietary state of the art electronic equipment.

Ten years later, you and your partner have built the business up to be a very profitable with $575,000 in EBIT on $4 million of sales. You decide to sell the business and you feel that you and your partner should each "gross" approximately $2 million on the business based on the prevailing seven multiple of EBIT for this type of operation. The company has been your major life's work, so the proceeds will be your long-term nest egg.

The Details of the Deal

Let's further assume that you are smart enough to confer with your trusted CPA to run the numbers. Your CPA points out the following:

- The valuation of seven times EBIT implies that the business is valued "before" interest and taxes, so one has to deduct out the interest-bearing debt to arrive at a net value.
- The closing costs are deducted from the gross proceeds.
- Phantom stock is not essential but in this case the owners failed to sign their key employees to a non-compete when they started their employment, so now the buyer insists that the six key employees be signed up with such agreements before the purchase; hence the need for a quid pro quo deal with the key employees.
- After federal and state taxes, the proceeds with the 50 percent partner are divided.
- Rarely are small entrepreneurial businesses of this type acquired without the owners signing non-compete and consulting agreements.

> The valuation of seven times EBIT implies that the business is valued "before" interest and taxes, so one has to deduct out the interest-bearing debt to arrive at a net value.

The Deal

EBIT:	$575,000
Price: 7 Multiple:	$4,025,000
Price: Settled for:	$4,000,000
Less Bank Debt:	($800,000)
Net Selling Price:	$3,200,000
Less Closing Costs:	($250,000)[1]
Less Phantom Stock:	($350,000)[2]
Sub Total:	$2,600,000

Case 1–All Cash At Closing

Sub Total:	$2,600,000	
Net After Federal Tax:	$2,080,000[3]	
Net After State Tax:	$1,980,000[3]	
50% Owner	$990,000	Net proceeds from sale

Case 2–Cash of $2m/deferred payments of $600k

Sub Total:	$2,600,000	
Cash:	$2,000,000	
Net After Federal Tax:	$1,600,000[3]	
Net After State Tax (a):	$1,520,000[3]	
Deferred Payments:	$600,000[4]	
Net After Federal Tax:	$372,000[5]	
Net After State Tax (b):	$353,000[5]	
Combine a + b:	$1,873,000	
50% Owner:	$936,500	Net proceeds from sale

While there are various income tax rates, this example is based on 38 percent federal and 5 percent state (varies by state).

[1] Closing Costs

Investment Banker	$180,000
Legal	50,000
Accounting	20,000
	$250,000

[2] Phantom Stock
for remaining employees $350,000

[3] Tax Computations–Capital Gains
Federal Rate at 20% with 0 cost basis
State Rate at 5% with 0 cost basis

[4] Deferred Payments

Non Compete	$300,000
Consulting Agreement	$300,000

[5] Tax Computations–Income Tax

The Bottom Line

In the above scenario, the two 50-percent owners sell their business that has a value of $4 million. In most cases, investment bankers and merger and acquisition advisors consider a valuation number to be debt-free. Depending on whether the transaction is all cash or cash with terms, the owners net-out less than $1 million each. In fact, in Case 2, the net proceeds from the sale are actually worth less than the $936,500 because the deferred payments are paid over a three-year period without interest, thus the buyer is paying the sellers with today's dollars tomorrow.

The purpose of this case study was to show a hypothetical situation in which two owners could have expected to have received considerably more for their business. For merger and acquisition advisors, the importance of analyzing each individual case is to avoid an embarrassing situation when the owner gets all the way to the Purchase and Sale Agreement before someone finally runs the numbers to see exactly what the net proceeds from the sale will produce. A number of deals have been aborted at that point.

This hypothetical example includes a number of variables that may not be applicable in other situations, such as investment banking fees, phantom stock, and a cost basis of zero. On the other hand, other corporate sales might incur costs such as unexpected environmental cleanup costs, disputed values on accounts receivable, and inventory figures.

Is this a doable deal for the owners? Are the proceeds going to be sufficient to provide the sellers with a reasonable nest egg for their future? If not, do the two owners turn down this offer and go back to work to build up the EBIT so they can sell the business at a higher price at a later date? In order to come to a conclusion on such matters, "Begin with the end."

Sell When Loose Ends Are Tied

There is a vast difference between selling a retail store with $1 million in sales and selling a manufacturer with $15 million in sales. No matter what the sales level of your business, one should ideally sell a company when all the loose ends are pulled together, so that the company is well positioned for acquisition.

> The importance of analyzing each individual case is to avoid an embarrassing situation when the owner gets all the way to the Purchase and Sale Agreement before someone finally runs the numbers to see exactly what the net proceeds from the sale will produce.

Here are some of the issues you should address in order to get your company in a good position to be sold.

Valuation. A market price range should be established by a professional corporate appraiser who utilizes numerous methodologies, such as comparables, multiple of earnings, and discounted cash flow.

Selling memorandum. As outlined earlier, this is a thorough description of the company, including its products and/or services, market, distribution, management, financials, competitive advantage, and strategy.

Management team. A one-man band is a major detriment. Key positions such as chief financial officer, sales manager, and plant manager should be filled.

Financials. Updated financials, preferably monthly, but minimally quarterly, should be available along with financial projections, ideally for five years but minimally one year.

Employee contracts. Create a complete file of documented non-compete agreements for key employees, especially for hi-tech companies. Also, stay agreements are often in order for the top managers to ensure they do not bolt before the company is sold.

Vendor contracts. Even before going to market, companies should develop written contracts with important vendors, customers, and suppliers.

Housekeeping. The plant and/or office should be organized and clean. Sloppiness portrays a poor attitude.

> Create a complete file of documented non-compete agreements for key employees, especially for hi-tech companies.

Conclusion

Determining when you should sell your business takes intuition, common sense, proper counseling from one's trusted advisors, and lots of preparation. Now that you are ready to sell, the following section will give you tools to help you execute your plan.

For more information on this topic, visit our Web site at www.businesstown.com

The Key Steps in Selling

Summary of Part III

- **Your financial records**
- **Non-price considerations**
- **Risk-taking**
- **Cultural fit between employees and buyer**
- **Mistakes made while selling**
- **Hiring intermediaries**
- **Hiring advisors**
- **Special steps for selling troubled companies**

Chapter 9

Key Steps in Selling a Business

In this chapter, you'll learn:

- **How to clean up your financial records**
- **How to prepare your management team**
- **The importance of valuation**

"The basic error made by most private companies is not beginning early enough to prepare themselves for an eventual sale. The result is untold millions left on the table, or worse, transactions never consummated. The seeds of a successful sale are sewn years in advance."

Those words were spoken by the experienced Valerio Giannini, who is with New Cap Partners, a private California-based investment banking firm specializing in mergers and acquisitions. Giannini knows well that proper preparation won't preclude the pitfalls that plague the process of actually finding buyers or negotiating a deal. Rather, important considerations in preparing the company sale are ones that can and should be taken long before the selling process begins. The following considerations are helpful in preparing the company for sale.

> Buyers are often suspicious of sellers, as they should be, and have a keen interest in investigating every item on the seller's balance sheet.

Clean Up the Balance Sheet

Buyers are often suspicious of sellers, as they should be, and have a keen interest in investigating every item on the seller's balance sheet. A seller may be perfectly innocent and even oblivious to balance sheet matters that will not only disturb the buyer but also cause him to question what else there is on the balance sheet that is questionable.

Once a seller shows the buyer the balance sheet, there should be no more adjustments. For example, the seller may have built up a surplus of assets over the years, including excess cash, stocks and bonds, real estate, automobiles, and life insurance policies. The seller should consult with his attorney and accountant and "dividend out" the excess cash and distribute the other items to himself before proceeding with the buyers. The buyer wants to be presented with a balance sheet that is not subject to drastic changes prior to closing.

Continuing down the balance sheet, if there are any accounts receivable from officers or shareholders of the company, they should be collected or finalized before proceeding with a buyer. If receivables are uncollectible, they should be written off and if receivables are over ninety days old, the seller should establish a reserve.

Inventory can be a substantial asset; the outdated portion should be sold or written off. The buyers' due diligence team will identify obsolete inventory very quickly.

If the seller has used unrealistic depreciation rates for the machinery and equipment, there should be an adjustment made. Also, if the seller has intellectual property that he wants to retain personally, the transfer should be made before the company is placed on the market.

If there are unrecognized losses or potential losses such as litigation, establish a reserve on the balance sheet in anticipation of losses. On the right side of the balance sheet, the seller should tidy up these items as well. For example, when accounts payable are in dispute, the matter should be settled. Shareholder loans either should be paid up or converted to equity. After all, such loans reflect poorly on the business and imply that family favoritism is the company norm. It is neater to consolidate various bank loans into one revolver note and one term note.

Audit the Financials

Most small businesses, except those that expect to go public, have their financial statements reviewed but not audited. Audited statements cost considerably more than reviews, perhaps $10,000 to $40,000 more depending on the size of the company. Audits verify the accounts receivable and payable and the inventory as well as some other items. Without an audit, you might just as well be selling a pig in a poke—there is no assurance that the figures on the balance sheet are totally accurate.

In the absence of audited financials, the buyer is apt to offer the seller less money for the company because he is not sure that financials are totally accurate. Alternatively, the buyer will insist that the seller have an audit anyway. Why give the buyer an opportunity to use the seller's unaudited statements as a negotiating tool to offer less?

Besides the audited financials, the buyer will expect to see real estate and machinery and equipment appraisals if the property and equipment are also being sold. The buyer will need such appraisals to line up his acquisition financing with his bank. Then, if the deal goes to a Purchase and Sale agreement stage, the buyer will probably get his own appraisals that he could use as negotiating tools.

Cleaning Up Your Balance Sheets

Whether it is a "stock" sale or an "asset" sale, a crucial reason for cleaning up the balance sheet is that the buyer will want to peg the purchase price to the selling company's book value or working capital.

As an example, let's say that the buyer and seller agree on a price of $5 million for the company on July 1, with a closing date of September 1. A lot can happen in sixty days, good or bad. If the book value was $2.5 million on July 1, then the purchase price is two times book value. If by September 1 the book value is only $2.3 million, then the purchase price is readjusted to $4.6 million.

Conversely, if the book value is higher, the purchase price is higher as well. If the buyer is not assuming 100 percent of the balance sheet, then both parties have to agree on a pro forma balance sheet that will address the adjustments at closing.

Cleaning up the balance will ultimately help the seller because the deal to sell a company often unravels when either the quality of assets or the quality of earnings are not verifiable.

Perform Tax Planning

Fred Corneel, the late Senior Partner of Sullivan & Worcester law firm in Boston, recently wrote: "Everyone involved in sales or mergers of businesses knows that there are important tax aspects which they will have to look at eventually. Unfortunately, eventually is often too late; the form of the transaction and its basic terms are no longer negotiable, important tax benefits are lost and major tax liabilities can no longer be avoided."

What does this mean in reality? If your company is a C corporation, for example, you better sell the "stock" instead of selling the "assets" because the latter will receive a double tax—once to the corporation and once to the shareholders. To defer capital gains taxes completely, consider a stock swap with a *Fortune* 500 company or an Employee Stock Option Plan (ESOP). On the other hand, you could consider a fully secured installment sale that would also defer the capital gains tax.

The point is to address the tax ramifications up-front so that a qualified tax attorney can help you alleviate the tax impact. As Fred Corneel said: "Taxes first."

> If your company is a C corporation, for example, you better sell the "stock" instead of selling the "assets" because the latter will receive a double tax.

Show Earnings

There are few apprehensions for a buyer greater than wondering if the company's earnings will continue after he has acquired the company. Have you ever seen a seller's projections that went anywhere but up? Furthermore, have you ever seen a company for sale that virtually shows no earnings until one "adds back" all the adjustments and bingo . . . the company shows a million dollars of cash flow?

Adding back excess owner's compensation is acceptable but when huge amounts of discretionary expenses are used to supplement lack of earnings, the buyer often becomes very uneasy. First, are these legitimate add-backs or did the entertainment add-backs really help make the "big-sales"? Second, is the seller really credible? If he cheats the government out of paying taxes, won't he also cheat the buyer, too?

There is nothing more powerful than showing solid, unimpeachable earnings to win the confidence and respect of buyers.

Round Out the Management Team

Many entrepreneurial owners who started their own business become accustomed to being a one-man band. Some of these smaller companies, between $5 to $20 million in sales, may be missing a chief financial officer, vice president of sales, or vice president of manufacturing. Without filling these positions either internally or externally, a buyer will perceive the management team to be thin. Buyers want to see a management team in place, not a retiring CEO who manages the company by himself.

Most buyers will want to talk to the management team before consummating a transaction. Therefore, the CEO/owner will have to confide with his senior managers about the probability of selling the company. Again, stay agreements for the management team should already be in place.

Establish a Valuation

A competitive valuation firm will do far more than to just place a price or price range on the selling company. The valuation process will enable the seller to receive industry comparisons of both private and public companies that will be helpful in the final negotiation process with buyers.

The valuation will not only give the seller a benchmark to use internally before the market ultimately determines the price, but it will also supply the seller with other information. For example, the valuation should highlight the value drivers and the risk factors, some of which might be addressed prior to selling the company. A value driver could be a successful joint venture with a *Fortune* 500 company or a unique patented technology. A risk factor could be customer concentration or a seasonal product.

Much of the valuation report, minus the actual concluding valuation assessment, can be used as part of the offering memorandum. It can also help position the company for sale by documenting the competition. This valuation report should have an objective comparison of the competitors' similarities and differences, strengths, and weaknesses. As someone said: "Information is all-powerful."

"Work Yourself out of a Job"

Geoffrey Dalton, author of *What Is Your Business Worth?*, has firm advice for the business owner who is halfway out the door:

"Your aim should be to work yourself out of a job, to become a non-executive chairman; ideally, by training others to take over most of your functions and decision-making," Dalton says. "You must insist that your managers, in turn, groom other employees to cover for them. A clear succession line in the company with well-trained, flexible employees is a significant advantage to offer a purchase."

Examine Long-Term Contracts

Take another look at long-term contracts. Where the timing is propitious, you should renegotiate the terms or extend these contracts if it is favorable to you. Where a particular contract could prove expensive, consider ways of minimizing or containing that risk.

Let's assume you own a restaurant chain in a major city. Obviously, the leases are the critical component to the value of the chain. If you can extend the lease on good terms and negotiate the leases to be transferable, then your chances of selling the chain at your desired price is far greater.

> Buyers are usually very experienced, knowledgeable, and excellent negotiators.

Assemble a Professional Transaction Team

Selling a business is no place for amateurs. Not only is there too much at stake financially but the process can be confusing, complex, and challenging. Additionally, buyers are usually very experienced, knowledgeable, and excellent negotiators. Furthermore, sellers are often approached by bona fide buyers before they are ready to go to market with their company.

Preparing yourself to sell your company should include a careful analysis of the best investment banker or merger and acquisition intermediary for your business, plus an experienced transaction attorney. Don't forget to check references, not just the ones the professionals recommend to you.

Conclusion

If you study what went wrong in business sales gone sour, more often than not you will find that the seller did not begin early enough to prepare the ground for the eventual sale. Preparation won't guarantee success but will likely translate into better original offers and fewer unpleasant surprises down the road.

For more information on this topic, visit our Web site at www.businesstown.com

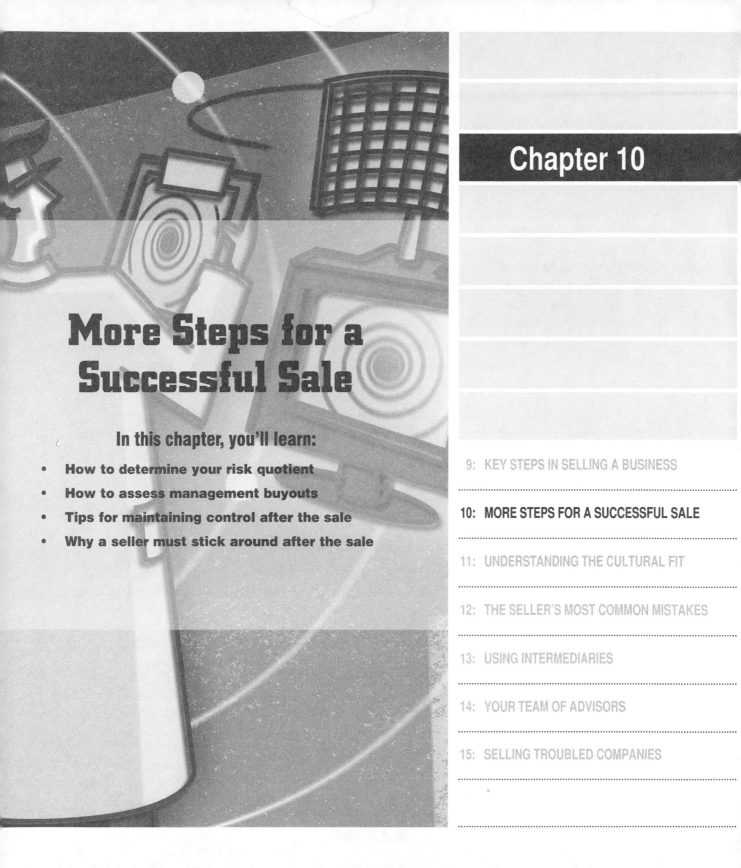

Chapter 13

More Steps for a Successful Sale

In this chapter, you'll learn:

- How to determine your risk quotient
- How to assess management buyouts
- Tips for maintaining control after the sale
- Why a seller must stick around after the sale

Chapter 10

ome years ago, a specialty materials company with proprietary products was brought to market by a prestigious investment banker. This selling company, with a $3 million EBIT, was very desirable. According to a survey published at that time by Securities Data Publishing, the average EBIT multiples for financial buyers was 7.1 compared to nine for strategic buyers. Based on the above, one might assume that a financial buyer would pay approximately $21.3 million compared to a strategic buyer's price of approximately $27 million.

Interestingly, the seller insisted that the investment banker approach financial buyers almost exclusively. So the banker contacted thirty-one financial buyers and only one strategic buyer. Why would the seller subject himself to the strong possibility of perhaps leaving $5.7 million on the table? While money was important to the seller, it was not paramount. The seller was very concerned about the future of his employees and management team.

Characteristically, financial buyers leave employees and the management team in place, while strategic buyers generally eliminate those who do not fit into the combined companies. This chapter is about the seven different implications—different objectives and different results—in selling a business.

> Characteristically, financial buyers leave employees and the management team in place, while strategic buyers generally eliminate those who do not fit into the combined companies.

Go for Top Price at All Costs

Conceptually, one would think that the main objective would be to receive the highest price for the company being sold. The highest price, however, may not be acceptable based on the currency and/or terms and conditions. As pointed out earlier, selling a business is unlike selling real estate in which the transaction is usually all cash at closing based on equity and a mortgage from the bank.

If you were willing to accept 100 percent stock from the acquiring company, you probably would be able to receive a price 50 percent higher than an all-cash offer. Furthermore, if you were willing to accept an offer with 50 percent cash, 25 percent in buyer's notes, and 25 percent in a non-compete and consulting agreement, then you probably would be able to receive a price 20 percent higher than an all-cash offer.

If you want the top price for your business, then you have to be open to terms that allow the buyer to pay for the company over time or with contingencies such as a partial earn-out.

Another scenario is to state up front that you want all cash at closing. If you want to receive the top price for an all-cash deal, there may be some other conditions you may find unpalatable such as the following:

- A strict Representation and Warranty Agreement
- An escrow account by the buyer withholding partial payment for a year or more until he is satisfied there is no breach in the Purchase and Sale Agreement
- The insistence that you remain with the company for another year to run it
- The acquirer's intent to move the company and discharge most of the employees

Keep Non-Price Considerations in Mind

The seller wants a full price, which normally means the company should be sold to a strategic buyer. However, one strategic buyer that offers $30 million and plans to move the business and replace management may be less desirable than a $27 million offer in which everything is left in place.

Many owners of private companies, particularly the founders, regard their business as their life's work. While receiving a full price is important, there are other considerations including the following:

- What is the chemistry between the principal of the acquiring entity and the perceived business philosophy and vision of the acquiring company?
- How willing is the buyer to retain most of the employees post-acquisition, particularly if some of them are family members of the seller?
- Will the buyer retain the owner as a consultant after the sale, respectfully acknowledging the importance of the owner's advice?

Public Stock, Private Cash

Have you noticed that when public companies acquire other public companies, they generally use cash or stock for currency, while small private companies are acquired with a variety of currencies including notes, consulting agreements, contingencies? There are a number of reasons for this difference.

Instead of audited accounting statements, small companies have "reviews" or "compilations" in which items such as inventory, receivables, and payables are not verified. As a result, the buyer is less sure of the accuracy of the financials so he is not as confident in paying all cash at closing.

Secondly, small companies are usually dependent on few key management people and are apt to have a customer concentration issue resulting in a less stable business. A buyer likes the security of holding back some of the cash payment at closing in case the business does not go well after closing.

What Is the Willingness to Take Risks?

The seller may be in an adverse situation in which there is extreme customer concentration, weak or retiring management, or other mitigating circumstances. In these cases, strategic buyers will often back off, but a large competitor will be less concerned with such matters when rolled into the total package.

Trying to sell to a competitor, however, is fraught with risk—risk that the buyer will renege on his initial offer, will walk away with a stack of competitive information, or will be turned down by an adverse antitrust ruling.

Some years ago, I was retained to sell a profitable bulletin board manufacturer that sold products to superstores and school supply distributors. The manufacturer had sales of about $20 million with more than 50 percent of its volume to one office superstore chain.

The owner wanted all cash at closing. While there were interested buyers, both strategic and financial, none were willing to pay a full price with all cash because of the high customer concentration. There seemed to be only one alternative left, which was to approach the manufacturer's number one competitor, albeit a much larger bulletin board producer with $125 million in sales. The company was of interest to the larger competitor because it gave the competitor immediate sales to the large superstore which it had been unable to penetrate. A nice bonus was that the competitor could eliminate the ongoing threat of my client.

We took the chance and approached the competitor regarding our interest in selling to them. The customer concentration issue was not much of an issue for a company that was six times the size. After one aborted attempt to sell to the competitor, the transaction was successfully completed at a satisfactory price, plus it was an all-cash sale. The moral: sometimes risks must be taken in selling a company, especially if the circumstances leave you with little other choice.

> Sometimes risks must be taken in selling a company, especially if the circumstances leave you with little other choice.

A Responsible Buyer but a Lower Price

A financial buyer traditionally does not pay the top price, but usually improves the company's profitability by making some changes, often including the replacement of some management. While the status quo is more or less the same, the financial buyer's modus operandi is to resell the company (usually to a strategic buyer) in five to seven years, during which the operating management may have obtained 20 to 25 percent ownership.

The advantages of selling to a financial buyer, commonly known as a private equity group, are as follows:

- They usually will consummate a transaction faster than other buyers.
- They are expert, experienced, and knowledgeable deal makers who are motivated to close deals. Their mantra is buying and selling companies that require them to be more acquisitive than other types of buyers.
- They are often receptive to leaving some equity with the sellers so the former owners can participate in the future upside or offer the new management team an ownership stake.
- They can invigorate the company with a fresh perspective by implementing a new board of directors.
- They have ready access to capital to support future growth.

Assessing Management Buyouts

A management buyout (MBO) yields the least monetary reward to the owner. However, if the company has significant customer concentration or acute technology dependence on management, the best alternative might be an MBO. Because existing management is usually underfinanced, it is common for the seller to take back paper as a majority of the purchase price.

The two critical aspects in a successful MBO are the competence and depth of the management team and the identification of the right sponsor (private equity group) to match the MBO's criteria. Private equity groups have changed in recent years, and many of them have industry specialties. If management solicits private equity groups to sponsor a buyout, management hopefully will have considered all the angles and developed a realistic exit strategy.

Through proper networking, the management team should be able to identify groups that focus on the particular industry. Other

> A management buyout (MBO) yields the least monetary reward to the owner.

important factors in considering a sponsor is their chemistry, integrity, and willingness to work through problems.

Management should try to work with the company's owners in a nonconfrontational way and both sides should try to reach a fair price. There is always the implied threat that if management cannot work out a deal with the owners, management will leave the company. The owners usually feel motivated to sell the company to management: It is an honorable exit strategy and management is more likely to retain the company's legacy with minimal disruption.

When the Seller Maintains Control After the Sale

Re-capitalizations are a way for the owner to pay out a significant part of the company's worth by leveraging the balance sheet. Of course, such financial engineering places considerable pressure on existing management.

The private initial public offering (IPO), originated by Heritage Partners of Boston, is a unique refinement of the regular re-capitalization. It works as follows: The owner is paid for 100 percent of the company but is then required to reinvest on a tax-deferred basis. Heritage invests a layer of preferred stock. The remaining cash is obtained through a modest layer of senior debt. Down the road, assuming that Heritage prospers, the seller gets a major "second bite of the apple," cashing out again at a substantial gain.

Another private equity group that specializes in re-capitalizations is Florida Capital Partners (FCP) of Tampa. Their structure for deals has three primary components: an all-cash price for the company, large equity participations for the owner/operators who continue to run the company, and access to non-dilutive equity from FCP to help the company grow.

The above structure allows the owner/operators to take cash out of their business without giving up operating control. FCP structures its re-capitalizations so that additional add-on equity from the fund does not dilute management's common ownership or require additional equity investments from the management team.

The Executive with the Right MBO Stuff

Here is a quick profile sketch of an effective management buyout leader, according to MBO consultants:

- He has a proven track record in a large company or major division as chief executive officer, president, or general manager, with bottom line responsibility.

- He knows the target company is available for acquisition.

- He has in-depth knowledge of the industry in which the acquisition is to be made.

- He can assemble a top management team to operate the acquired company.

- He has a burning desire to build a successful business.

When the Seller Must Stick Around After the Sale

Michael Selz, a staff reporter for the *Wall Street Journal*, once wrote: "The only way the owners are going to get a premium for their companies is to hang in there for a while and make sure everything goes well. Many prospective sellers want to cash out and walk. Some buyers will not acquire a company unless the owner has a substantial stake in the company's performance for at least two years."

The unwillingness or inability of many buyers to come up with all the cash at closing is forcing a growing number of sellers to stick around for years after a sale so they can ultimately receive a higher price for the companies. In a survey of more than fifty relatively small deals by the Institute of Mergers and Acquisitions Professionals, nearly three-fourths of sellers said they stayed on as consultants.

For some private equity groups, small businesses will be purchased only if the owner has a substantial stake in the company's performance for at least two years.

> For some private equity groups, small businesses will be purchased only if the owner has a substantial stake in the company's performance for at least two years.

Conclusion

A good rule of thumb to keep in mind is that financial buyers leave employees and the management team in place, while strategic buyers eliminate those who do not fit into the strategic direction of the combined companies. On the other hand, selling to a financial buyer will leave a business seller with the least amount of cash at the end of the day.

Besides money, cultural compatibility is a major factor to consider when putting a business on the market. The next chapter will deal with culture clash, and how to avoid it.

For more information on this topic, visit our Web site at www.businesstown.com

Understanding the Cultural Fit

In this chapter, you'll learn:

- How to look for cultural differences
- Hidden reasons why mergers and acquisitions fail
- Deciding whether or not cultures fit

It's Easier to Swallow a Guppy

When a large company such as General Electric acquires a small company with $10 to $20 million in sales, the small company is expected to accept the culture of the significantly larger company. Larger acquisitions, and mergers or acquisitions of companies of near-equal size, pose a much larger problem in terms of culture and integration.

"We've made three or four small acquisitions over the course of the last couple of years, technology and corporate acquisitions," says Katherine Catlin and Jana Matthews in their book *Leading at the Speed of Growth*. "The small ones were really easy. We just absorbed them into the company. That was no problem. Then we made a big one last year. And we have required massive doses of Pepto-Bismol to digest that acquisition. It really has accelerated a transformation in the company that we intended to go through, but I think we didn't realize just how large and how difficult that was going to be."

It is common knowledge that too many mergers and acquisitions fail to produce the expected synergies and results, and "culture" is usually cited as the problem. John Chambers, Chief Executive Officer of Cisco Systems, has overseen seventy acquisitions, and he clearly states that he will not do an acquisition unless there is a cultural fit with the seller. But, as a seller, why should you care if there is a compatible cultural fit or not?

The importance of the cultural fit depends on the characteristics of the seller and the structure of the deal. One scenario is that you sell the company for 100 percent cash and do not care what subsequently happens to the company, its employees, customers, or vendors. In other words, you take the money and run. In this case, this is little concern about cultural compatibility.

Another scenario is that you sell the company for mostly cash so you feel secure that you have been able to get the best deal, from your point of view, at the time of the sale. You are, however, very concerned about the future of your employees and the likelihood that they will be let go under the new ownership.

The third and final scenario is that you merge your company or receive stock in the acquirer's company. Assuming your company is a meaningful entity in the combined business, the value of your compensation is somewhat dependent on how well the cultures mesh. As I mentioned earlier, the success or failure of a merger or acquisition is greatly affected by acceptance of the dominant company's culture or the ability to meld the two different cultures.

The classic case of how cultural friction erodes the ability of two companies to effectively work together is the infamous Daimler-Chrysler merger. Promoted as the "merger of equals," in which Daimler owned 53 percent and Chrysler owned 47 percent of the combined entity, the Germans completely took control and the American management team left in droves.

Some of the obvious cultural disparities included huge compensation packages for the American executives while the German executives were paid rather modestly but received enormous company perks. Perhaps the greater rift between the two cultures was the different management styles: decentralized versus centralized; quick decisions by management versus methodical decisions by committee; supplier rivalries versus supplier partnerships. The Daimler-Chrysler merger will be a case study at many MBA programs as to how the two companies were unable to resolve their cultural differences, which led to enormous loss of shareholder value.

Looking for the Cultural Differences

One way to determine whether the cultures of the two companies are compatible or not is to spend some time with the potential acquirers asking questions and probing accordingly. For example, here are some questions and considerations:

How do you go about making important decisions: by presidential edict, consensus of senior management, consulting a few employees?

How do you compensate employees: arbitrarily, defined salary, salary and bonus combined?

What is the nature of the business: entrepreneurial or hierarchal, team- or individually oriented, customer- or policy-driven?

What is your product return policy: lenient or strict?

There are some companies whose cultural styles are so different that it is not feasible to try to work out a common ground. There are a few companies whose cultural styles are so similar that a union between both businesses is idyllic. And then there are a majority of the companies that have different cultural styles; in those cases, extensive communication and proper counseling can make a merger or acquisition possible.

Assuming that you decide to sell or merge with another company, the critical stage of blending the cultures is during the integration period. Culture is considered one of the "soft" issues in the merger and acquisition process, which includes the following: marketing and customer focus; style of communication; corporate mission; methods of problem-solving; company values; constructive leadership; overall strategy; collaborative work habits, cultural environment; and continuous learning.

> Assuming that you decide to sell or merge with another company, the critical stage of blending the cultures is during the integration period.

Deciding Whether or Not Cultures Fit

Let's suppose that you are selling your relatively small family business. While you have taught your employees skills, you have not taught them values. Your company's cultural values of how people behave and operate have spread by example. You are very concerned about how the two companies will collaborate when and if you sell to the larger corporation.

Knowing that it is almost impossible to communicate too much, you spend as much time as you can negotiating with the acquiring company, particularly the decision makers. Ideally, the acquirer has completed other acquisitions so you can personally visit the managers of these companies to understand how well or poorly their cultures meshed with your prospective acquirer. If you are in a niche industry, chances are that the industry acquirer has created a particular reputation among its peers. Determine your acquirer's reputation through peers.

Deconstructing Corporate Culture

There are several models that attempt to explain the dynamics of a company's culture. The Hofstede Cultural Orientation Model classifies cultures based on where they fall on five continuums:

1. Individual versus Collective Orientation: Level at which behavior is appropriately regulated.
2. Power-Distance Orientation: Extent to which less powerful parties accept the existing distribution of power and the degree to which adherence to formal channels is maintained.
3. Uncertainty-Avoidance Orientation: Degree to which employees are threatened by ambiguity, and the relative importance to employees of rules, long-term employment, and an obvious career path.
4. Dominant-Values Orientation: Nature of dominant values, such as assertiveness, monetary focus, and gender roles, versus concern for others, focus on quality of relationships and job satisfaction, and flexibility.
5. Short-Term versus Long-Term Orientation: Short-term time frame involves more inclination toward consumption and saving face. Long-term time frame involves the preservation of status-based relationships, thrift, and deferred gratifications.

If you expect your company to be left alone as an autonomous unit in which your sales force is given incentives on your terms, then you have to specifically nail down items of this nature post-acquisition. Generally, merging companies that run into cultural differences have rushed to closing too quickly in order to complete the transaction expeditiously.

For example, let us assume that you are talking to the chief executive officer of the acquiring company and your major concern is the process in which certain issues will be resolved. You ask these questions:

- What happens if we make different assumptions on critical issues such as the best market to pursue?
- What happens if we have different perceptions as to the best technology for certain applications?
- What happens if you have different ways to offer incentives to employees?

The response to these questions will in part tell you if the process, also considered the culture, will be compatible with the way you are accustomed to handling these matters.

> Generally, merging companies that run into cultural differences have rushed to closing too quickly in order to complete the transaction expeditiously.

Conclusion

Hopefully, cultural harmony will be successfully achieved. There are some consulting firms that advise and orchestrate the integration of businesses with emphasis on cultural issues. Often it is beneficial to have a third-party consultant lead the two entities in blending their operations harmoniously to achieve full potential.

For more information on this topic, visit our Web site at www.businesstown.com

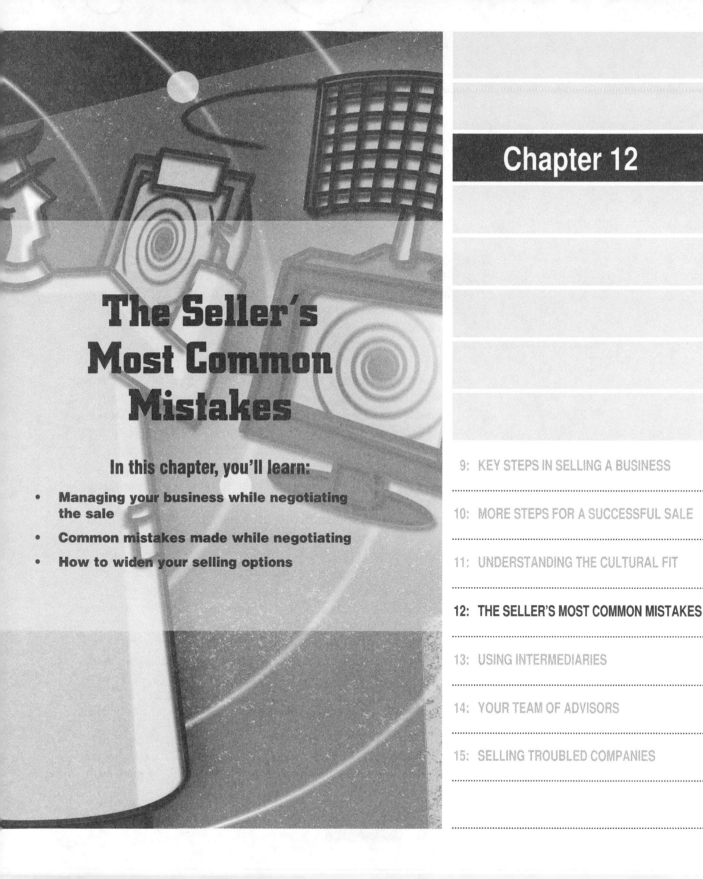

The Seller's Most Common Mistakes

Chapter 12

In this chapter, you'll learn:

- **Managing your business while negotiating the sale**

- **Common mistakes made while negotiating**

- **How to widen your selling options**

As emphasized in Chapter 2, sellers who are often inexperienced in selling companies are prone to making mistakes. Here are some potential bloopers, including how to avoid them and what to do if you make them.

Neglecting to Run Your Business

Selling your business is emotional and distracting. It is very important to retain professional advisors, including an investment banker to do the "heavy lifting" when selling a business. Do not neglect to run your business, or sales and earnings will deteriorate and the potential buyers will back off.

Sellers should anticipate the buyers' intensified interest in tracking the company's performance, particularly after the Letter of Intent has been signed by both parties. Most buyers are apprehensive about their impending purchase, wondering if sales and earnings will continue upward as assured by the seller. In fact, many transactions are aborted between the Letter of Intent and the closing if, during the short span of sixty to ninety days, the business deteriorates. The buyer often gets cold feet and loses faith in the viability of the business. For his part, the seller feels the pressure of the buyer during the due diligence phase, which results in careful scrutiny by the acquirer's advisors. Prior to the Letter of Intent, buyers are usually content to receive quarterly financials from the seller, but as the due diligence commences, the buyer puts the company under a microscope and often requires monthly financials to be sure the company is on track, and will then often ask for weekly sales figures.

There are a number of ways to avoid neglecting your business at the same that you are trying to sell it:

> **Do not rush the decision to sell your business.** Instead, wait until you have both your personal life and business sufficiently organized so that when you decide to sell the company, you can devote the necessary time to focus on this very important project.

> **Realize that while selling a company is usually a clandestine event, it is too difficult to do successfully by yourself.**

> Sellers should anticipate the buyers' intensified interest in tracking the company's performance, particularly after the Letter of Intent has been signed by both parties.

Make one or more of your trusted senior managers, particularly the chief financial officer, your confidant in the selling process and award him monetarily with a stay agreement if he keeps all confidential matters confidential, and if he stays with the company until it is sold. Customarily, stay agreements amount to an equivalent of three to six months of annual salary.

Retain an investment banker to represent you in the sale of the company so that the major part of the selling process is the role of the investment banker. Aside from the need to keep the sales confidential, the investment banker is charged with doing most of the work, thus allowing you to focus on running the company.

Understand that if you allow too many prospective buyers to visit your business, it will be a huge distraction and will affect the way you run the business. You also risk a break of confidentiality. Make sure the investment banker screens the buyers properly so that no more than three to six candidates visit the facilities, usually after receiving an indication of their valuing of the business based on the offering memorandum.

> Understand that if you allow too many prospective buyers to visit your business, it will be a huge distraction and will affect the way you run the business.

Suppose that, for whatever reason, you have neglected your business, and sales, earnings, and backlog have dropped off. There is no set answer to this problem because it depends on various factors, including how far along you are in the selling process, how badly the business has deteriorated, the circumstances related to the downturn, and whether or not you are willing to compromise on the price or terms.

Hopefully, you can persuade the potential buyer that this is just a short-term matter and that the situation will be corrected shortly. If the buyer does not accept this reasoning, you can lower the price or adjust the terms of the sale with a performance clause based on increased sales or earnings. If all else fails, simply take the company off the market until the business turns around.

Placing Too High a Price on Your Business

Many sellers dream about their company's worth based on their "sweat equity" or Wall Street comparisons. The merger and acquisition marketplace is fairly efficient, although it is not formalized like the real estate industry in which all sales are public knowledge and all properties have assessed values.

Placing too high a price on the business, however, can be a mistake. If the company does not sell in a reasonable period of time, the business becomes shopworn and tarnished. There is a greater risk of confidentiality being breached the longer the business is on the market. A higher price often requires the buyer to use greater leverage, thus possibly jeopardizing the debt payments or the seller's notes. For a variety of reasons, it is usually best for the seller to arrive at a win/win arrangement with the buyer.

One way to avoid placing too high a price on your business is to initially receive a formal valuation by a competent business appraiser. Of course, setting a price on your business is not to be announced to buyers but rather to be used in your negotiating process. Surveys show that half of the time owners have an unrealistically high asking price, and the other half of the time it is far too low. Without a professional opinion for reference, owners cannot begin to discuss or justify a selling price that makes sense.

A thorough valuation will probably cost between $10,000 to $20,000—maybe more, maybe less, depending on the size of the company. The valuation should include comparisons of other companies in your specific industry, adjusted to equalize the comparison such as size or growth rate. The valuation should use different methodologies and should include value drivers and risk factors of the business.

If you have set too high a price on your business based on offers you are receiving from potential buyers, there are a number of choices for you. You can lower your price or become more generous on the terms by offering some sort of "earn-out." Alternatively, you can take the company off the market until your company's earnings have improved and then go back to market with the same price. Or, you can reassess your buyer's list and go further afield to seek out buyers abroad on the assumption that they may be willing to pay more than those buyers whom you have already contacted.

The Not-So-Overnight Success

Once your business is placed on the market, it will take about one year to find a buyer and complete the deal. If you are planning to sell to family members or key managers, the creative methods to save money and taxes can take up to five years to put into place.

For these reasons, planning for a business sale should begin two years in advance, if possible. The quickie, six-month deal is possible, but it is more likely that without sufficient leadtime, you will not receive market value for the business but instead feel pressured to cut a deal, any deal.

Not Reminding the Buyer of the Confidentiality Requirement

Maintaining confidentiality should be more than just having the buyer sign a confidentiality agreement. A premature breach of confidentiality can blow the deal. The seller should continually remind potential buyers of the confidentiality requirement and take all precautions accordingly. For example, the relevant mail should be addressed to his or her home instead of the office.

One can never overemphasize the importance of confidentiality with the buyer. There are ways to mitigate the possible breach of confidentiality, such as only approaching a handful of buyers or only contacting financial buyers or buyers outside a certain geographic area. Another way to lessen the chance of a confidentiality leak is to shorten the time frame in which the company is on the market. Sellers should realize that it is not just the buyer who might reveal that the company is for sale; it may happen internally when a secretary inadvertently opens a letter marked "personal and confidential." A precautionary step is to tell the buyer to dress down when visiting the company and to visit under the aegis of a potential customer.

There is the distinct possibility that in fact word does leak out that the company is for sale. It should not happen if the precautionary steps have been adhered to, but mistakes do happen. Here are a few suggestions that may apply to certain breaches:

> Speed up the selling process.

> Take the company off the market.

> Publicly announce the company is for sale but will definitely not go out of business, and that under new ownership to a larger entity the company will be stronger.

> Deny the company is for sale but that you are seeking minority investors for a re-capitalization in order to strengthen the company financially.

One can never over-emphasize the importance of confidentiality with the buyer.

Selling Impulsively

The purported number one reason for owners of private companies to sell their businesses is burnout. The tendency is for the owner to work like a dog until he or she "hits the wall"—then to sell out immediately. Time out! Do not sell impulsively.

Ideally, the owner will plan ahead carefully by cleaning up the balance sheet, settling all litigation, solving environmental problems, and paying the extra money for audited financial statements one or two years in advance of selling. As discussed earlier, the latter move could increase the company's value by up to 20 percent by generating "believable" financials.

To avoid selling impulsively, start thinking of your exit strategy almost as soon as you either start or either buy the company. While we all change our minds from time to time, the mere process of trying to think through how and when you might exit the business gives you a better chance of arriving at a pragmatic decision than to just leave the outcome to fate.

Not Anticipating the Requests of Buyers

Many sellers will not anticipate the requests of the buyers. Lack of anticipation in most endeavours is dangerous, whether it is in warfare, sports, chess, or business. Selling a business is no different.

Put yourself in the buyer's shoes. He or she would probably want to see a complete description of the company before he or she determines whether to spend the time and effort pursuing this opportunity. As a seller, you anticipate this need, so you retain an investment banker and have him prepare an offering memorandum. As a seller, you anticipate that the potential buyer will want to visit the facilities. You know that first impressions are very important, so you clean up the plant, warehouse, and office to project the image of pride and efficiency. As a seller who owns a manufacturing plant, you anticipate that the potential buyer will be concerned about environmental matters, so you have an environmental assessment of the property.

Widening Your Selling Options

Selling the company to a third party is not your only existing strategy, so consider the following options so as to avoid selling impulsively:

Sell the company to your employees through an Employee Stock Option Plan (ESOP).

Sell the company to your management team, commonly known as a Management Buyout (MBO).

Sell the company to your family heirs.

Keep the company but hire a professional management team.

Keep the company, recapitalize it in order to take some "money off the table," and hire a professional management team.

Go public and retire.

Neither sell nor keep the company but liquidate it.

Acquirers usually require bank financing and that means appraisals of the property–the machinery and the equipment. Both of these items take time, so have it done before the seller goes to market.

Negotiating with Only One Buyer

Negotiating with only one buyer at a time is frequently the choice of the seller who finds it too confusing to negotiate with two or more potential buyers at one time. This is a big mistake because the seller loses the leverage of competitive offers when only dealing with one buyer at a time.

To avoid dealing with only one potential buyer, consider retaining an investment bank that is charged with the role of surfacing multiple buyers in order to create competitive bidding. "Many owners think the best buyer is a local competitor, customer, supplier, or employee," says Lawrence Marziale, partner in Kostin Ruffkess & Co., in West Hartford, Connecticut. "Often, the best buyer is someone looking to enter a marketplace. Thousands of very quiet, private investment groups and offshore investors are interested in acquiring profitable, private, U.S.–based companies."

If, however, you have failed to negotiate with more than one buyer, then your fallback position is to be coy and imply that, while you would like to sell the business, you do not *have* to sell it, and that you will just hold out until you get a deal that is the right price and terms.

Not Sticking Around After the Deal

Sellers usually want to retire after selling their business, although that is often not in their financial self-interest. According to Michael Selz, staff reporter of the *Wall Street Journal*, owners will receive considerably more money if they are willing to stick around after the deal. Selz cited a specific example of a seller receiving 20 percent more for his business because, by staying aboard, it helped reduce the risk to the new owner.

> Thousands of very quiet, private investment groups and offshore investors are interested in acquiring profitable, private, U.S.–based companies.

The implication is fairly obvious: if you would like to retire at sixty-five years old, you should plan four years ahead of the retirement date. For example, it will take one year to prepare for the sale, in order to arrange for audited statements, various appraisals, and stay agreements. It will take another year for the investment bank to sell the business, and up to two years of your continued employment.

Being Inflexible with the Structure of the Transaction

Naturally, most sellers want all cash at closing, but it is estimated that only one-third of middle-market transactions are structured that way. In many deals, the structure is more important than the price, so if a seller is inflexible on structure, it can be a major obstacle and most likely a deal breaker.

Another way to analyze whether you should be flexible with the structure of the transaction is to look at the alternatives. Suppose you were to receive offers by the same buyer as follows, which would you accept?

$10 million for the acquirer's stock

$9 million (half in cash; half in unsecured notes)

$8 million (half in cash; half in secured obligations)

$7 million (all cash but hefty escrow accounts and tight representations and warranties)

$6 million (all cash, no escrow accounts, no representations and warranties)

The above is a hypothetical case whereby a buyer might offer ten times EBIT of $1 million, or $10 million for stock and as low as six times EBIT, or $6 million for all cash. As a seller, you will be faced with a decision on a risk/reward basis: the higher the risk, the higher the reward. There is no correct answer; it depends on the individual seller.

> Another way to analyze whether you should be flexible with the structure of the transaction is to look at the alternatives.

A seller could charge the buyer more for the C corporation if it is an asset sale in order to allow for the additional capital gains tax. The buyer usually will want to acquire the company's assets, not its stock, in order to avoid prior liabilities and to be able to mark up the assets to fair market value for depreciation purposes.

Being a Nitpicking Negotiator

Negotiating every item, or almost every item, is much less effective than keeping your powder dry for the more important issues. If a seller tries to win every point of contention, the buyer may just walk away from the deal. Most successful transactions are a win/win scenario for both parties.

There is an old expression in the merger and acquisition business that says the buyer usually pays more for the company than he or she intends; and the seller usually sells for less than he or she expects. Another way to look at it for buyers: "You may be paying more than you think it's worth, but you'll find that you're actually getting more than you pay for."

About ten years ago, the chief executive officer of the prestigious BankBoston was charged by his board of directors to acquire other regional banks during the height of the bank consolidations. The executive tried on numerous occasions to acquire other banks, but ultimately failed. The rumor was that BankBoston's CEO was inflexible and insisted on prevailing on each and every issue of the negotiations. Soon after, the CEO was asked to retire and Fleet Bank acquired BankBoston.

It is almost impossible to win every point in a negotiation and if one does win every point, the deal could eventually haunt the entity that prevailed. Just remember the Treaty of Versailles, which ended World War I but led to World War II.

> If a seller tries to win every point of contention, the buyer may just walk away from the deal.

Letting the Deal Drag

Some sellers want to take their time throughout the selling process, probably because they equate length of time with being careful.

Jack Kellogg, an experienced transaction attorney, states that deals that drag tend not to close. When the company is in play, move quickly for the close.

There are a number of reasons why closing quickly is advantageous to the seller. By entering into a Letter of Intent with the buyer, the seller by agreement takes the company "off the market" and cannot discuss the situation with any other potential buyer. If, for any reason, the deal is aborted, it is difficult to entice the previous suitors to regenerate their interest. Therefore, the Letter of Intent should be in the thirty to forty-five day period, and not over sixty days.

Furthermore, the longer the deal takes to close, the more likely it becomes that the buyer will discover items that he or she does not like about the company and either want to renegotiate or kill the deal. Remember that only 50 percent of deals close after the Letter of Intent is signed, so do not dilly-dally.

Remember that only 50 percent of deals close after the Letter of Intent is signed, so do not dilly-dally.

Not Using Experienced Professional Advisors

According to Chris Mercer of Mercer Capital Advisors of Memphis, Tennessee:

Naïve sellers often make mistakes, and mistakes cost far more than the expense of competent advisors. The objective is to make the right deal including both price and terms. Your advisors can keep sellers informed about what the comparable sellers are doing, both from direct experience and research. Their knowledge of the market can be invaluable in helping close transactions successfully. A seller and/or his or her advisors should be able to articulate the valuation rationale and negotiate from it—rather than merely arguing 'higher' and 'lower,' which is a loser's game. In other words, if comparable companies are selling at six times EBITDA and the buyer is offering 4.5 times EBITDA, that is a substantial difference. The common mistake is often that the seller is not fully educated to the market conditions.

Failing to Conduct Proper Due Diligence on the Buyer

Due diligence is not only legal and financial research but also operational. The last thing a seller wants is for the new owner to run the business into the ground, because that would make it more difficult for the seller to collect the outstanding amount of the purchase price.

Conclusion

Realism and clear-eyed thinking must rule. The seller must be realistic about the value of the company, and his or her ability to handle both the negotiations and the daily running of the business. Professional help is available and should usually be exploited.

Professional help is available and should usually be exploited.

For more information on this topic, visit our Web site at www.businesstown.com

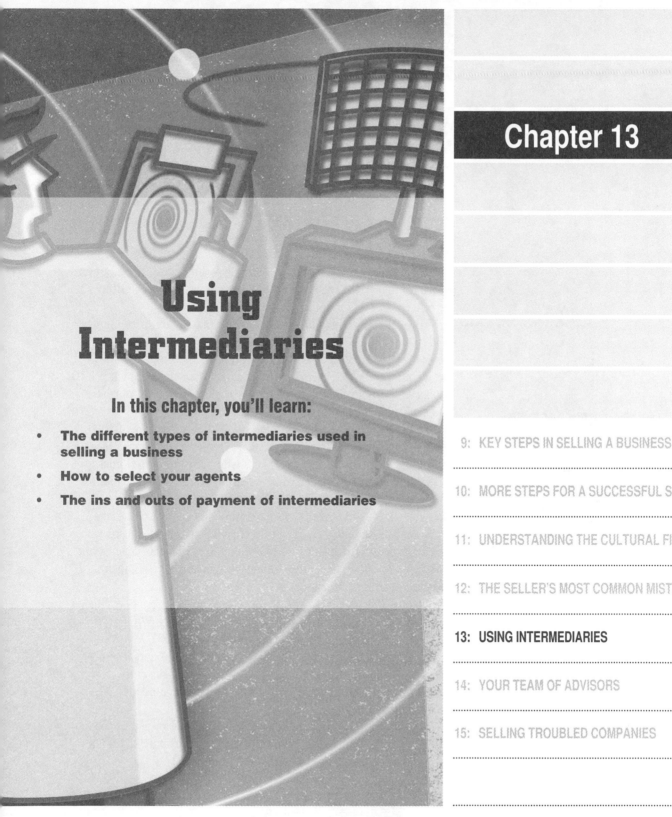

Chapter 13

Using Intermediaries

In this chapter, you'll learn:

- The different types of intermediaries used in selling a business
- How to select your agents
- The ins and outs of payment of intermediaries

*I*ntermediary*, in the merger and acquisition business, is a broad term for an agent, someone who represents the buyer or seller in the purchase or sale of a business. The following are my explanations of the various categories:

The Business Broker

A business broker is a person engaged in selling small businesses—those with sales under $3 million annually—who operates without an up-front retainer but with a fairly high accomplishment fee (10 to 12 percent) if the transaction closes.

Brokers serve the market in which businesses are priced under $500,000 with annual revenues of less than $750,000, and with fewer than ten employees. This category, which is commonly known as "Main Street USA," is comprised of small retail stores, quick print shops, landscapers, liquor stores, caterers, electricians, restaurants, and cleaners, among others.

American Business Information has estimated that as of 2000, there were about 3,400 business brokers in the United States. If we were to include the real estate brokers who occasionally sell businesses, the figure is substantially increased. The *Business Reference Guide*, published by Business Brokerage Press (BBP) of Concord, Massachusetts estimates that 40 percent of all business brokerage firms are sole practitioners, and that they sell about eight deals per year on average. The balance of the brokerage firms have agents, and BBP's survey shows that these offices have on average 4.5 agents completing six deals per year.

These brokers almost always represent the seller on an exclusive basis and have qualified them as bona fide sellers. While the financial information for these small businesses usually do not include formal balance sheets or reports from accountants, the brokers will provide an "asking price" usually based on the rule of thumb for that particular type of business, updated annually by the *Business Reference Guide*.

Inasmuch as these small businesses might sell for as little as $200,000, then the $20,000 plus commission is certainly justifiable,

> Brokers serve the market in which businesses are priced under $500,000 with annual revenues of less than $750,000, and with fewer than ten employees.

considering the effort and service the broker provides in the transactions. Since the broker is paid by the seller, his or her allegiance is with the client. Invariably, however, the broker seems to represent the deal because without a retainer, the broker must sell businesses in order to be paid.

How to Select a Business Broker

Just like a real estate agent, the business broker almost always represents the seller without an obligation of a retainer from either party. As a seller, you want to be very careful whom you select as a broker, especially if you are obligated under contract to give the broker an exclusive for more than three months at a time. The following six points represents a due diligence checklist which you should follow when selecting a broker:

1. **The office.** Is this a one-person operation, is it staffed by five or six people as "backups," or is it part of multi-office brokerage businesses? Look around the office to see if they have a secretary, computers, and faxes, as well as a conference room, literature, and other indicators of success. Can you select the broker in the office who you would like to represent you or is that not an option? Is the office geographically located near you?

2. **Experience.** Has the particular broker been trained in this business or has he or she learned the profession by observing others? Has the broker worked with other firms in this business, and if so, for how many years? Is the broker or rookie at age twenty-five or a professional at age fifty? How many clients does the broker have now? How many deals does the broker complete in a year?

3. **Quality of listings.** Ask to see a list of companies the brokerage firm sold last year and for a blind list of the companies they are now selling. If the list is predominantly retail stores and you are selling a small manufacturer, beware.

4. **References.** Usually every business has a couple of good references, so go beyond those suggested by the broker to find

As a seller, you want to be very careful whom you select as a broker, especially if you are obligated under contract to give the broker an exclusive for more than three months at a time.

out as much as you can about the broker's competence, reliability, and honesty.

5. **Valuation methodology.** Ask the broker to explain in detail how he or she values companies to see whether it is logical and whether you agree with the methodology. If the broker's valuation of your company is unrealistic, whether it is too high or too low, then you should probably find another broker.

6. **Licenses.** Depending on the state in which your business is located, there are different requirements for brokerage licenses, and if property is being sold then a real estate license is required. Check out the license requirements.

The M&A Intermediary

A merger and acquisition intermediary is a person engaged in both buying and selling businesses, usually with a relatively small retainer. This person usually focuses on the smaller size companies of the middle market with sales between $2 and $10 million, and will conduct corporate valuations but probably will not raise capital.

The process of selecting a merger and acquisition intermediary is virtually the same process as selecting an investment banker, discussed in the next section. The major difference between the two entities is that intermediaries work on smaller-sized transactions, receive smaller retainers, and have a different fee structure.

The Investment Banker

Often known as an I-banker, this person represents buyers and sellers, and offers related services such as conducting valuations and raising capital. I-bankers probably will receive higher retainers than M&A intermediaries, will belong to a firm of at least a half-dozen deal makers, and will work with companies ranging from $5 million in sales to *Fortune* 500 size.

You should be careful and pragmatic in selecting an intermediary. Often the selection of an investment banker, particularly if the

---

Where to Find Brokerage Firms

International Business Broker Association (IBBA): A national association that can refer you to various brokers in your geographic area. Telephone: 1-888-686-IBBA.

The New England Business Brokers Association (NEBBA): This is an example of one of many regional associations. Telephone: 978-263-5559.

Sunbelt Business Brokers is an example of one of many brokerage chains. Sunbelt is the largest chain with 200 offices in thirty-nine states. Telephone: 1-800-771-7861.

business is being sold, is by the board of directors, the company's advisors, and the principals of the business. Such a decision is frequently determined after a formal presentation is delivered to this group by each of the individual investment bankers. Usually three firms have been selected and quite often these firms have been recommended by the company's attorneys.

How to Select an I-Banker

The process for selecting an investment banker seems logical and straightforward. On the other hand, the selection of the investment banker is so critical to the success or failure of the impending transaction that often certain aspects of the decision are overlooked. The following ten points represent a due diligence checklist that you should follow when selecting an investment banker:

1. **The firm.** General reputation, number of years in existence, number of principals and support staff, international connections, and other outward signs of competence are considerations in selecting an investment banker. Of particular importance is the normal range of deal size the firm completes—a small transaction for a large investment banker might not get a buyer's attention, and a big transaction for a small investment banker could be beyond their expertise.

2. **The lead player.** Often the investment banker will state that the project is a team effort. However, there inevitably is a lead person who understands the bulk of the project. Of the ten criteria for selecting an investment banker, this is probably the most important. It is no different than selecting an attorney at a law firm, for example. Beware of an investment banker who customarily represents an acquiring company when your assignment is to sell a company. A deal is a deal, right? Wrong!

    Some investment bankers are better at acquiring companies than at selling them and vice versa. The techniques on the buy-side often take a more aggressive approach. The difference between buying and selling can be compared to offense and defense in football. A key question to ask the

> The selection of the investment banker is so critical to the success or failure of the impending transaction that often certain aspects of the decision are overlooked.

lead investment banker is how much of his or her time are they going to spend on your particular account—20 percent, 30 percent, 50 percent?

3. **References.** Do not be satisfied with just a few references. Almost everybody has at least a few good ones. Beware of references that may be for a transaction that took place four or five years ago. Six to ten references on the individual would not be too many. Also, ask for names of his or her clients in which the deal was not consummated. Ask questions aimed at revealing the individual's shortcomings as well as his or her strengths. Does this person communicate often and well and also follow through? Does he truly represent your best interest or is he so anxious to do a deal that in essence he represents the transaction?

4. **Tombstones.** The outward mark of a firm's success is the listing of tombstones. A tombstone is an announcement of a completed transaction, almost like a wedding invitation in which the buyer and seller (groom and bride) are announced as a merger and acquisition transaction. In this case, the I-banker is also mentioned at the bottom of the tombstone as the agent in the transaction. Ideally, these tombstones will be listed both by the year and the type of business.

   If the firm can only produce a few tombstones for the past few years, beware that the best deal makers may have left the firm. Which is more impressive, a firm of five that completed ten transactions last year, or a firm of twenty that completed twenty transactions last year? The former did more deals per person than the latter. The larger firm, however, may utilize half their people for valuations, fairness opinions, and consulting assignments, all of which may not have been represented by tombstones.

5. **Industry experience.** Clearly there is an advantage if a firm has an industry specialty or sub-specialty in the client's specific industry. For instance, Broadview Associates of Fort Lee, New Jersey, specializes in information technology; Veronis, Suhler & Associates of New York City specializes

> Ask questions aimed at revealing the individual's shortcomings as well as his or her strengths.

in media and communications; and O'Conor, Wright Wyman, Inc. of Boston specializes in the office products industry.

The latter firm has a broad practice as an investment banker, but has a sub-specialty in office products. The office products industry knowledge includes the extensive database of likely buyers and sellers, the understanding of industry valuations, and the key relationships that have been sustained over the years. Notwithstanding these advantages, if the same firm represents several buyers in the same industry, it could be a conflict of interest, unless their client's criteria are substantially different.

6. **Pricing, packaging, and processing.** Whether the client was a buyer or seller, it is important to review, on a "no-name" basis, the recent transactions of the firm as to the pricing the investment banker is able to achieve. It is even more important for an investment banker to apprise the potential seller, you, of the anticipated selling price. Additionally, the investment banker should be prepared to show how he will package your business in a most convincing way, often by demonstrating selling memorandums of other clients to see how they described or represented acquiring clients. Of equal importance is the process the investment banker will use to contact the numerous target companies. Ask the banker to show you examples of how the target referrals are reported, logged, and followed up on.

7. **Contract.** There are a number of elements of the engagement agreement between you and the investment banker that are easily comparable: the amount of the retainer and whether it is deductible, the amount of the accomplishment fee, the minimum compensation, exclusivity, exclusions if any, and the cancellation period. Investment bankers' terms and conditions vary, and their willingness to compromise also varies. Beware of investment bankers who are too compromising for their compensation, because it might reflect poorly on their services. On the other hand, higher compensation does not necessarily guarantee superior performance.

> Beware of investment bankers who are too compromising for their compensation, because it might reflect poorly on their services.

8. **Intermediary style.** Investment bankers must monitor a transaction's progress and be prepared to intervene when necessary. Clients often value investment bankers who allow them to meet independently with the other party. The investment banker must be able to sustain the momentum, put the deal back on the tracks when derailed, never give up, and have grace under fire. James Bond with a briefcase.

9. **Chemistry.** All the other reasons for selecting an investment banker are objective. When it comes to your gut feeling or chemistry, it is important to weigh the subjective feeling as part of the decision-making process.

10. **Location.** In most cases, it is preferable that the investment banker is located near you, for the frequent and necessary interaction. The advantage of selecting an industry specialist, however, can offset the advantage of being close.

The chances of completing a successful transaction are obviously increased by selecting the best investment banker for your particular situation. The best investment banker for one company may not be the best one for another. Therein lies the challenge in the selection process.

The Retainer

Often the question arises as to why a corporate seller should pay an investment banker a retainer. It is uncommon for retainers to be paid to real estate brokers, while on the other hand, most executive search firms require retainers. Here are some reasons why you should pay a retainer:

- It shows that you are committed to selling your business. The first question a buyer asks is, "Why is the seller selling?" The second question the buyer asks is, "Is the seller committed to selling?" The best way investment bankers have found to prove your commitment to sell is to tell the buyer you have paid them (retained them) to represent you.
- It indicates your commitment to work with your intermediary. Investment bankers feel that if you are committed to

Wanted: I-Banker with World View

When deciding on which investment banker to hire, you may want to consider the extent of the banker's contacts in countries other than the United States.

George D. Shaw, a certified public accountant and partner in charge of corporate finance advisory services at Grant Thornton LLP in Boston, told *Inc.* magazine, "It also makes sense to look for an investment banker with the capability to sell your company internationally, because that's a growing outlet for many entrepreneurial firms."

Shaw warns, however, "there is a big difference between an investment banker who just has an international database of prospective leads and one that has real distribution capabilities overseas." You are looking for an I-banker with international offices and relationships with foreign investment banking firms.

selling your business, you show this commitment by paying them to retain their services. When you hire an employee and give them a paycheck, you expect them to produce. When you retain an investment banker, you can expect and will receive results from their firm.

- It shows your intermediary is committed to the deal. If your investment banker takes your money, they have a responsibility to give you a 110-percent effort on the deal. With no retainer, how do you know if your intermediary will be fully committed to giving his or her best effort to the transaction?

- The retainer payments give the intermediary clearly defined milestones to achieve. The retainer schedule usually calls for three separate payments. This sets up a schedule for you and your investment banker to work with.

- Writing checks to the firm you choose forces you to review that firm's results on a regular basis. Every time you write a check to them, you'll want to be sure they earned your money. By paying the retainer over three payments, it forces you to review what they have produced on your behalf.

- The retainer is credited against the success fee. A firm would not take on a project unless they were reasonably sure they could be successful. Thus, your retainer is really nothing more than a non-refundable down payment toward the ultimate success fee.

- Investment bankers will earn their fee in the services they perform for you. And most important: You get what you pay for. Getting that next retainer payment can be great incentive for an investment banker to work hard. If you don't pay much, you may not get much back.

I-Banker's Fee

The commission is based on the value of the transaction. Let's assume that the company is losing money, has a negative net worth, and has $2 million of interest-bearing debt. You, as the seller, negotiate to sell the company for one dollar plus the assumption of the debt. Your fee agreement with the I-banker states that he or she will

> The retainer payments give the intermediary clearly defined milestones to achieve.

receive a minimum commission, no matter what the ultimate selling price, of $50,000. What does the investment banker receive for an accomplishment fee?

The answer is $90,000 (based on Lehman Fee of 5-4-3-2-1 percent, that is 5 percent of the first $1 million, 4 percent of the second million dollars, etc.). Assumption of interest-bearing debt, usually bank debt, is part of the company's capitalization. In this case, you sold the company's "stock," which includes all the assets and all the liabilities.

Another scenario is an "asset" transaction in which you acquire certain assets and assume some liabilities of the balance sheet. Let's assume that you sell the company for $30,000 and the buyer takes over the receivables, the inventory, and the payables. The seller keeps all the other items, leases the machinery and the equipment, and rents the real estate. What is the I-banker's fee? Would it be the $50,000 minimum as stated in the I-banker's fee agreement?

The answer is no, not if the I-banker has properly included a commission, like a broker, for equipment leased or real estate rented instead of acquired. If the seller leases the equipment and real estate and rents the real estate for five years at $50,000 per year, the commission would be based on the $250,000 value, normally paid at closing and not spaced out over the entire period but discounted to present value, plus the commission on the $30,000 sales price mentioned previously.

> Brokers, merger and acquisition intermediaries, and investment bankers make their living smoothing out the business-selling process.

Conclusion

Brokers, merger and acquisition intermediaries, and investment bankers make their living smoothing out the business-selling process. Well chosen, they are worth every penny they make. But they are not your only advisors. It is now time to look closely at other members of your team.

For more information on this topic, visit our Web site at www.businesstown.com

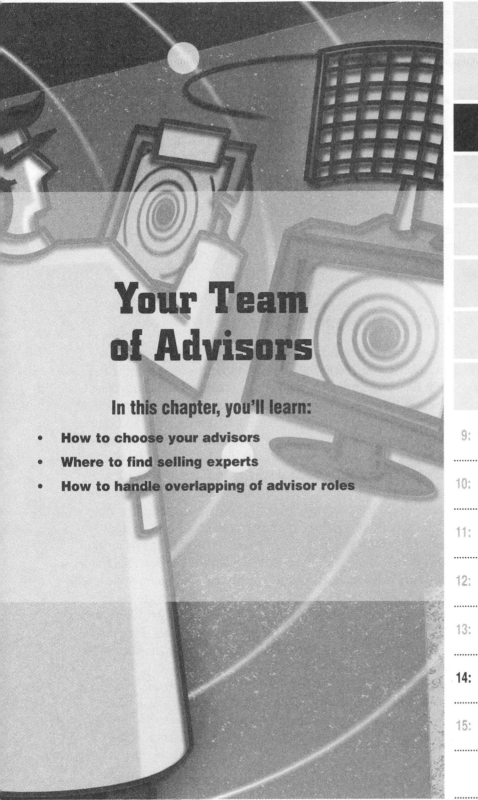

Your Team of Advisors

In this chapter, you'll learn:

- **How to choose your advisors**
- **Where to find selling experts**
- **How to handle overlapping of advisor roles**

Chapter 14

Chapter 15

9:   KEY STEPS IN SELLING A BUSINESS

10:   MORE STEPS FOR A SUCCESSFUL SALE

11:   UNDERSTANDING THE CULTURAL FIT

12:   THE SELLER'S MOST COMMON MISTAKES

13:   USING INTERMEDIARIES

14:   YOUR TEAM OF ADVISORS

15:   SELLING TROUBLED COMPANIES

If I were asked by a seller of a company to select just one chapter to read before selling his or her business, I would be tempted to suggest, Chapter 3, "Important Points in Selling a Business," or Chapter 8, "The Seller's Most Common Mistakes." Upon further reflection, though, I would say the most important chapter is this one: "Your Team of Advisors."

Selling an operating company is complicated. If you are dealing with a middle-market sized business with family interests, numerous shareholders, and various tax ramifications, it is essential to be advised properly by a variety of people. Here is the cast of characters.

Advisor 1—Board of Directors

Outside directors customarily concern themselves with corporate governance, which historically has been the stewardship of the company. Hiring and firing the CEO and overseeing the various committees, such as audit, compensation, and nominating, are the directors' primary focus, in order to be sure the company doesn't go off course.

In the case of a merger, acquisition, or sale, the first objective of the board, particularly of an outside director, is to assess whether there is enough horsepower and skill to successfully complete a transaction and, if not, to retain an experienced investment banker and a transaction attorney.

The board of directors' primary responsibility is to do what is best for the shareholders, and secondarily to do what is best for the other stakeholders. The directors should analyze the potential transaction not only from the financial perspective but also from the business perspective. There are many variables for directors to consider. For example, if the company merges with another, what is the human element? In a merger, one management wins, the other loses; one pension plan prevails, and maybe one plant is closed and consolidated with the other.

The director's role is to help the chief executive officer through the process of the impending transaction, or conversely to be the devil's advocate in questioning the merits of the deal. Often inside management becomes so enamored with the transaction that an

> The board of directors' primary responsibility is to do what is best for the shareholders, and secondarily to do what is best for the other stakeholders.

outside perspective can challenge the management's rationale. Conversely, the director can be the catalyst to get the deal done if the negotiations drag on or if communications between the two parties break down. Many times it is the outside director who influences the owner/CEO to overcome seller's remorse at the later stages of selling the company.

Ultimately, the CEO has to be the driving force, but often it is the outside director who has enormous influence on whether the transaction is a success or failure.

Advisor 2—Tax Attorney

Frederic G. Corneel, former senior partner in the tax department of Sullivan & Worcester in Boston, wrote an article a number of years ago on mergers and acquisitions entitled, "Nothing Has Changed . . . Taxes First." The point of his article was that a seller must understand the tax ramifications to the shareholders before a discussion takes place about selling a business.

You should take the time to compute the net proceeds to each shareholder depending on whether it is a stock sale, asset sale, or a tax-free exchange, and also explore how a good tax attorney can legitimately save you from paying unnecessary taxes. While you are calculating the tax impact on the sale of the business, you should also deduct all related expenses to the transaction: stay agreements, all closing costs, environmental cleanups, escrow accounts, among others.

Advisor 3—Transaction Attorney

There are generalists and there are specialists. If you need to have a brain operation, you engage a neurosurgeon—hopefully one of the best. If you sell your company, you engage a transaction attorney; not a country lawyer that handles everything from divorces to collecting delinquent accounts receivable. There is a place for both types of attorneys, but when it comes to selling your company, you

> If you sell your company, you engage a transaction attorney; not a country lawyer that handles everything from divorces to collecting delinquent accounts receivable.

want a real professional, even if it costs you two or three times more for the best legal advice on corporate transactions. Bad advice could cost you millions of dollars.

A transaction attorney knows the nuances of successfully completing a deal and is charged with the role of protecting his client from entering into an unfavorable contract. According to Andrew Sherman, a transaction attorney at McDermott, Will & Emery in Washington, D.C., "The classic mistakes are a lack of adequate planning, lawyers and other advisors who did not understand the underlying goals of the transaction, misrepresentations by one or more key

Help Is On the Way

You needn't be alone in selling your business. Consider making use of some of these experts.

Association for Corporate Growth International
Headquarters
1926 Waukegan Road, Suite 1, Glenview, IL 60025
Tel: 800–699–1331 or 847–657–6730
Fax: 847–657–6819 or 847–657–6825
www.acg.org
Email: acqhq@tcaq.com

Corporate Finance Associates
Locations in the United States, Europe, and Canada
Tel: 303–296–6300
Fax: 303–294–9411
www.cfaw.com

International Merger and Acquisition Professionals
525 SW 5th Street, Suite A, Des Moines, IA 50309
Tel: 515–282–8192
Fax: 515–282–9117
www.imap.com
Email: imap@imap.com

M&A International s.a./n.v.
Chaussee de Louvain 88, 1380 Lasne (Brussels), Belgium
Tel: +32 (0)2–627–5120
Fax: +32 (0)2–640–7375
www.mabrussels.com
Email: info@mabrussels.com

IBBA Headquarters
401 North Michigan Avenue, Suite 2200, Chicago, Illinois 60611-4267
Tel: 888–686–IBBA (4222)
Fax: 312–673–6599
www.ibba.org
Email: admin@ibba.org

parties to the deal, and overly aggressive timetable to closing. It is extremely important that the owner of the selling company attend the drafting sessions of their attorney. The attorney needs to know the business implications for all facets of the deal and therefore needs the businessman's knowledge and input accordingly, especially on such matters as the Representations and Warranties. Sellers and buyers have different objectives. Simplistically, the seller wants to be sure he receives all the money or considerations for the company and its assets as purported . . . and therein lies the potential hurdles in reaching a harmonious resolution in the Purchase and Sale Agreement."

Advisor 4—Accountant

As with attorneys, there are specialists within the accounting community who are experts in mergers and acquisitions. They can help you clean up the balance sheet to make the company more presentable—for example, by taking long overdue write-offs or settling disputed receivables and payables. If the financials are not audited, your accountant would probably recommend that you spend the extra $10,000 to $40,000 to have an audit to verify the financial statements so that the buyer will have more confidence in his or her offer. An audit for a service company with a relatively low inventory will cost far less than an audit of a retail, distributor, or manufacturer that might have extensive inventory, all of which has to be counted and verified.

Accountants can also advise you on the price range you can expect from potential buyers and how to best present the current, historic, and future financials of your company. Financial projections are a critical element in the valuation process because many buyers heavily rely on the Discounted Cash Flow (DCF) model in determining their price. (DCF is a valuation technique that assigns a value in today's dollars to the cash flows that are expected to occur in the future.) And, finally, the accountant can advise the seller on the best structure of an impending transaction with emphasis on how to mitigate capital gains taxes.

> Accountants can also advise you on the price range you can expect from potential buyers and how to best present the current, historic, and future financials of your company.

Advisor 5—Business Appraiser

I could not imagine selling a business without having a professional opinion as to the market value of the company. If you overvalue your business, there is a real possibility that the company will not sell because it is considered overpriced. If you undervalue the business, there is a strong possibility of leaving too much money on the table.

Proper valuations conducted by corporate valuation experts or investment bankers may be submitted in a tight range to allow for the fact that offers by buyers differ according to whether the price is 100 percent cash or, perhaps, 50 percent cash and 50 percent some sort of payout.

A business appraisal helps in the negotiating process because the appraisal can be used for the seller's rationalization of price. Furthermore, buyers will expect to see current appraisals on machinery and equipment and real estate. If a seller does not have appraisals on the latter before going to market, it will certainly slow down the entire selling process. Often the business appraiser will subcontract out the non-business valuation portion, which specifically addresses machinery/equipment and real estate because these skills are highly specialized.

I have seen people's lives shattered because they simply did not bother to have a professional value the business. Remember, valuing a business properly does not just mean reviewing the financials. All aspects of the business have to be reviewed: the industry, the customers, the vendors, the employees, and the competitors.

Advisor 6—Investment Banker

Usually the way to obtain the best price and terms is to receive competing offers from numerous potential buyers. To orchestrate competing bids normally requires an investment banker. The mere presence of an I-banker involved in the transaction will psychologically increase the price.

Advisor 7—Investigator

Business intelligence is becoming more of the norm nowadays in the M&A business, particularly when selling to buyers who are not well known by reputation.

Let's suppose you are selling a business for $8 million—$5 million cash, $2 million notes, and $1 million on a contingency basis. Additionally, the buyer has negotiated that certain funds are withheld in escrow for six months and that there are substantial representations and warranties. As the seller, you don't know whether or not the buyer has reneged on former deals, or if the principals of the buying company are honorable.

In order to conduct due diligence on the buyer, a firm can be retained that specializes in investigations. The importance of investigators should not be overlooked.

When Roles Overlap

The roles played by these advisors can certainly overlap. As the seller, you have to decide how well these advisors can work in concert. For example, the accountant, the business appraiser, and the I-banker are all qualified to do a business valuation on the selling company. Accounting firms are more apt to do an academic evaluation, while an I-banker is apt to have the pulse of the marketplace and rely more on comparable sales. The business appraiser who may be part of the I-banker's office could be best utilized prior to totally committing to the sales process.

Having two valuations may sound excessive, but it may also allow you to have the benefit of a second opinion. Since the market ultimately determines the price, one has to realize that valuations are not an exact science but rather a rational business analysis.

Other overlapping roles with advisors could involve whether tax advice is received from the attorney or the accountant or both. Also, who will be the lead negotiator: you, the I-banker, or the attorney? These are some of the matters that must be determined up front.

> As the seller, you have to decide how well these advisors can work in concert.

One protocol that the seller needs to be aware of is that his attorney communicates with the buyer's attorney, his I-banker communicates with the buyer's I-banker. Seldom is there a crossover in which, for example, the seller's attorney communicates directly with the buyer. Obviously, if the seller's team and the buyer's team are together in a room, the crossover communication is acceptable.

Further, the seller must decide who will be the lead negotiator in the final discussions of the purchase and sale agreement. At this point, there is no protocol as it could be the I-banker on one side and the attorney on the other side; or it could be the owner on one side as the lead negotiator and the buyer's attorney on the other side.

> Selecting a group of advisors is one of the most critical aspects of the entire process.

Conclusion

There are other potential advisors, like family business consultants who work with the family to evaluate and advise whether family management succession should be chosen rather than selling the company outright. A trusted business friend who has had experience in buying and selling companies would also be recommended as an advisor.

At any rate, your team of advisors is a critical element in accomplishing a successful transition of a business. Selecting a group of advisors for the purpose of selling a business is one of the most critical aspects of the entire process.

For more information on this topic, visit our Web site at www.businesstown.com

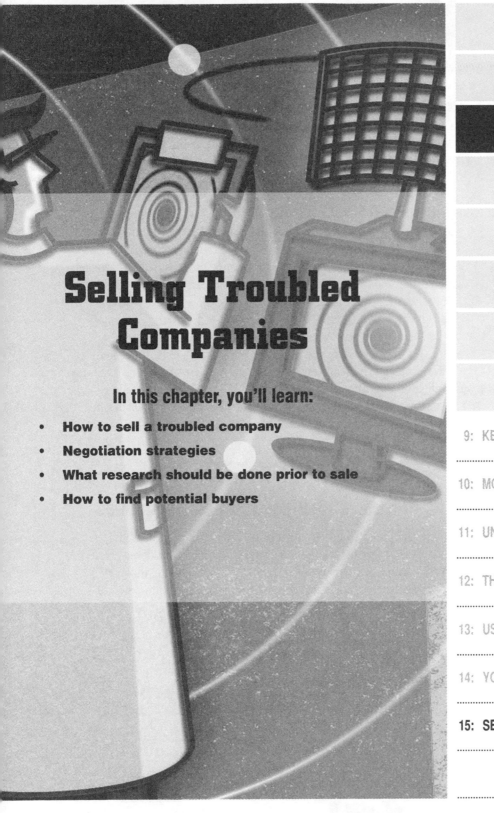

Selling Troubled Companies

In this chapter, you'll learn:

- **How to sell a troubled company**
- **Negotiation strategies**
- **What research should be done prior to sale**
- **How to find potential buyers**

It is well known that most owners of unprofitable companies wait too long to address their problems. The alternatives are to fix the problems, sell the company, or liquidate the business. In all cases, time is the enemy because it takes numerous months to either fix the ailing company or to sell it.

A few years ago, Linda Mertz and Ward Wickwire spoke to the Association for Corporate Growth's InterGrowth Conference on the topic of selling troubled divisions and companies. In working with a troubled company, they agreed, time is the crucial commodity. While the normal sales process can take six to nine months, Mertz has completed the sale of a troubled division in less than three months. Speed was essential to capturing the remaining value that was quickly eroding.

Next, Mertz and Wickwire said that it is important to find and focus on prospective buyers who can recognize opportunities and solve problems. It is also essential to maintain credibility and candor in all communications with prospective buyers. Interest should be developed based on knowing all the facts, either positive or negative. If negative factors are not disclosed up-front, their later disclosure can compromise the entire effort.

Lastly, identify key assets and develop a plan to sell.

> If negative factors are not disclosed up-front, their later disclosure can compromise the entire effort.

The Process of Selling Troubled Companies

Before the process of selling troubled companies is addressed, it is important to first determine whether, in fact, it is considered "troubled." Obviously, there are different degrees of how one might classify troubled companies, but some of the following characteristics would indicate that the company is in trouble:

Negative book value

Rapidly declining earnings or negative earnings

Default of the bank loan covenants

Inability to meet debt obligations

Rapidly running out of cash

By determining that the company is in a state of trouble, the owner can substantially accelerate the process of selling the company as time is of the essence. Additionally, the owner of a troubled company will be far less concerned about confidentiality and be willing to contact direct competitors that otherwise might be avoided.

Owners of healthy companies are trying to maximize the selling price through a very controlled and confidentially orchestrated selling process. The objective in selling a troubled company is to get out of the situation with the least amount of debt obligations as quickly as possible, before the company further deteriorates.

The following is an overview of the process of selling troubled companies as seen by Stuart W. Cohen, Managing Director of Ascendant Capital LLC of Andover, Massachusetts, a private equity group focusing on branded consumer product companies.

The process includes four basic steps.

1. Understanding why the company is in trouble
2. Determining what you would be selling and what realistically you can expect to obtain for the business
3. Deciding whom the company should be marketed to and how it should be marketed
4. Developing the negotiating and transaction structure strategy to be employed

> The objective in selling a troubled company is to get out of the situation with the least amount of debt obligations as quickly as possible.

Why Is the Company in Trouble?

The critical first step of understanding why the company is troubled is instrumental in determining how you will proceed throughout the remainder of the sale process. This analysis might lead you to conclude that the business is not saleable and should be exited, with the process ending right there. As I mentioned earlier, time is of the essence in this type of transaction, and you cannot afford to use it inefficiently or unproductively. Some common reasons a company may be in trouble include the following:

- Poor management
- Loss of key people
- Lack of focus

- Inappropriate or inadequate financial structure (could be overleveraged or undercapitalized)
- Product problems, including quality, functional, or technical obsolescence, or lack of responsiveness to market needs
- Operating problems or inefficiencies, such as capacity under-utilization and unfavorable business economics due to raw material prices, labor rates, geographic locations of plants and warehouses, and an unreasonable burden of parent company overhead
- Customer problems, including a loss of a key customer or poor or deteriorating customer relationships
- Market problems due to a declining market or market price level or a paradigm shift in the market
- Litigation problems, which could be environmental or patent-related

> You need to highlight the strengths of the company and, where possible, turn the reasons for the company's problems into an opportunity for the potential buyer.

What Are You Selling?

What you are selling goes beyond the stock of the company or the assets on the balance sheet. It's really the business attributes of the company that you are going to sell in order to obtain the maximum value for the company. You need to highlight the strengths of the company and, where possible, turn the reasons for the company's problems into an opportunity for the potential buyer. Here are a few examples:

You might have a company with good products and a good customer base but with inefficient manufacturing operations. This type of situation could be attractive to a potential buyer having strong manufacturing capabilities and looking to expand its product line and customer base.

Your company could boast good products and gross margins that haven't reached the size necessary to realize the economies of scale required to make it profitable. This kind of company could be attractive to a potential buyer with an interest in the company's business, one that can absorb the company within its existing infrastructure.

As a final example, you may have a company that has the basic fundamentals to be successful but whose major flaw is its leadership or focus, shortcomings that a potential buyer may be willing and able to remedy.

What Can You Get for the Company?

In most instances, you will find it easier to maximize value for a company whose problem is related to its costs or expenses rather than its marketplace performance. Determining what you could possibly get for the business should reflect what you believe you have to sell, including the company's strengths, as well as the buyer's opportunity to enhance value. Recognizing that, the buyer is more likely to share some of the expense-related improvements with the seller than to share nothing at all.

I try to create a pro forma income statement that closely mirrors the general economics of the business I'm selling. I then apply a range of multiples to the pro forma operating income to get a potential range of values. The range of the multiples used will depend upon the actual operating performance of the company compared to its pro forma level. Simply said, a company whose actual performance is below the pro forma level will get a lower multiple than that which is above it. The potential purchase of the company as a going concern is then compared to the value that could be realized through its liquidation. If the potential purchase price is not significantly higher than the net liquidation value to reflect the time and risk of selling the company and receiving the anticipated proceeds, the decision will then be made to liquidate the company.

To Whom Should the Company Be Marketed?

I learned a valuable lesson a while ago when I sold an eight-year-old Datsun 280Z sports car–in mint condition–that I owned when I lived in southern Connecticut. I placed an ad in two newspapers, one a highly prominent local newspaper that ran the ad daily for a week, and the other in the *New York Times* that ran the ad once in its Sunday edition. I received sixteen responses to my ad in the local paper but only one to my ad in the *Times*. On the surface this would appear disappointing because my one-day ad in the *Times* cost more than my weekly ad in my local paper. The car, however, was eventually sold to the single respondent from the *Times*. What I learned was getting the best price for what you are trying to sell doesn't mean you need to get a lot of interest, but rather you need to get the right interest.

> The potential purchase of the company as a going concern is then compared to the value that could be realized through its liquidation.

The right potential buyer should be familiar and experienced with turnaround situations; have a high tolerance for risk; have competence in the industry in which your company participates; have the ability to move quickly; and have the proven ability to finance and close the transaction.

Potential buyers should be further qualified as someone who you believe would have the most interest in what you are trying to

The M&A Online Meet Market

The following is a list of business-to-business online services for listing businesses for sale. Some also list advisors.

MergerNetwork
Web site: *www.mergernetwork.com*
Seller listings: 9,328
Buyer listings: 1,481
Exclusive listings: 2,104
Done deals: 779

NVST
Web site: *www.nvst.com*
Investor capital: $136 billion
Capital sought: $170 billion
Opportunities: 9,102
Investors: 43,339
Advisors: 27,990

BiZ Trader Online
Web site: *www.biztrader.com*

BizBuySell
Web site: *www.bizbuysell.com*
Updates or adds over 6,000 listings a month
Breakdown of sectors listed:
Manufacturing (15%), wholesale/retail (40%),
    services (30%)

Businessesforsale
Web site: *www.businessesforsale.com*
Lists more than 12,000 businesses for sale

Business Resale Network
Web site: *www.br-network.com*

National Business Multiple Listing Service
Web site: *www.listbuysell.com*

USBX
Web site: *www.usbx.com*
More than 14,000 businesses "market themselves."

MoneyZone.com
Web site:
www.moneyzone.com/BusinessesForSale.cfm
More than 11,000 businesses for sale

sell, and be willing to pay the highest price. Essentially, look for buyers who have the best opportunity for extracting the most value out of the transaction. Many times you will find that the most logical buyers are not necessarily the right buyers.

How Should the Company Be Marketed?

There are various approaches to marketing a troubled company. Here are a number of them:

Should the company be sold in a formal sealed bid auction or in a flexible auction? If you are selling a company in bankruptcy, the courts require a sealed bid as all the buyers are bidding on the same entity—a package of all the assets and all the liabilities. On the other hand, you want a flexible auction when the company is not in bankruptcy because the various buyers will undoubtedly have a wide variety of offers based on different terms, conditions, and structure. A few buyers could make an offer on all the assets and none of the liabilities, while other buyers will make an offer on assumption of some of the assets and some of the liabilities. Therefore, you need to be flexible in order to negotiate the best deal for yourself.

How confining should the confidentiality agreement and the information you are willing to provide potential buyers be? An underperforming company is usually in a survival mode and therefore speed to market is absolutely essential. The confidentiality agreement should be very simple, perhaps one page. If it is too legalized it will hold up the potential buyers, especially corporate buyers who often have to receive approval from their legal department. The purpose is to go to market quickly; a lengthy sales process can jeopardize the company's market position and unfavorably impact its already precarious perceived value.

Should an offering document be prepared or should information be communicated in a more informal and unstructured manner? With a troubled company, the offering

> The confidentiality agreement should be very simple, perhaps one page.

document will make awful reading and only show a company with red ink for financials. Therefore, as a seller of a troubled company, you must sell the sizzle, the products, the future–the potential. Such a sales pitch should be done in person, especially if you can show the benefits of the combined companies.

Should the company be marketed internally or by a third party? There are so many problems and issues in dealing with a troubled company that if there is sufficient cash to hire an I-banker to handle the sale of the company, do so. Hire an I-banker who either has industry expertise or one who has had experience in selling troubled companies.

What Should the Negotiating Strategy and Transaction Structure Be?

You need to know what your key objectives are before beginning your negotiations. Are you looking to obtain the maximum up-front cash for the business? To obtain the highest value, which in most instances will require some seller financing? To obtain a meaningful premium over liquidation value? To get out from under certain debt, labor, plant, or environmental liabilities? Or to get out and get out quickly?

I've found that the following two factors are key to achieving the objectives that you have established for the transaction. First, you must believe that the dog you are selling could be someone else's diamond and that they might want to buy it as much as you want to sell it. There are few hard and fast rules for setting pricing for troubled companies and attitude can be important. The optimum scenario is when the buyer believes he or she stole the company and the seller believes he or she got more for it than anticipated. Second, you need to get more than one interested party bidding on the company. No matter how poor the property, competition will help drive the transaction and give you some leverage in the negotiations.

Given that timing is of the essence in these transactions, you need to be credible, responsive, creative, and flexible in your

> You need to know what your key objectives are before beginning your negotiations.

negotiations with potential buyers. You may need to lead the potential buyers to where you want them to go as well as show them how to get there. In many instances, you might end up structuring the deal for them. You almost need to think what you would do if you were buying the business, including what and how you would pay for it.

The Advisor Team

As with any sales transaction, it is important to have an experienced team of advisors for the legal and investment banking aspects of the project. Being specialists in the process, they will be able to advise the owners and executives during the process. In addition, they will take some of the burden off the shoulders of operating management. In the case of a troubled company, freeing operating management for day-to-day duties is especially important. It may even be necessary to augment the advisory team with turnaround experts.

Once the attorney has been selected, he has to get involved in the process earlier than he would have in a non-troubled context. While this may involve extra costs, bringing the attorney up to speed or dealing with preliminary issues that could have been dealt with at an earlier stage is extremely important.

It is also important to resolve issues regarding how the advisors will be compensated early on. Perhaps the investment banker should be paid a monthly retainer three months in advance. Otherwise, the I-banker's commitment to the project may be at odds with his desire to be compensated.

When selling a troubled company, keep in mind from the beginning that you will sit at the negotiating table not as equals but as virtual supplicants with no leverage. You are counting on the buyer living up to the agreement in the Letter of Intent, because if you have to re-shop the company, you will probably have to take less money since the company is deteriorating quickly. Therefore, it is critical that you hire an attorney who is not just competent in buying and selling companies when everything is going well but one who is also willing to subordinate his need to show his smarts in favor of building a team between buyer and seller and the respective counsels and advisors.

> Being specialists in the process, they will be able to advise the owners and executives during the process.

Identifying Problems

Early detection of problems is critical. The earlier they are identified and recognized, the more options you are able to offer to the potential buyers. A complete assessment of the business's strengths and weaknesses needs to be made immediately.

Indication that a business is having problems includes: operational challenges (inability to deal with problems), sales decline, marketing uncertainty, pricing, competition, and margin erosion. The lack of cash is also one of the key indicators that there is a severe problem. Unfortunately, it is also one of the last indicators to surface.

Problems with banking relationships can severely undercut the ability of a business to function. A good banking relationship, including a credit facility, is key for most businesses to continue with their operations. If a business is not functioning within the terms of its loan agreements or is violating loan covenants, its ongoing operations are at risk. Understanding the banks' concerns regarding these covenant violations is key to understanding the depth of the company's problems and the time it has to correct them.

Some problems are so significant that they should be resolved before initiating a sale. These could include product liability claims, environmental cleanup, and ownership disputes. Depending on exactly what the problems are, it may be important to solve them before the seller is shopped or while the company is being shopped, but they should definitely be solved before a buyer is found.

Ownership disputes within a seller group, in particular, can be a significant problem. No buyer wants to get between owners who cannot agree, because the negotiating process then becomes difficult, if not impossible, to complete. If owners cannot agree, it will be very difficult to assemble a team of motivated advisors.

> A good banking relationship is key for most businesses to continue with their operations.

Sales Issues

The qualities that buyers seek in a good turnaround include the seller's channels of distribution, an established track record of sales growth, and the availability of quality information about the company. The problem of getting good, quality information can be especially difficult when a division of a larger company is being sold. In such cases, we are typically confronted by questions and issues regarding intracompany charges and allocations.

For everyone's benefit having a motivated seller is a must. The owner, whether an individual or parent company, must have a realistic understanding of the situation the company is in and the options to improve the situation. Some owners may change their minds if the company begins to turn around or they see interesting ideas advanced by potential buyers. The owners may then decide to pursue those options themselves. If they decide not to sell, everyone will have wasted a lot of time, energy, and money.

In addition, owners need to be realistic when renegotiating their price expectations and transaction structure. Prospective buyers do not particularly care about seller's expectations. A proper valuation of how long the company can survive without a sale is critical to the process.

Preparing for a Sale: Research

Factors to consider in positioning the company for sale include the conditions in the seller's industry and served markets, and the state of the capital markets. In spite of major problems, a company may still have excellent value in proprietary technology, products, customer relationships, and so on. Preparation for the sale will require studying these factors and incorporating them into the documentation and marketing plans.

Intangibles, whether listed on the balance sheet or not, can present some challenges. In a number of cases, it may be necessary to share some intangibles through license agreements with "field of use" of restrictions for patents and trademarks.

Documentation

In many cases where a troubled company is being sold, an offering document is not assembled as a single coherent document. Rather,

> Owners need to be realistic when renegotiating their price expectations and transaction structure.

it evolves as a series of exhibits prepared in sequence. For example, Linda Mertz was hired by Morgan Products to sell a wood-molding division. During the first week of their engagement, they began preparing a sequence of exhibits to document the business and develop interest, while at the same time initiating mail contact with more than 1,500 strategic buyers and 1,000 attorneys, accountants, and bankers. Using this aggressive approach, where confidentiality was of minimal concern, Mertz obtained five Letters of Intent in five weeks. During any sale process, it may be necessary to maintain periodic communication about the status of the company with key constituencies, such as bankers, trade creditors, key customers, or employees. It is especially true in the sale of a troubled company. Communications may be either proactive, or in response to rumors that surface.

Be up front in dealing with buyers, and address problems with suggested solutions. Keep in mind the different prospect groups and then position the company favorably with respect to each potential group. Holding back information, even though it may be detrimental, risks wasting everyone's time. If the company being sold is not troubled, it is often a better strategy to let the buyer come forward with problems and questions, and respond as they are brought up. If the company is troubled, however, it may not have time to investigate and respond to potential problems and issues raised by a buyer in the middle of the process. In such a case, a thorough disclosure up front is called for.

> Be up front in dealing with buyers, and address problems with suggested solutions.

Working with the Advisors

It is critical that both you and your attorney understand the differences in the attorney's role when selling a troubled business rather than in a normal deal. Typically, your attorney can negotiate material points and not delay progress in attempting to win on many of these points. Ultimately, with your permission, they might walk away from the negotiation table.

But these practices rarely work when you are selling a troubled company. You will only want to walk away over the most fundamental impasses, since there is no guarantee in this context that you will be able to bring a buyer back (or find another buyer at the same price). Since you can't walk away, however, you have to avoid drawing lines in the sand to begin with. Therefore, when selling a troubled company, you need a lawyer who can treat negotiation as a partnership rather than a contest, and try to move the negotiations forward by putting differences on the table and explaining the seller's position as best as it can be explained. The attorney must be able to force the clients, on the basis of their original handshake, to resolve issues fairly (where one side has a point) or by splitting the difference where there are no right answers.

Even though most states have repealed their bulk sales laws (the bulk sales act still exists in approximately twenty states), an array of legislation regulation and judicial decisions make it difficult, if not impossible, to leave certain types of liabilities behind. The theories of successor liability may impose upon a buyer not just responsibility for product liability claims against a seller, but the seller's unfulfilled contractual obligations as well—whether or not the buyer has assumed them in the purchase agreement.

Also, environmental law makes all owners and operators of a facility responsible for any cleanup, regardless of whether the firm then owning the facility caused the problem. Finally, buyers of plants with collective bargaining agreements will, at the least, have to bargain in good faith with the union about their post-closing role.

> A good buyer for a troubled company must have confidence in their ability to complete a turnaround.

Identifying Potential Buyers

A good buyer for a troubled company must have confidence in their ability to complete a turnaround. They should either have experience with turnarounds (basically financial buyers) or competence in industry (a synergistic/strategic buyer). And they should also be able to demonstrate that they have the necessary financial resources.

A recent development we have observed is that many private equity groups can move much more rapidly than corporate buyers. Equity groups are sophisticated and typically do not have the layers of management involved in the decision-making and approval process that corporate buyers have. In the interest of time, it is important to make assessments about buyer capabilities early on, so energy is not wasted on prospects of low probability of coming through.

Selecting the Approach

Selecting the marketing approach can affect the success of a project. While the time and resources available to continue operations are considerations, the relative attractiveness of the entity to be sold is also important.

In general, a flexible auction process is preferable to a structured bid auction process. Many buyer prospects will refuse to participate in a formal bid auction unless the seller is particularly attractive. In general, the best value for a troubled company can be obtained by remaining flexible and responsive to a buyer's needs and perception of synergy.

The type of marketing campaign should also be considered. In the case of a troubled company, where time is of the essence and confidentiality is of less concern, a mass campaign is preferable. In certain situations, however, a selective approach (contact only a limited number of top prospects) or even a pre-emptive approach (approach a single buyer prospect) can work effectively.

I used a pre-emptive approach when engaged by a public company to sell a division that made overhead bridge cranes. The market was extremely thin. We sold the unit to a foreign buyer at more than two times book value. I believe that the transaction was completed more rapidly and at a higher value than would have been possible with an auction-type process.

In my experience, a formal bid auction process is appropriate only for very strong sellers. Rarely is a bid auction process appropriate for a troubled company. Some buyers and buyer groups will refuse to participate in an auction process. Whenever possible, I prefer to develop alternates and competition. And, during the due diligence process, I have found that we can maintain a discreet but appropriate level of contact with a backup alternative in the event that the primary one falters.

Hire a Turnaround Specialist

Position the company for sale by first hiring a turnaround specialist to stabilize the business. He or she should be able to identify the major problems, concentrate on raising enough cash from operations

> Selecting the marketing approach can affect the success of a project.

for short-term survival, and help prepare a selling memorandum. This will enable the seller to present the "sick" company to potential buyers with perceived solutions, thus preparing financial projections that show profitable future operations. The consultant's opinion will be more credible than the owner's projections because the consultant does not have a vested interest in the company.

In one example, an aircraft parts manufacturer with $2 million in sales was on the verge of having its loan called in by the bank. The owner-operators, who were also husband and wife, were not capable of stabilizing the company's finances in order to hold off the bank until the company could be sold. A turnaround specialist recommended by the bank was hired. Halfway through the consultant's engagement, the husband was hospitalized with cancer. The consultant implemented the stabilizing measures and engaged an intermediary who sold the business several months later.

With the business crisis compounded by the owner crisis (the husband died before the business was sold), it is highly unlikely the business would have survived long enough to be sold. In this case, the success of selling the unprofitable company was properly positioning the company for sale by first stabilizing the business financially.

Identify Potential Buyers

Very carefully identify potential buyers who will find the acquisition of the unprofitable company strategically advantageous. While buying a profitable company is obviously desirable, it is not necessarily essential. Take the example of a manufacturer of industrial automation with unprofitable sales of $7 million. The company was sold a few years ago for $12 million—all cash at closing. A careful look at the company's financials revealed their development efforts in industrial process controls resulted in temporary, but necessary, exorbitantly expensive charges. The successful sale was largely a result of the perfect synergism between the foreign buyer and the proprietary selling manufacturer.

Contact Experienced Buyers

In selecting an experienced buyer, one has to be sure that such a prospect has a successful record because it is likely that much of

> Very carefully identify potential buyers who will find the acquisition of the unprofitable company strategically advantageous.

the seller's payment will be in notes or contingency payments from the buyer based on his ability to turn the company around. Let's take a look at Peter Alcock of Alcock Ltd. Partners as an example of a qualified buyer.

In the early 1970s, Alcock joined a small management consulting company called Innovative Management. Under a consulting contract in 1972, Alcock, aged thirty-three, became acting president of Worcester Baking Company, which was beset by problems including a teamsters' wildcat strike. This was Alcock's first successful turnaround: In only six months, he resumed profitability and helped the family owners to re-establish their control.

Word quickly got out that this young fellow was an effective turnaround specialist. His next assignment was to become acting president of Educator Biscuit Company in Lowell. Alcock walked right into a hornet's nest: Educator was losing $175,000 per month from an operation with annual sales of $15 million, 450 union employees, and a 350,000 square foot antiquated plant. There were more than labor problems at Educator. Vendors had been short-shipping, previous management was not accountable, and within months, the price of flour doubled. Working fourteen hours per day, seven days a week, Alcock completed his year's contract having brought the company to a break-even level.

For several years, Alcock performed a number of consulting and investment banking assignments until 1980, when he acquired controlling interest in M.B Claff and Sons, formerly the world's foremost shoebox manufacturer. Claff's bank financing had been called due to excessive losses. Alcock quickly restored the company to profitability and sold part of the business at a substantial premium.

It was in the fall of 1987, however, that Alcock embarked on his most dramatic turnaround. He acquired U.S. Repeating Arms Co. (USRAC/Winchester) out of Chapter 11 bankruptcy, leading a group of American investors and Fabrique National de Belgique (FN). Serving as underwriter, Alcock pursued complicated negotiations for the acquisition of USRAC/Winchester with teams representing the city of New Haven, the state of Connecticut, creditors, labor unions, and Olin Corporation, licenser of the Winchester trademark.

Alcock's reorganization plan succeeded over those presented by investment bankers from the United States, Austria, and Belgium.

> Working fourteen hours per day, seven days a week, Alcock completed his year's contract having brought the company to a break-even level.

He was subsequently named president and CEO of this New Haven-based manufacturer of Winchester-brand firearms. In three years, he became known as the man who restored the quality in Winchester firearms, improved market share, and substantially increased the productivity of both the work force and the administration. In December 1990, after the successful sale to FN of his and three American-investor interests, Alcock left USRAC/Winchester to pursue further turnaround opportunities.

Sell a Portion of the Company

Sell part of the company that is unprofitable and keep the profitable portion. Merchants Tire Company in Boston was struggling in the very competitive tire retail/distribution business. It sold its large five-storey building, located next to Fenway Park, to a nearby hospital, and also sold six of its unprofitable tire stores. Merchants kept the profitable truck tire sales/service business, and eliminated the car tire business.

Do a Valuation Analysis

Proper valuation analysis for unprofitable companies is critical in justifying the price for the buyer. Many unprofitable companies sell for book value, adjusted book value, book value plus goodwill, or less than book value. If all of the above methodologies are unsatisfactory and the correct valuation is perceived to be higher, then one can capitalize EBIT, EBDIT, or Gross Profit, even though the Net Before Tax figure shows a loss. The capitalization rate on EBDIT, or the Gross Profit, is substantially less as one goes up the levels of profit on the income statement. The capitalization rate selection can be chosen from a comparable company in the same industry. The seller can rationalize that under new ownership much of the overhead figures will change and that the most objective valuation should be based on the direct manufacturing profit.

> Many unprofitable companies sell for book value, adjusted book value, book value plus goodwill, or less than book value.

Be Creative with the Structure of the Deal

Concentrate on the structure of the deal to entice the buyers. For example, one manufacturer of large machines, which had an average selling price of $200,000, ran into financial difficulty when its largest customer went bankrupt without paying its sizable invoice. Selling the company was the only viable solution at the time, but none of the competitors made an offer.

The successful solution was to sell to a different industry buyer—all the assets plus some goodwill for the brand name—but leave the liabilities with the seller. By itself, this transaction would not have been a good deal for the seller; however, he additionally signed an exclusive five-year nationwide sales representatives contract for the line of machines. This contract practically guaranteed him $750,000 more on level sales volume.

Another seller of a capital-intensive manufacturing business made the purchase price more reasonable by keeping the numerous and expensive CNC machines and leasing them, and by renting the real estate to the buyer. This change in the structure of the Purchase and Sale Agreement substantially reduced the risk to the buyer and vastly reduced the cash outlay.

> The seller's M&E appraisal may be outdated or one may not even exist.

When the Deal Hinges on the M&E Appraisal

For a capital-intensive manufacturer such as an injection molder or metal or woodwork producer, the machinery and equipment (M&E) usually is a significant part of the assets, and if you include the plant, then the value of these assets is a very important part of the overall valuation. The seller's M&E appraisal may be outdated or one may not even exist.

The buyer quite often is trying to get maximum leverage for the acquisition financing and the structure of the deal may hinge on the appraised values. The use of appraisals can also be helpful in determining the replacement value for insurance and determining the appropriate value for depreciation. The purpose of the appraisal will dictate the methodology.

There are five different categories used for valuations.

1. *Auction value* is based on a forced liquidation (auction sale). Based on experience, appraisers are able to estimate the actual selling price within 5 to 10 percent.

2. *Orderly liquidation value* accounts for the equipment being disposed of in a reasonable period of time.
3. *Fair market value* is a figure agreed upon by a willing buyer and a willing seller. This valuation does not include the foundation, wiring, plumbing, or transportation costs.
4. *In-place value* is the fair market value up-and-running in the plant.
5. *New replacement cost* is the cost of replacing the same or similar item with a new one today.

Often appraisers are called in to give a preliminary valuation and submit a formal proposal. Their proposals will include either an outright purchase of the assets, a guaranteed minimum dollar amount with a split of sales generated above that minimum, or a sale on a commission basis and expenses as agreed.

The equipment must be properly prepared for sale, which includes cleaning, arranging, tagging, and cataloging. Promotion and marketing will include a pictorial brochure as well as trade magazine and newspaper ads. Appraisers supervise an inspection period, conduct the sale, and supervise the removal of the equipment. It is not unusual to have hundreds of companies in attendance, with international buyers at larger sales.

Conclusion

I have learned that successfully selling a troubled company requires a well-defined sales process supported by a well-thought-out sales strategy. Sticking to these disciplines should lead to a timely sale of the troubled company. It should also significantly boost your chance of finding the right buyer who can see enough value in what you are selling to pay you the price that will enable you to attain maximum value.

Plan for the Long Goodbye

Whether you plan to sell out in one year, five years, or never, you need an exit strategy. As the term suggests, an exit strategy is a plan for leaving your business, and every business should have one, if not two. The first is useful as a guide to a smooth exit from your business. The second is for emergencies that could come about due to poor health or partnership problems.

Exit strategies may allow you to get out before the bottom falls out of your industry. Well-planned exits allow you to get a better price for your business.

For more information on this topic, visit our Web site at www.businesstown.com

Pricing Your Business

Summary of Part IV

- Techniques used to value your company
- How to position your company for the best offer possible
- The facts about goodwill

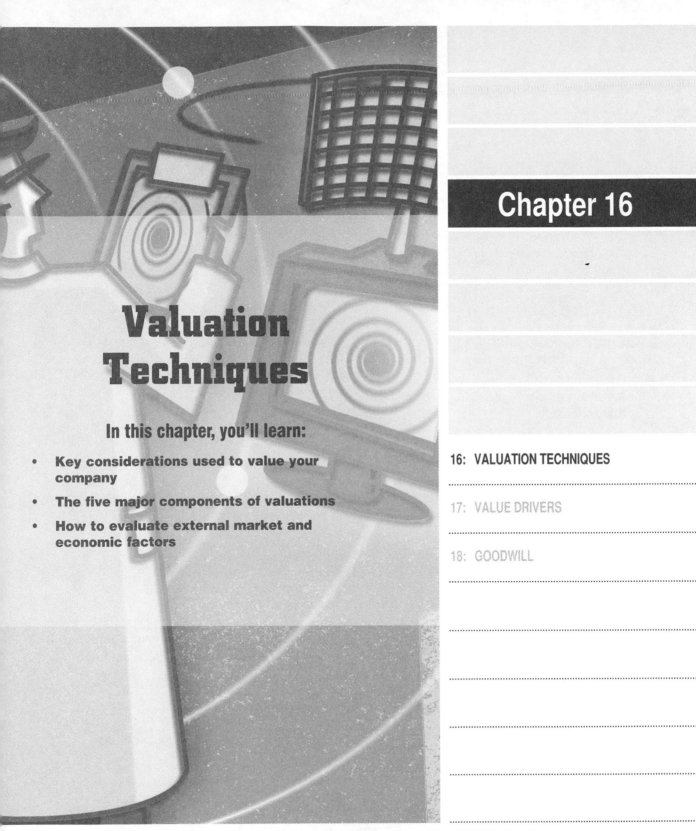

Valuation Techniques

In this chapter, you'll learn:

- Key considerations used to value your company
- The five major components of valuations
- How to evaluate external market and economic factors

Chapter 16

A seller should not even consider selling his or her business without professional advice about the company's valuation. In fact, a second opinion would not be considered out of line. Valuing a company involves a lot more than just studying the firm's financial statements.

Part of determining a company's value is based on timing, and that is influenced by the state of the economy, the specific industry, the banking environment, and the stock market. It is customary for a valuation expert to use a blend of various methods to determine a price range for the seller, in order to prepare for negotiations. Such methodologies would include a multiple of earnings, a discount cash flow analysis, comparables of other similar companies, cost of capital to cash flow comparison, among other factors. It is important, however, to not only analyze the financial aspects of the business but also the non-financial aspects, which can be both objective and subjective.

> It is customary for a valuation expert to use a blend of various methods to determine a price range for the seller.

Basic Factors

Valuing companies may be more of an art than a science, but there are three basic factors that buyers seek when trying to establish a price for a target company:

1. **Quality of earnings.** Do not have a long list of add-backs or one-time events, such as the sale of real estate, that do not reflect on the true earning power of the company's operations. It is not unusual for companies to have some non-recurring expenses every year, whether it is a new roof on the plant, a hefty lawsuit, or a write-down of inventory. Beware of the investment banker that restructures your company's earnings without any allowances for extraordinary items.

2. **Sustainability of earnings after the acquisition.** Two key questions buyers often asks themselves: Is the company that is targeted at the apex of its business cycle? And will earnings continue to grow at the previous rate?

3. **Verification of information.** The concern for the buyer is whether the information is accurate, timely, and relatively unbiased. Has the company allowed for possible product returns or for uncollectable receivables? Is the seller above-board or are there skeletons in the closet?

The multiple of corporate earnings varies with aspects of the business, including the company's history, the industry, market, management, the company's potential, proprietary products, niche, growth rate, and size. The multiple of earnings also depends on the buyer's desired rate of return. For example, a five multiple represents a 20 percent return on investment while a four multiple represents a 25 percent return on investment; the higher the perceived risk, the higher the desired return on investment.

The effect of the size of a company, as it relates to value, is demonstrated by a 1998 survey of 150 companies by the group IMAP/FINET. For companies with more than $50 million in sales, the multiples averaged 6.5 times EBIT, while companies with sales less than $10 million averaged a 4.5 multiple. Based on the EBIT of $1 million for one company with $50 million versus another company with $10 million in sales, the difference in price is equivalent to 44 percent more for the larger company.

> Has the company allowed for possible product returns or for uncollectable receivables?

Measuring Earnings

When a seller talks about earnings, what does he or she really mean: EBIT or EBITDA; 2002 earnings or 2003 projected earnings; EBITDA-CAP X; reinstated without prerequisites but with add-backs? Sometimes crafty investment bankers will submit a selling memorandum and the earnings will be recast to include all of the owner's salary and compensation; that is certainly one way to boost earnings.

When measuring your company's earnings you must also ask yourself: When a buyer is analyzing earnings, is it for one year or three years, interim earnings annualized or a combination of reporting periods? What is the time frame for measuring earnings and what is the trend of earnings?

Another concern when making such measurements is to determine what changes could affect earnings in the future, such as increase in rent, family members off the payroll, or loss of key customers or vendors. If your company is locked into long-term contracts in which you are unable to raise prices, or if your company is in a commodity business in which there is unrealistic market pricing, be aware that such factors could affect the measurement of your company's earnings.

Key Considerations

The following questions will help you to understand your business and thereby value the company more prudently.

What's for sale? What's not for sale? Does it include real estate? Are some of the machines leased instead of owned?

What assets are not earning money? Perhaps they should be sold off.

What is proprietary: formulations, patents, software?

What is your competitive advantage? Is it a certain niche, superior marketing, or more efficient manufacturing?

What is the barrier of entry: capital, low labor, tight relationships?

Are there employment agreements or non-competes? Have you failed to secure these agreements from key employees?

How would someone grow the business? Perhaps it can't be grown.

How much working capital would someone need to run the business?

What is the depth of management and how dependent is the business on you, the owner/manager?

How is the financial reporting undertaken and recorded, and how do you, or management, adjust the business accordingly?

> What assets are not earning money? Perhaps they should be sold off.

A Valuation Worksheet

Here is a handy worksheet that consolidates many of the factors that need to be considered when trying to place a value on a company.

1. Start with the business.

Value drivers	Value detractors
Size	Customer concentration
Growth Rate	Poor financials
Management	Outdated M&E
Niche	Few assets
History	Lack of agreements with employees, customers, suppliers
Poor exit possibilities	
Small market	
Potential technology changes	
Product or service very price sensitive	

2. Conduct financial analysis.
   - Market Value—comparables
   - Multiple of Earnings—based on the rate of return desired
   - Discounted Cash Flow—based on expected growth rate
3. Set structure and terms. 100 percent cash at closing could reduce price 20 percent.
4. Get a second opinion. Even professionals need a sounding board.
5. Consider indicators of high value.
   - High sustainable cash flow
   - Expected industry growth
   - Good market share
   - Competitive advantage—location, exclusive product line
   - Undervalued assets—land/equipment
   - Healthy working capital
   - Low failure rate in industry
   - Modern well-kept plant
6. Consider indicators of low value.

Poor industry outlook	Company liabilities
Foreign competition	Distressed circumstances
Price cutting	History of problems—employees, customers, suppliers, litigation
Regulations	Heavy debt load
High taxes	
Material costs	

Private Company Considerations

Valuing private companies is more difficult than valuing public companies because most private companies do not have audited financial statements, which forces a buyer to spend considerable effort to dig out the accurate information on true earnings. Historically, closely held companies sell for one-third less than publicly held companies.

EBIT buyers, those who value sellers based on a multiple of EBIT, will not pay more or less than five times the earnings for a company that is left as bare bones. The buyer will expect at least 50 percent or more of the purchase price to be supported by working capital and net tangible machinery and equipment. Also, the buyer usually wants to buy a going concern particularly if he or she is paying full price. And the buyer expects to be able to run the company without additional infusions for working capital or capital equipment.

In analyzing what would be a reasonable price to acquire a private company, the potential buyer should scrutinize the seller's facilities list to assess its capital needs and the adequacy of its working capital. In today's sophisticated marketplace, professional buyers are very pragmatic. They want to be sure that the budgeted depreciation will exceed the necessary capital expenditures and that EBIT will hold up for the ensuing years.

A lot of discussions are based on the current EBIT multiple, but just like price earnings multiples of public companies, its relevance is often tied to the growth rate. One possible scenario for determining the EBIT multiple for private companies is the following analysis:

Growth Rate	EBIT
10%	4.5 to 5.5
15%	5.5 to 6.5
20%	6.5 to 7.5

The above example is a theoretical approach to valuations, but in the real world buyers have to be conscious of the prices at which businesses are being bought and sold. Unfortunately, there are

> The potential buyer should scrutinize the seller's facilities list to assess its capital needs and the adequacy of its working capital.

numerous solid and well-financed buyers, but excellent companies for sale are hard to find. Therefore, it is difficult to buy companies at a reasonable price in today's market.

According to Howard Smith, former Managing Director of Baldwin & Clarke Corporate Finance, Inc. of Bedford, New Hampshire, it is a myth to believe that growth for growth's sake is what drives the EBIT multiple upward. The real index for determining a reasonable price for a business is the cost of capital. If the cost of capital exceeds EBIT growth, then growth for growth's sake does not add value and does not increase the company's price.

The following chart illustrates how to compute the cost of capital. If a company's after-tax cost of debt is 6 percent and its estimated cost of equity is 16 percent, and it plans to raise capital 20 percent by way of debt and 80 percent by way of equity, it computes the cost of capital at 14 percent as follows:

> It is a myth to believe that growth for growth's sake is what drives the EBIT multiple upward.

	Weight	Cost	Weighted Cost
Debt	20%	6%	1.2%
Equity	80%	16%	12.8%
Cost of Capital			14.0%

The cost of equity is based on equity risk premiums published by Ibbotson Associates. The Ibbotson analyses make extensive use of the rate-of-return data basis compiled by the Center for Research in Security Prices at the University of Chicago Graduate School of Business. In this case, the common stocks annual total return (growth plus dividends) "arithmetic mean" is 12 percent plus a risk premium of 40 percent, which leads to a cost of equity of 16 percent.

Therefore, in this example, unless the EBIT is growing at a rate of greater than the 14 percent of the cost of capital, many prudent corporate acquirers would not acquire the target company.

What does a multiple of earnings really mean? If we use a five multiple and divide it into one hundred, it inputs a return on capital of 20 percent. A seven multiple, by contrast, results in 14.3 percent return. Based on the risk/reward considerations of buying and running a business, if you paid ten times EBIT, your return would be

10 percent before tax, or approximately 6 percent after tax, compared to a tax-free and risk-free treasury of 5.2 percent.

The above analysis begins to fall apart if applied to a hot mergers and acquisitions market. In order to buy a good company, an acquirer probably has to pay an unreasonable price. The alternative to buying good companies at inflated prices is to buy companies that are underperforming at reasonable prices (four times EBIT), and then fix them.

Valuations of private companies are much more subjective than public companies because there is no free trading marketplace for the stock of private companies. You could argue that a reasonable price for some private companies could be ten times EBIT but, just like a champion figure skater, the performance has to be flawless. Get out a piece of paper and see if you can answer "yes" to all of the following questions about the selling company:

Is it in a stable market?

Historically, has your company had a stability of earnings?

Do you have a realized cost savings after purchase?

Are there no significant capital expenditures pending?

Are there no significant competitive threats?

Are there no significant alternative technologies?

Is there large market potential?

Do you have a reasonable market position?

Do you have broad-based distribution channels?

Do you have a synergy with the buyer?

Is sound management to remain with the company?

Do you have product diversity?

Do you have a wide customer base?

Are you not dependent on only a few suppliers?

> The alternative to buying good companies at inflated prices is to buy companies that are underperforming at reasonable prices (four times EBIT), and then fix them.

The above list is not complete, but it is the type of analysis that should be compared or benchmarked to other companies. Of course, in the real world, the market sets the price. The seller usually settles for a lower price than originally desired, and the buyer pays more than originally expected.

The Five Major Components of Valuations

Corporate valuations are highly complicated. Unlike real estate valuations that are fairly straightforward with the help of comparable transactions, assessed values, and current capitalization rates, corporate valuations have many more variables and components. Trying to understand the various components of the corporate valuation is like peeling back the layers of an onion. Here are the five major component parts: outside influences, financials, business, structure, and benchmarking.

Outside Influences

The euphoric or depressed condition of the marketplace has a considerable impact on the price of a company. The state of the economy, the healthiness of the stock market, interest rates, the availability of capital, the cost of capital (debt and equity), and the prevailing EBIT multiples in general will all influence a company's valuation.

Before the stock market accelerated in 1998 through 2000, EBIT multiples of good middle-market manufacturers ranged from five to six times EBIT. With the booming stock market during those two halcyon years, the EBIT multiples rose accordingly for middle-market companies up to six or seven. Based on a $1 million EBIT, the increase in multiples could mean a $7 million purchase price compared to $5 million. That's no small potatoes. Conversely, when the stock market tanked in 2001, the EBIT multiples eroded.

These multiples are based on the previous year's EBIT. Buyers using aggressive multiples have no trouble justifying their actions; they say, for example, that while they are paying six times

2001 EBIT, it is five times "projected" 2002 EBIT. Based on a calendar fiscal year (December 31), this logic is reasonable since the year is half over. So the real question is: What EBIT are we using; 2001, an estimated 2002, or a blend based on the last four quarters?

The driving force for the continuing keen interest in mergers and acquisitions is the low cost of capital, the need for most industries to consolidate, the race for technology, and the excess cash in most corporate accounts. Furthermore, much of the corporate restructuring has been accomplished. Future profits must come from top-line growth. Many aggressive companies have the mandate to grow 10 percent internally and 10 percent externally. The culture of most mature companies is to grow at least partly by acquisition. There isn't a day that goes by when the *Wall Street Journal* does not report another company being gobbled up.

Most business professionals understand that good businesses sell for a premium in spite of the stock market declines in 2001. It is worth noting that most public companies sell for a 20 to 40 percent premium to their market valuation (the number of shares times the price per share). If one believes that the market capitalization is a fair valuation for public companies, a good argument could be made that a solid middle-market private company should sell for a 20 to 40 percent premium over an independent corporate enterprise valuation. Such a premium is based on the nature of competitive bidding. Private company valuations compared to public company valuations should be discounted 25 to 50 percent.

In summary, the above factors are the outside influences affecting valuations.

Financials

Perhaps no other component of the business will be scrutinized as carefully as the company's financials. Aside from all the obvious factors—trends of top- and bottom-line growth, percentage of gross and operating income, debt ratios—the size of the company affects the valuation considerably.

> The culture of most mature companies is to grow at least partly by acquisition.

VALUATION TECHNIQUES

The larger the company in sales and EBIT, the more robust buyers will chase after it. Many strong buyers will not consider companies with sales under $20 million or EBITs below $2 million. Companies with EBITs over $5 million receive the lion's share of attention from buyers. Unfortunately, small companies do not have management, infrastructure, national distribution, or proper reporting systems. And small companies under $20 million in sales are usually dependent on the CEO, so the valuation is discounted accordingly. A one-man band is great for the CEO's ego, but it adversely affects the valuation.

Most non-technology companies with EBITs under $1 million will sell for substantially lower multiples, maybe five instead of 7.5, or a 50 percent difference. And if the company is just barely profitable, the valuation will be based on book value, not a multiple of earnings. So size makes a difference, both in sales and EBIT.

Many middle-market companies are not positioned to grow and, in fact, have either barely grown more than the inflation rate or are not really positioned to grow under the current management. Some family businesses and/or S corporations take out most of the profits instead of reinvesting them, thus inhibiting growth. There is plenty of truth to the general guideline that a company growing at 10 percent is worth a five multiple of EBIT, one growing at 15 percent earns a six multiple, and one growing at 20 percent is rewarded with a seven multiple. While this analysis is broad, the point is that growth rates are important, particularly if they are sustainable. In addition to the company's ability to grow internally, consider whether an industry is conducive to growth: buggy whips or biotechnology?

One of the key factors of growth is the company's commitment to reinvestment in fixed assets (cap-x), in other words replacing old equipment with new. Further, be aware that S corporations pay out most of earnings while C corporations are building the net worth each year of profitability. It is not uncommon for a profitable C corporation with $10 million plus of sales to be worth several million dollars more because of the S corporations' flow-through of earnings to the individual stockholders.

> One of the key factors of growth is the company's commitment to reinvestment in fixed assets.

Other major considerations from the financial perspective are:

- The stability of earnings over time
- The realized cost savings after purchase
- The capital expenditures (excessive or normal)
- The add-backs prerequisites of owners or unusual circumstances
- The projections
- The pricing of earlier investment rounds

> While add-backs are part of "other major financial considerations," it is important to elaborate on this item.

While add-backs are part of "other major financial considerations," it is important to elaborate on this item. There are some investment bankers who have honorable intentions that are unrealistic because they add back in general about 50 percent more than is truly justifiable. Let's say the owner of a company with $20 million in sales is paying himself $300,000, including a leased BMW. The investment banker would rationalize that a buyer could pay a replacement CEO $100,000 total compensation with no leased BMW valued at $10,000 annually. So we have now identified a $210,000 saving for the new CEO, which is immediately added to the add-backs. Using a six multiple, the investment banker has just added $1,260,000 to the corporate valuation.

As a buyer, are you going to accept the above analysis? Chances are that to attract a topnotch CEO for a company that size, a $200,000 total compensation with a $10,000 leased luxury car is not unrealistic. The new CEO will also want stock or stock options, so that at the end of the day, including the executive search firm's fee (33 percent) to recruit the new CEO, there will be no add-backs for the replacement CEO.

Other areas in which add-backs are too aggressive are the "one-time events" category. The seller's investment banker might list extraneous events as add-backs, such as unusual attorneys' fees, accounting fees, consulting fees, or promotional expenses. In reality, there are extraordinary circumstances every year, so to add back all these expenses to adjusted earnings and use the prevailing multiple is plain wrong.

When it comes to analyzing the financials for valuation purposes, it is important to question the validity of every item.

Business

Some of the major issues in evaluating a company relate to how to determine whether or not the sales and profits are truly sustainable. Many factors contribute to these results:

- Proprietary products and services
- Market share
- Customer concentration versus broad distribution
- Cyclicality versus seasonality
- Sophisticated financial systems
- Management depth
- Current appraisals on equipment, real estate, and insurance coverage

A potential buyer often tests the return on investment by applying the larger company's tax rate (40 percent) to various scenarios, such as some growth, no growth, negative growth, and with various gross margins.

Much of the business valuation is confirmed or denied during the due diligence phase. For example, is the company's market position weaker than purported, is the competition tougher, is the market in general struggling? Pre-acquisition evaluation of the company should encompass factors such as customer loyalty, status of contracts, and employee retention.

The business component is the most difficult of all the parts to analyze because it may be, in part, subjective.

> Pre-acquisition evaluation of the company should encompass factors such as customer loyalty, status of contracts, and employee retention.

Structure

One might think that every seller would prefer all cash at closing, but that is not necessarily so. A buyer's bid price is almost meaningless unless you have some sense of the terms of the deal. Deferred payments, for example, postpone tax payments and shelter the remuneration until sometime in the future.

Without delving into details, which is the better of the following two deals: $4 million cash at closing or $6 million comprised of $2 million cash, $2 million unsecured note, and a $2 million earnout? The question forces you to consider the risk versus the reward, which in turn affects the valuation.

Another critical factor in the valuation is whether an owner of a C corporation can convince the buyer to acquire the stock instead of the assets of the corporation. With thorough "reps and warranties," covenants, and escrow accounts, stock transactions should be doable.

If a seller wants to net $1 million after taxes, there would be a different price depending on the structure of the deal. For example:

If C Corporation:	Price	$2.0 million
To Corporation	After Tax (30%)	$1.4 million
To Stockholder	After Tax (30%)	$1.0 million
If S Corporation	Price	$1.5 million
	After Tax (30%)	$1.05 million

> Many large corporations determine the valuation of the target company by relating it to their own cost of capital.

Many large corporations determine the valuation of the target company by relating it to their own cost of capital. Unless there is a compelling reason to acquire a target, many large companies will not pay a price that exceeds their own cost of capital. For example, if the buyer's cost of capital (debt and equity) was a blended rate of 15 percent, then a company with a $1 million EBIT would have to be purchased for less than $7 million to exceed their cost of capital ($7 million $\times$ 15 percent = $1.05 million).

Benchmarking

The last major component of the valuation analysis is benchmarking. There are various types. One is based on comparables with other companies in that specific industry, such as injection molding, machine tools, and software. The other forms of benchmarking relate more to whether the acquirer is a financial or a strategic buyer.

Financial Buyer

Let us assume that the equity investors of a buyout fund have stipulated an 18 percent return on equity (ROE). Furthermore, the seller wants all cash at closing—no seller financing and no contingent payments. Additionally, the only bank source for this buyout fund has a strict covenant that during a recession, financing may be possible only at a 1:1 debt/equity ratio, and during good economic times financing may be possible at a 2:1 debt/equity ratio.

In the following example, the buyout fund's offering price is dictated by the investor's requirements, the seller's stipulation on terms, and the covenants of the bank.

VALUATION IN RECESSION PERIOD

Price $12,500,000
(figures below in thousands)

EBIT	$ 2,500	$ 2,500
EBIT Multiplier	5	
Purchase Price	12,500	
Financing Debt	6,250 × 10% interest	(625)
Equity	6,250	
Pre-Tax Profit		1,875
Taxes (40%)		(750)
Net Profit		$1,125
Return on Equity		1,125/6,250 = 18%

VALUATION IN GOOD ECONOMIC TIMES

Price $15,000,000
(figures below in thousands)

EBIT	$ 2,500	$ 2,500
EBIT Multiplier	6	
Purchase Price	15,000	
Financing Debt	10,000 × 10% interest	(1,000)
Equity	5,000	
Pre-Tax Profit		1,500
Taxes (40%)		600
Net Profit		$ 900
Return on Equity		900/5,000 = 18%

Strategic Buyer

Let us assume that a public company wants to acquire a competitor. Both are importers of proprietary products. Aside from the obvious synergies, the buyer's requirement is that the acquisition must lead to immediate growth. Again, the seller wants all cash at closing. The seller's minimum price is $8 million. Let's go through a hypothetical case study.

Sales (thousands)	$10,000		
Gross Profit	4,200		
Operating Expenses	(2,800)		
EBIT	1,400		
Add Backs	500		
Reconstructed EBIT	$1,900		
After Tax (40%)	1,140	Return on Capital	
		$1.140M ÷ $8M =	14.25%
Net After Tax	$1,140		

As an investment, 14.25 percent is not a stellar return on capital. On the other hand, the upside potential and prospective cost savings under the new ownership may substantially improve the return.

In the above two examples, we benchmarked or compared the companies' financials with certain standards, which in turn either set the price or justified the price.

Floors, Ceilings, and Reviews

Each of these five components must be analyzed separately but viewed in its entirety in order to set a price range—a floor and a ceiling price. In the negotiations, the seller should not go below his or her floor price and the buyer should not go beyond his or her ceiling price.

Most corporate valuation experts use a blend of numbers derived from discounted cash flow, capitalization of earnings, and multiples of book value—which would include a weighted average of the past, present, and future.

Modeling is helpful to test what happens in various worst-case scenarios, such as declining sales and margins. Of course, a banker wants to be sure that his cash flow model covers debt; 1.8 to

> The seller should not go below his or her floor price and the buyer should not go beyond his or her ceiling price.

1.0 gives banks the necessary debt coverage under adverse conditions ($1.8 million of cash flow compared to $1.0 million of principal and interest obligations).

How you value a company will depend on how you finance the acquisition and the business going forward. That is why many buyers will receive a general financing commitment from a bank before the buyer commits to a firm price with the seller.

Pricing and structuring a transaction are extremely difficult and prudence often requires a second or third expert opinion.

Remember the five major components of valuation; they are equally important.

Difficult Issues in Business Valuations

Corporate valuations are often difficult, complex, and subject to the appraiser's interpretation of the relevant facts and circumstances. The appraiser's judgments are based on as much information, both objective and subjective, as he or she can obtain. The appraiser often has to assume that the information received is accurate.

In merger and acquisition transactions, due diligence will frequently reveal additional facts that may alter the value of the company. While it is common for the buyer and seller to discuss a range of values for a company, a corporate appraiser's assignment is usually to arrive at a precise number for a valuation at a given date, which can be defended in court under the toughest of scrutiny. Since valuation experts labor over myriad factors that affect the ultimate outcome of the valuation, roundtable discussion groups are a way for two experts to share the factors that they incorporate into their valuation process.

Due diligence will frequently reveal additional facts that may alter the value of the company.

Distinctive Business Characteristics

Key person(s). It is not unusual for a private company owner to be the CEO, CFO, and COO. The owner may pay himself $200,000 per year to handle all these duties. If a larger company bought this business, they might insist on hiring a CFO and COO and pay the management team $400,000. In this case, a buyer would subtract the difference ($400,000 minus $200,000) to arrive at a lower reconstructed EBIT. In other situations, it is not clear whether the key person's skills, experience, and personal relationships can really be replaced.

Lack of product diversity. Single-product companies are inherently subject to greater risks, such as competitive products and competitive pricing, than are multiproduct companies.

Critical supply source. If a company's competitive advantage is to have low costs resulting from single sourcing all the nuts and bolts from one supplier in China, or buying all their adhesives from one supplier with proprietary formulations, then the company is vulnerable to change in supplier relations or interruption of supply.

Customer concentration. Many small companies have one or two key customers that account for 50 percent of their total sales. The loss of one or both of these customers could adversely affect the company's survival.

Reliance upon short-term contracts. Tracking major customer orders annually over a five-year period indicates the dependability of the business. It costs substantially less servicing regular customers than opening up new accounts.

Franchises/Third party approval. The opportunity to buy a franchise may be obvious, but what about the restrictions on reselling the franchise? Restrictions on resale will affect purchase value.

Inventory and currency risks. Inventory, good or bad, affects the company's value dollar for dollar. Inventory that hasn't sold for a year is often deemed nearly worthless. Buying foreign companies always has currency risks, up or down.

Company-/Industry life cycle. In general, companies that produce consumer products are particularly vulnerable to life

> Many small companies have one or two key customers that account for 50 percent of their total sales.

cycle issues. One obvious industry that appeared to reach maturity and then decline is the bicycle industry, which was reborn with the advent of mountain bikes.

Intangible assets. Off-balance sheet items, such as patents and goodwill of respected brand names, will increase valuation but can be difficult to quantify or negotiate.

ESOP ownership. A company that is partially or totally owned by the employees requires an employee vote before the company can be sold. The company's marketability may thereby be restricted, possibly reducing the attractiveness to a buyer and reducing the company's value.

External Market and Economic Factors

The following are examples of the parts external market and economic factors play:

Changes in markets. It is extremely important to change with the market. Wang Laboratories produced one of the finest word processors but the company failed to change as the market changed, which was one reason why the company failed.

Changing competition. When Home Depot moves into the backyard of a lumber retailer, the value of the latter usually decreases substantially. Home Depot's mass volume allows the retail chain to price goods at near unbeatable prices.

Cyclical industry. Investors and buyers will pay a premium for steadily rising earnings through good and bad economic times, and conversely will discount the valuation for cyclical industries.

Real Estate and Environmental Factors

Most acquirers of manufacturers would rather lease than buy the plant. Therefore, for realistic valuation purposes, it might be

> Off balance sheet items, such as patents and goodwill of respected brand names, will increase valuation but can be difficult to quantify or negotiate.

necessary to discount the fair market value of the real estate in offering a package deal that includes the business. Environmental issues are one of the major deal breakers primarily because an unresolved environmental problem can be a bottomless pit, which can exceed the entire principal invested.

Conclusion

We covered quite a bit of ground in this chapter. You now have some grounding on the theory behind business valuation, but it is worth emphasizing that theory is one thing, the real world quite another. In the real world, of course, buyers have to be conscious of the prices at which businesses are being bought and sold, as well as of the subtle issues at play when a business is brought to market.

Environmental issues are one of the major deal breakers.

For more information on this topic, visit our Web site at www.businesstown.com

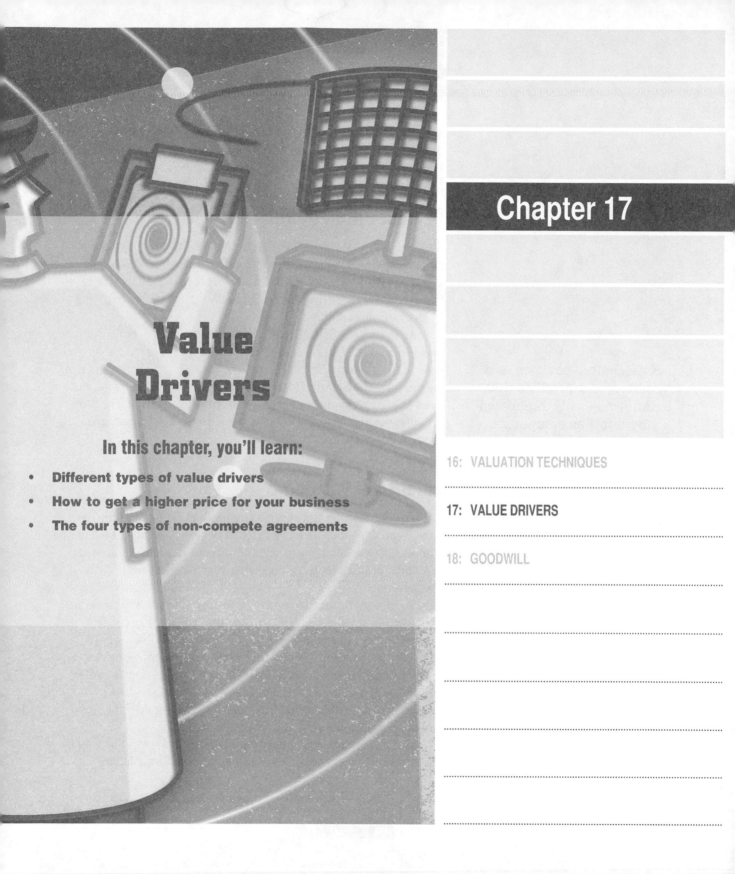

Value Drivers

In this chapter, you'll learn:

- Different types of value drivers
- How to get a higher price for your business
- The four types of non-compete agreements

Chapter 17

It is imperative to identify the value drivers of the selling company, substantiate them, and, if possible, position them so they are transferable to the buyer.

Product Differentiation

A special taste, a unique formula, a distinctive appearance, and a particular image are characteristics that differentiate products from one another that, in turn, differentiate the company. These characteristics are called value drivers and will usually result in a buyer paying a higher earnings multiple.

An example is SmartFoods cheddar cheese coated–popcorn that took the market by storm about fifteen years ago. It seemed that none of the popcorn companies could duplicate the addictive taste of the product. The SmartFoods company sold out to Frito-Lay for four times sales, a premium price for a small regional company. The product differentiation was SmartFoods' value driver—the unique, and popular, popcorn.

Defensible Position

> A defensible position is a service or a product that cannot be easily replicated by another company.

A defensible position is a service or a product that cannot be easily replicated by another company. It may be a government license that allows your company to operate without the likelihood of any additional licenses issued, thus giving your business no or little competition.

To provide an example unrelated to special licenses, your defensible position could be similar to Dispenser Services, Inc. (DSI), which operates outside of Boston. DSI sells items such as coffee, orange juice, and yogurt to major institutional cafeterias—such as those in hospitals and universities—at prices that are often 30 percent higher than the competition. The hook, however, is that DSI loans, not leases, coffee, juice, and yogurt dispensing machines supported by twenty-four-hour guaranteed service.

DSI has been in business for twenty years with sales and profits increasing annually. The company had more than $1 million of dispensing equipment on loan with the top institutions in the Boston area. The key value driver is that immediate service and maintenance of the dispensing machines is more important to the institutions than the lowest price for coffee, juice, or yogurt. For a competitor to replace DSI, they would have to start by investing in $1 million worth of machines that would be loaned out.

Dominant Market Share

An important value driver is for a company to command a position so strong in the market that, by default, it has few or ineffective competitors. One private equity group, FCP Inc. from Tampa, Florida, has a strategy to consolidate subsets of industries, but in niches where there might be only five companies left within that product area, such as lariats, aquariums, and fire hose couplings. This strong market share is the value driver for these companies.

Technology

Proprietary technology does not always have to be patented to be effective. For one thing, it can also be a secretive process. Take the example of a small Massachusetts adhesive company. The company develops custom adhesives for specialty purposes, usually in small batches. The applications are often critical to the overall situation, which means the adhesive might have to resist high temperatures, withstand extreme pressure, or be totally waterproof. Overall, though, it is a small cost to the entire project. When the new owner took charge of the company, his first order of business was to double the prices of all the custom adhesives. The owner figured out that if he lost 50 percent of his business because of the price increase, he would still be even. As it turned out, he did not lose any customers. Their technology is their value driver.

Protection of engineering talent, intellectual property, and proprietary information are paramount in the successful transfer of ownership in the high-technology industry. Pre- and post-sale agreements with key employees are essential to have in place. The loss of assets

> Proprietary technology does not always have to be patented to be effective.

previously mentioned would greatly diminish the value of the company. Conversely, the retention of the assets, both people and intellectual property, enhances the company's value. The validity of the confidentiality agreements and non-compete agreements depends on the ability of the company to enforce them.

Let's assume that Technology Inc. has obtained confidentiality agreements down to the lowest employee level. In the case of the non-compete agreements, the company granted stock options as part of the contractual agreement. Further, Technology Inc.'s top ten management team members were willing to sign a three-year employment contract with Newco to help assure continuity going forward. These agreements, pre- and post-sale of Technology Inc., are value drivers for selling the company.

Cost Advantage

Whether it was John Rockefeller's oil empire or Wal-Mart, the advantage of being a low-cost producer is obvious. Even small companies can have a cost advantage, particularly if they are serving a relatively small market. For example, Walden Paddlers was a virtual kayak company with all its employees leased and all its manufacturing subcontracted. Walden was only the sixth largest kayak company in the industry, but it was one of the most profitable. It had aligned itself with one of the largest roto-molding manufacturers in the world on an exclusive basis—a manufacturer that was truly a partner. The value driver was the ability of the founder, Paul Farrow, to become a low-cost producer even though it was not the largest company in the industry.

Customer Lists

Some businesses, such as magazine publications, have built their company by repeat sales, year after year, like an annuity. Another example would be a residential oil company where customers usually remain loyal in spite of a small price differential by a competitor. The purchase of such companies would be the acquisition of accounts, hence the value driver is the customer lists.

Converting Value Drivers to Higher Prices

While there may be other possible value drivers, you now have a good idea of their characteristics. It often takes more time than the normal modus operandi in the selling process to identify all of your value drivers. Whether it is the impatient client or the overzealous investment banker, if you want to receive a higher price for the business you need time to verify the value drivers. Slow down and take your time to develop a compelling case.

When I learned the details of the SmartFoods transaction, I could see how the owners developed a scenario that significantly increased the value of the company based on a discounted cash flow valuation. Since SmartFoods was a regional brand in New England, operating from one factory in Marlborough, Massachusetts, its distribution was limited. Fortunately, it is relatively easy to track and measure branded consumer products through various reporting services—Neilson, IRI, SAMI.

Let's assume that these reports showed that SmartFoods had 30 percent market share in New England of the supermarket retail business for popcorn in 1990, which was when they sold out to Frito-Lay. Knowing that New England makes up about 8 percent of the total U.S. population, and assuming that SmartFoods could grow within five years to $40 million on a national basis under Frito-Lay's ownership, the price at the time of sale in 1990 was justifiably $12 million—based on various factors for branded food companies. Obviously, the case was made on projected market share. The valuation was derived based on discounted cash flow. This example shows precisely how to incorporate value drivers to reach the highest price.

Identifying the value drivers is one aspect of determining the value of your business, but converting the value drivers into a higher price—deal drivers—is the objective. The following are several examples of deal drivers.

> Identifying the value drivers is one aspect of determining the value of your business, but converting the value drivers into a higher price—deal drivers—is the objective.

Retail

Superior locations and long and competitive renewable leases are deal drivers in the retail business above and beyond multiples of

EBITDA. A very desirable contract might be a ten-year lease with interim escalators based on the consumer price index with the right to renew for another ten years based on certain conditions. Now, the value driver in the retail business could be the attractiveness of the assumable leases.

Consumer Products

Brand recognition and the power of the brand name are value drivers. Several years ago, I was retained as an investment banker to sell a sporting goods manufacturer. When I approached the large sporting conglomerates such as Brunswick, K-2, and Johnson Worldwide, they were not interested in acquiring my client because the company was not one of the leading brands within its product category.

> Brand recognition and the power of the brand name are value drivers.

Franchise

Whether it is a Sir Speedy printing company, Roto-Rooter sewer and drain service, or a Dunkin Donut coffee shop franchise, the value driver is the highly visible name coupled with a protected geographic territory.

Conclusion

The seller's challenge is to sell the company at a price that exceeds the norm for its industry peer group. Measuring financials is straightforward but capitalizing on the power of the company's value drivers is the best way to maximize the sales price.

For more information on this topic, visit our Web site at www.businesstown.com

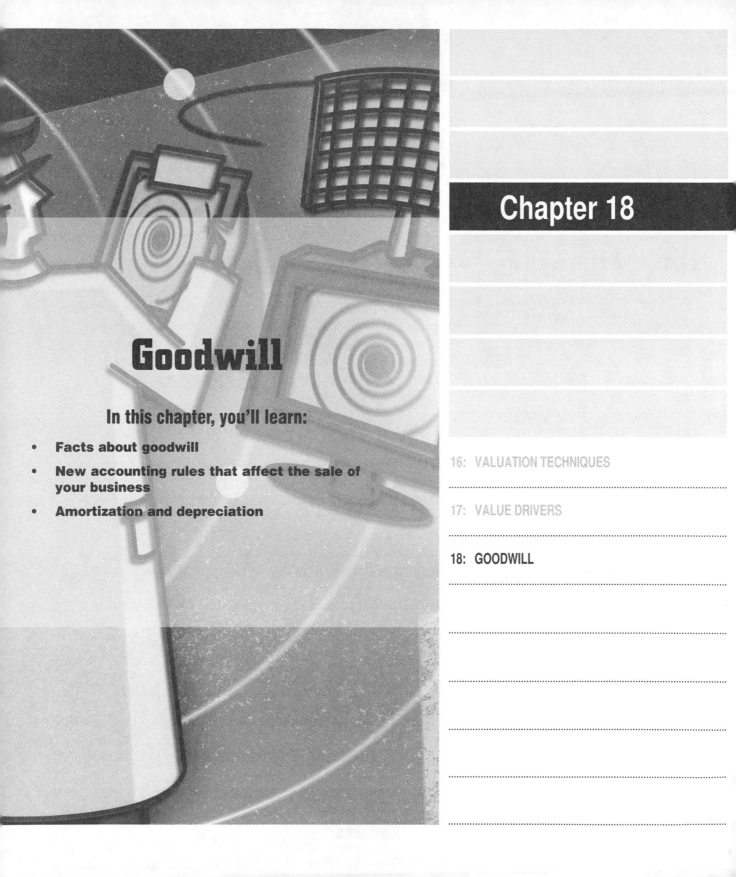

Goodwill

In this chapter, you'll learn:

- **Facts about goodwill**
- **New accounting rules that affect the sale of your business**
- **Amortization and depreciation**

Chapter 18

Goodwill is the price a buyer pays for a business over and above the economic value of its tangible assets, and/or the amount over book value. Important accounting changes by the Federal Account Standards Board (FASB) were implemented on July 1, 2001, which changed the way goodwill is treated on the income statement. Before the accounting rule change, if you sold a company for $10 million but only had assets of $6 million, the buyer would inherit $4 million of goodwill if the transaction was an asset sale. The buyer would then amortize the $4 million of goodwill over fifteen years, thus diluting earnings.

Depending on the circumstances, the acquisition could be dilutive, not accretive, which was a huge burden for public companies because of the negative effect on their stock price. Prior to the accounting change, many sellers, particularly high-technology or service companies, were passed over by buyers because the acquisition would give them a hit to earnings.

The new FASB rule is good news for sellers because goodwill does not have to be written off, except if and when it is being carried on the books at too high a value.

The acquirer or merged company must periodically assess the items that go into goodwill, such as brands, customer relationships, and other intangibles, and take a write-off if their value is impaired. The new accounting rules will promote write-downs at companies with overvalued assets. Before the start of 2002, companies must assign a certain amount of goodwill to each of their reporting units. They must get an outside auditor—not their usual accounting firm— to put a fair value on each unit's goodwill.

It should be noted that companies who have developed most of their sales and profits internally have little or no goodwill. Since private company valuations are principally based on Earnings Before Interest and "Depreciation" (EBITDA), there will not be a change in valuation. Public company valuations, however, could increase because their value is based on earnings per share and their earnings will read higher without the old charges for goodwill.

The new FASB ruling has eliminated the pooling-of-interest accounting, which avoided goodwill when shares of two companies were exchanged.

> The new FASB rule is good news for sellers because goodwill does not have to be written off.

Negative Goodwill

One has to ask: Does goodwill exist in this business? According to Chris Mercer of Mercer Capital of Memphis, Tennessee, a leading corporate valuation firm: "Many people believe that there is an implicit goodwill with all companies. On the contrary, there is no automatic goodwill. In fact, in many situations if the company's earnings are not sufficient to justify a reasonable return on its assets, then there could be negative goodwill.

Under these circumstances, if a company with a minimal multiple of operating income (like four) does not equal book value, then it's arguable to say that the earnings are not sufficient to support the assets. Therefore, the selling price for such a company could be at book value or less, which would negate any goodwill."

Examples of ill will, or no goodwill, show up quite frequently with small to medium size distributors with sales under $20 million—particularly distributors of commodity products that have an abundance of outlets, such as plumbing, electrical or heating ventilating, and air conditioning in the same area.

Some years ago, Watertown Electric Supply in Massachusetts retained an intermediary to sell the fourth generation family business with profitable sales of $5 million from three outlets. The intermediary conducted an exhaustive search for buyers. The rule of thumb for purchasing this type of business has been book value. Offers, and eventually a Letter of Intent, were submitted to the owner of Watertown Electric—all at book value with no goodwill.

Unfortunately, the owner wanted a higher price for his business and withdrew it from the market. In April 1995, the *Boston Globe* published a front page article entitled, "After 60 Years, A Family Business Goes Under." In the attempt to save the overleveraged business, the owner pumped in more money from his personal funds, all for naught. The results were devastating as the owner's and his mother's home were repossessed by the banks. Furthermore, the owner had cashed in a life insurance policy, individual retirement accounts, stocks, and bonds.

While everything is clear with hindsight, this dramatic story is meant to accentuate the fact that sometimes it is unwise to hold out for goodwill when the industry or business does not justify it.

When Goodwill Is Bad for Business

We usually think of goodwill as the sum of good products, good service, and good follow-through—the reputation a company works hard to build. In accounting, goodwill takes on a whole new meaning, a financial meaning. Goodwill is valued as that part of a company's earnings that are over and above the earnings attributable to assets alone, or, the portion of a company's earnings over and above what would be a reasonable return on its assets.

Some Facts about Goodwill

As you place some value on goodwill, consider the following:

Depreciation recapture. Some buyers who want to avoid having a significant goodwill on the newly acquired company's books may try to shift a greater portion of the valuation to the tangible assets, thus reducing the intangibles. The seller no doubt would object because such an allocation of assets may increase the capital gain to the point that the gain may exceed the depreciation which has already been taken, resulting in the seller paying a depreciation recapture tax on that amount at the ordinary income rate (which is a higher rate).

Amortization of goodwill. Prior to July 2001, goodwill was amortized over a period of fifteen years to recover the cost of intangibles, including goodwill and customer lists. Since July 2001, the Statement of Financial Accounting Standards eliminates amortization of purchased goodwill and requires annual testing to determine if goodwill has been impaired.

Asset purchase. Buyers are particularly motivated to complete an asset purchase in this case because they can increase the allocation of tangibles in the term sheet and fully amortize such items as computers, machinery equipment, and vehicles in just five years. On the other hand, the seller of a C corporation might prefer having the goodwill portion allocated to non-competes and consulting agreements to avoid the "double" taxation on tangibles. The intangibles in this case would be taxed "once" as ordinary income.

Stock purchase. In a stock purchase, if the cost of the acquisition is less than the fair value of the net assets, the purchase discount is negative goodwill.

Some buyers who want to avoid having a significant goodwill on the newly acquired company's books may try to shift a greater portion of the valuation to the tangible assets, thus reducing the intangibles.

Assets not identified on the balance sheet. A goodwill item might be a customer list or, for a publisher, a backlist of titles. Such items should be identified and assigned a value; however, if these items were already expensed, the buyer cannot resubmit them. While most businesspeople focus on goodwill items on the balance sheet, there is also *ill* will, or negative intangibles, such as unfavorable, long-term leases or unprofitable contracts.

Valuation of companies with sizable goodwill. The valuation methodology of capitalization of excess income was originally adopted to compute the value of goodwill that brewers and distillers lost because of Prohibition. Today this valuation method is used with companies that have created a sizable goodwill factor, such as service companies. The technique is based on the theory that the value of goodwill is equal to a business's excess earnings on net assets over some appropriate industry average return on net assets. The excess earnings are capitalized at a rate that reflects the risk inherent in the target company's business.

Minimizing goodwill. Excessive goodwill is basically the buyer's concern. On the other hand, if goodwill is such a large component of the transaction, the buyer may want to renegotiate the deal. Therefore, the seller has a vested interest in trying to help the buyer minimize the impact of goodwill.

Walter Morse, CPA and vice president of the accounting firm Tonneson & Company in Wakefield, Massachusetts, has the following advice regarding the treatment of goodwill in an asset purchase: "One should make sure that they have captured all the costs needed to be allocated under the purchase price. Some costs that may be forgotten are professional fees: appraisers, lawyers, accountants, marketing experts, etc. These are costs incurred in acquiring the assets and should therefore be capitalized and not expended. This is important to remember, since the discovery of additional costs to be allocated

> If goodwill is such a large component of the transaction, the buyer may want to renegotiate the deal.

to the assets once you are well into the transaction, may leave you inflexible and create unwanted goodwill."

Now that we have quantified the purchase price to be allocated up-front, the allocation is a simple process of making a list of all the assets to be acquired at their fair market values and assigning dollars according to these values. The excess of the purchase price over these listed assets is our potential goodwill. Since we have identified the potential goodwill early on in the transaction, however, we have the flexibility to minimize it.

Goodwill Hunting

Alfred King, chairman of Valuation Research Corporation of Princeton, New Jersey, believes that the new FASB rules on goodwill may encourage more transactions. As King states: "Since goodwill no longer has to be amortized, this is certainly a plus, both for existing goodwill but for new business combinations."

The good news does not stop there, says King. Here are other positive developments arising from the new FASB rules.

Many, if not most, intangibles probably will not have to be written off.

Trademarks and brand names can have an indefinite life.

The value of an assembled workforce does not have to be calculated.

Most customer lists will be valued at zero and included in goodwill.

If the acquisition is included in an existing profitable reporting unit future impairment losses can be minimized if not eliminated.

Existing goodwill can probably be written off immediately and treated as a change in accounting, thus not affecting operating results.

Many existing intangible assets, not now classified as goodwill, can be reclassified and thus no longer amortized against earnings.

The new accounting rules are tax-neutral, thus not increasing taxes paid.

Companies will have a lot more flexibility in disposing of unwanted segments of the target.

Companies will no longer be precluded from buying back their own stock before or after a merger.

How to Minimize Goodwill

There are different guidelines for accounting and tax allocations but for discussion purposes we are looking for additional "assets" to assign to the purchase price. The following tools, if properly structure and documented, should help us to minimize goodwill.

Non-competition agreements. This item is a regular expense for a determinable period of time. While the basic intent is to create a binding contract with the seller, a substantial non-compete agreement can help bridge the gap when the deal appears to have too much goodwill.

Consulting agreement. An off-balance sheet agreement requires the seller to consult over a specified period of time, which helps reduce the total purchase price needed to be allocated. Services must be performed and the agreement is usually not guaranteed unless a corresponding letter of credit is written for this item.

Patents. These are assets that have a determinable life and an economic benefit to the buyer.

Customer lists. The allocation of the purchase price can still include the customer list, although scrutinized more diligently by the Internal Revenue Service. Make sure you document how you determined the value and life of this asset.

Bargain lease. As a buyer, one may have a benefit of a sub-market lease. Allocation of the purchase price to bring the remaining portion of the lease up to market rates may be available.

Royalty agreement. This is a payment to the seller if certain volume levels are met. Like the consulting agreement, a royalty agreement needs to be carefully structured and properly documented.

> An off-balance sheet agreement requires the seller to consult over a specified period of time.

Additionally, beware that there may be some assets not on the books such as office supplies and inventory that were previously written off. At the same time, watch out for obligations that are not on the books such as warranties, pensions, and employment contracts.

Conclusion

Plan your transaction up-front in order to maximize the flexibility and minimize the potential of goodwill. Once you have satisfied yourself that the business has been valued properly, it is then time to turn your attention to negotiating the deal, the subject of the following six chapters.

> Plan your transaction up-front in order to maximize the flexibility and minimize the potential of goodwill.

For more information on this topic, visit our Web site at www.businesstown.com

Negotiating the Deal

Summary of Part V

- **Negotiating techniques for selling your business**

- **How to put a deal together**

- **Common buyer concerns**

- **What information should be included in the Letter of Intent**

- **The elements of representations and warranties**

- **Factors that can derail a deal**

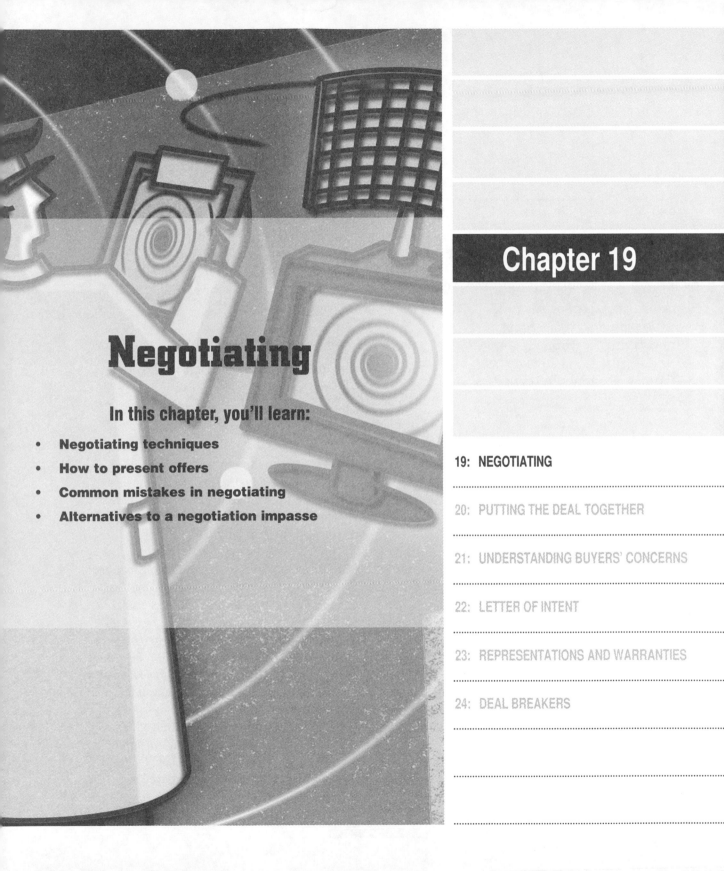

Negotiating

In this chapter, you'll learn:

- **Negotiating techniques**
- **How to present offers**
- **Common mistakes in negotiating**
- **Alternatives to a negotiation impasse**

Chapter 19

For all its importance to a successful transaction, the art of negotiation is often overlooked by sellers. Owners will take over the responsibility themselves, whether or not they have experience in selling companies.

As a seller, if you are inexperienced in selling companies it would be prudent to defer the negotiating to your mergers and acquisitions advisor or your transaction attorney. It may be also prudent to spend time fine-tuning your own negotiating skills. One of the better books on the subject is *Dealmaker . . . All the Negotiating Skills and Secrets You Need* by Robert Lawrence Kuhn. Some of Kuhn's words of wisdom are:

"Thorough preparation is critical in negotiating."

"Get all the items to be negotiated on the table early."

"Forward movement is vital for deal success."

"Price is usually the number one 'sticky wicket,' so plan your rationale early on."

"Strive to boil down the issues to one major item to be resolved at the end of the discussion. Usually price is the most difficult item on which to reach final agreement. If there is one outstanding issue, often it is best to initially bypass it and then circle back to the item later on."

Every dealmaker has a different attitude toward negotiating. In many cases, the difference is in the style or technique. One deal maker might use bravado, self-assurance, and cockiness as scare tactics to humble the other side. Another deal maker might use an entirely different attitude—complimentary, consensus building, humor—to establish a cooperative relationship.

My favorite style is to be "dumb like a fox," commonly portrayed by Lieutenant Columbo on television. In this instance, you pretend to be dumb and ask for most items to be explained and re-explained until even the other party has difficulty keeping a straight face.

In negotiating, usually one should not give up something without taking back another consideration. For example, if the buyer is pushing for a lower price and the seller concedes, the

> If you are inexperienced in selling companies it would be prudent to defer the negotiating to your mergers and acquisitions advisor or your transaction attorney.

seller should require more cash up-front. When compromising on an issue that is not important to you, pretend that, in fact, it is a meaningful sacrifice. Your counterpart will believe that item was painful for you to give up. However, if you are in a strong bargaining position but unable to move the process to closing, then make one final concession on the idea that the other side will move to closing immediately.

Don't be the first to concede a major issue because it is a sign of weakness. Offering minor compromises first is fine. This tactic will most likely not bring out the shark in your opponent. Be prepared to move the price up in smaller sequential increments; for example, start with $500,000 and then go to $200,000, instead of starting with $200,000 and trying to go to $500,000.

Crucial Considerations

Negotiating the sale of a business is the most dramatic segment of the transaction. Inevitably, as we've said earlier, the buyer ends up paying more for the company than originally planned and the seller ends up receiving less than expected. In negotiating the sale of the business you have the opportunity to place yourself in a position of strength if you can achieve the following:

1. **Information.** The power of information should not be underestimated. Not only must you be knowledgeable about all aspects of the company and its intrinsic value, you should have information on your company's industry such as specifics of other transactions, including the prevailing multiples of earnings.
2. **Predetermine the anchor price and terms.** With proper advice from your advisors, decide the lowest price and most lenient terms prior to the actual negotiating.
3. **Project an image of calmness.** Try to convey the impression that you do not have to sell the company and that you are not under pressure to do so. While the situation may be just the opposite, you should be coy and not imply that the company must be sold.

> Negotiating the sale of a business is the most dramatic segment of the transaction.

4. **Contact numerous qualified buyers.** Creating competition among buyers increases your negotiating power, particularly if you have competing offers. The presence of other buyers creates the greatest leverage for the seller.

5. **Set a time frame for the selling process.** By orchestrating the procedures from beginning to end within a predetermined time frame, you obviate the chance of deals failing because they drag on too long.

Winning Techniques

The preferred technique for negotiating the sale of a company is to establish a controlled bidding process with the buyers. For example, you can tell the interested parties to submit their term sheets by a certain date. A term sheet merely states a price range with a basic structure of the deal and whether or not it includes the real estate. From the submissions, you can then narrow the list of prospective buyers to three or five finalists. This is when the negotiating really begins.

Up to this point, the buyers have made their assessment of the company by thoroughly studying the offering memorandum and asking pertinent questions over the telephone. Now, the finalists are invited to visit the company for the first time, followed by a management presentation that might be held at a nearby hotel conference room.

As the seller, you, along with your vice president of sales and vice president of finance, should take the opportunity to present your company's attributes and competitive advantages. The second part of the meeting will be to respond to questions by the buyers. The thrust of the discussion should be "forward looking" as to why the acquisition will be positive, particularly if the buyer is from the same or similar industry.

Once the discussion of price and terms starts, you then have an opportunity to negotiate by utilizing your information and knowledge about both the company and the industry. In the case of the first buyer, his initial offer is $6 million, which equates to six times EBIT. Your target selling price is $7 million, so you have a gap of $1 million. Furthermore, the buyer has offered you 50 percent cash and 50 percent other considerations, and you want 80 percent cash at

> A term sheet merely states a price range with a basic structure of the deal and whether or not it includes the real estate.

closing. Your technique in this negotiation is to bring out favorable attributes of the business in order to justify a higher price.

The following are some examples:

- Brand equity of your products
- Long-term contracts with numerous customers
- A high number of customers
- Important alliances with other companies
- Intellectual property that includes three patents
- A highly trained and experienced workforce
- Non-compete agreements signed by all the employees

The technique is to persuade the buyer of both the tangible *and intangible* reasons why your company is worth more than their original offer. Furthermore, if there are synergies between the two companies, explain how the combined entities can significantly increase revenues and reduce costs. The objective is to have the buyer reconsider his offer and submit a Letter of Intent in the $7 million range. In the meantime, you are still talking with other buyers.

There are a number of negotiating techniques that can be used in selling a company, and for a full discussion I would recommend Philip Baguley's book *Negotiating*. Here are five major points to keep in mind.

1. **Preparation.** While it is important to know what you want to achieve in the negotiations, it is just as important to be clear about what you are willing to give up. During the negotiations, you will nearly always encounter times when the burden falls on you to offer a compromise or concession. When this occurs, check over your list and make a counteroffer that effectively reduces your demand one notch on your lowest-priority objective.
2. **Concessions.** Negotiation is essentially a process of giving things away to the other side. After all, if the other side does not want anything from you or if it wants something you don't mind giving away, there is no need for negotiation. Some tips on concessions are as follows: First, offer your concessions in reverse order, with the least important ones first.

> Your technique in this negotiation is to bring out favorable attributes of the business in order to justify a higher price.

Second, make every concession contingent on getting something in return from the other side. And third, behave as though every concession is a loss of something vitally important to your side in the negotiations.

3. **Focus.** One way experienced negotiators try to get more from the other side is by trying to confuse the main issue with minor points, unrelated matters, and distinctions that do not really make a difference. That's why it is important to assemble an agenda and use it to keep discussions on a central path.

4. **Beware.** There are several disturbing developments that should show up on your radar. If your opponent is unyielding, inflexible, and unwilling to compromise, for example, beware that you probably will not be able to work out a give-and-take negotiated transaction that would be in your favor:

   - If you rule out discussion on any particular issue without even the pretense of negotiating, it generally inflames the passions of your negotiating opponent who often will fight harder on other fronts.
   - If you are negotiating from weakness, be prepared to put a positive spin on these issues in order to mitigate your opponent's ability to capitalize on them.
   - If you think you understand the terms of the transaction, do not agree too quickly because it will acknowledge your opponent's skill and expertise.
   - If you discuss two related points as if they will be agreed on simultaneously, beware that your opponent will suddenly dump the second one as soon as they get your agreement to the first.
   - If your negotiating opponent too quickly accepts a compromise on a point that has previously been the subject of much discussion, beware that your opponent may be intentionally or unintentionally misunderstanding the compromise you have proposed.

5. **Time Savers.** One good way to save time is to write your main negotiating targets on a single 3" x 5" card and keep it with you during the negotiations.

That's why it is important to assemble an agenda and use it to keep discussions on a central path.

When you enter into the negotiation process, make sure you are dealing with an individual who can legitimately assume decision-making power for the organization. As you listen, don't limit your focus on just points of disagreement. Note areas where both sides agree, as well.

Ask the other party, up front, what they want. It's far faster to ask and answer this question than to play a cat-and-mouse guessing game. And whenever you and your negotiating opponent can't move forward on the present topic, switch to the major issue that has received the least attention so far.

At the Starting Point

Before getting into the best practices of negotiating, let's explore what negotiators do that harms their chances of success:

One, they arrive at the negotiating meeting unprepared because they are overconfident, overworked, or just plain sloppy.

Two, they make incorrect assumptions regarding their counterparts' goals, deal process, or price expectations.

Three, they do not know which person has the ultimate authority to do a deal.

Four, they set the wrong tone for the meeting by speaking abruptly and jumping into the business at hand without taking a few minutes of cordial conversation to simply talk about a few pleasantries.

Five, they come into the negotiation still "fighting the last war." If a previous unrelated negotiation was an acrimonious affair, don't start this engagement with a similar attitude.

Six, they jump right into the substantive issues without first discussing the objectives and needs and agreeing on the process to be pursued in the negotiations.

Other Warning Signs

In the heat of negotiations, be sensitive to the following situations:

- If you sense that the other side has reached its limit of interest, tolerance, and movement in the direction you want to go, back off.

- If you sense the other side is using a deadline as one more weapon to force you into an unfair agreement, be ready to counterattack with an earlier deadline of your own.

- If you expect and ask for too much, you'll just anger the people on the other side and possibly destroy any chance for an agreement.

- If your opposing negotiator gives in too easily, beware that the person is either naive or knows something you don't.

- If the other side becomes too demanding, too difficult, or just plain uncompromising, be ready to step off.

- If you use a threat, do so judiciously and only as a last resort, and be prepared to follow through.

- If you find yourself in an irreversible losing trend in the negotiations, it's better to call off the negotiations.

Seven, they let the other side set the agenda. It is better to have a consolidated agenda in which both parties contribute.

Eight, they come to the meeting without any preliminary discussion of price and terms. The use of a price range implies that the seller would consider an all-cash, no-contingencies deal on the lower figure, and liberal terms and contingencies with the higher figure.

Presenting Offers

There are two schools of thought as to who goes first with the offer. The buyer worries that if his offer is too high, he has left money on the table but that if the offer is too low, the seller will be insulted and walk away from the deal.

On the other hand, if one has thoroughly analyzed the deal with logic, extensive comparables, and a professional presentation, then going first with an offer is often recommended because it is considered the "anchor" price from which both parties must negotiate. For example, if the buyer makes a compelling case that the business is worth $5 million but the seller was hoping for $10 million, the seller has to move the price upward by twice the amount on the table. That movement may be insurmountable.

Know When to End Matters

By the time you have arrived at the closing, most of the issues should now be resolved and, by previous agreement, not subject to renegotiation. Again, there is a fine balance between fighting for concessions and being too obstinate by holding out on a $50,000 item in a $50 million deal.

It is important to remind your counterpart how much you have compromised and how much you have moved in their direction. Equally important is to not overlook the details. It is important to document all phases of the negotiations so you have reference to all

Open Ears, Button Lips

It may sound like an oversimplification, but often the party that fails to focus on their counterparts' needs will lose.

It is of paramount importance to carefully structure questions and to offer a corresponding amount of thoughtful listening. If you talk too much, you obviously cannot learn the primary concern of the other party. Conversely, just because you have said something, do not assume that you have been either heard or understood. Some people may lack the confidence to admit that they do not understand a certain issue, which may be critical to the deal.

There is a fine balance of revealing too much information or too little. Often, in order to get information you have to give information. But you must also convey that you have other alternatives than this particular deal, even if you do not.

previous discussions, facts, and matters agreed upon. Otherwise, in the spirit of closing the deal, you could make unnecessary and costly concessions. Also, the deal could abort if the two parties try to renegotiate items previously agreed upon. Documentation is not only important, but continual acknowledgment from the other side is equally important.

As you prepare for your next negotiation, learn as much as you can about the other party, research the alternatives to the deal you have at hand, but understand also your own motivators, emotional buttons, and habits. As a detached observer, think over your past negotiations, noting your patterns and the manner in which you responded. Ask colleagues to tell you about yourself as a negotiator.

Mistakes in Negotiating Deals

Once the negotiations begin, you are likely to present more of a challenge to your own success than anything the other side does to you. By considering what you do and how you do it, you will avoid many common pitfalls, and as a negotiator you will likely be happy with the outcome of your negotiations.

Thinking Win/Lose

People often view negotiations as a win/lose competition in which they are competing with the other side for a larger share of a fixed pie. Adopting this attitude, they generally damage the relationship with the other party and forego collaborative opportunities that would enlarge the pie for both of them. Of course, there is a distributive component to nearly every negotiation, but approaching it as a purely competitive game will likely leave you holding less in your hand at the end of the day.

Setting the Wrong Goals

Many times negotiators have preconceived notions of the results they want without really understanding *why* they want them. They get fixated on a particular number at which they want the deal

> By considering what you do and how you do it, you will avoid many common pitfalls.

to close or particular terms they want included. In many cases, that number turns out to be less meaningful than they thought, or the terms less relevant. By focusing on those positions rather than on their underlying interests, they lose sight of their real objectives and may end up either regretting the deal they end up with or walking away from a deal that would have been favorable to them.

Coming to the Table Unprepared

Negotiations are built on information. The better and more comprehensive your information is, the more likely you are to be satisfied with the results you achieve in the negotiation. This includes information not only about the material context of the deal but also about the people involved on both sides.

Failing to Prepare an Alternative

In any negotiation, the results you achieve at the table should be better than those you can achieve away from the table or with no deal at all. In many cases, people do not even know what their alternatives are and have a tendency to underestimate or overestimate the quality of their alternatives. Preparing a strong alternative and knowing your realistic choices determines your walk-away point and gives you a strong hand in negotiations.

Making Assumptions About the Other Side

Very often, your personal knowledge of and your communication with the other side will be limited, leading you to make erroneous assumptions about their intentions and actions. Take the time before the negotiation to learn about the other parties, and spend the early part of the negotiation getting to know their real intentions. Relying on your assumptions is likely to cause you problems in the negotiation.

Talking Rather Than Listening

Negotiators sometimes spend most of their time stating and defending their own position and attacking the other party's

> The better and more comprehensive your information is, the more likely you are to be satisfied.

positions, and not enough time listening to what the other party has to say. The other party will give you invaluable information to benefit your side, as well as ideas for expanding the pie that will benefit both of you if you simply listen.

Communicating Poorly

Negotiators often state their demands from the other side with no explanation, leaving the other party with no choice but to reject them. Always explain your reasoning and ask the other party for their reasoning as well. You will get less resistance to your ideas and plenty of valuable insight.

Conceding on Issues Improperly

In the heat of bargaining, negotiators often make concessions they do not have to make at all, concede too much too soon, concede on issues without getting anything for their concessions, or make concessions in the name of closing a deal without achieving closure. First, look for ways of trading your important issues for their issues so you do not have to concede in the first place. Second, remember that concessions are the currency of negotiations, and that each concession should achieve an objective that ultimately leads you to an agreement that meets your interest.

Rushing the Process

Either through their own discomfort or pressure from the other side, negotiators often rush through negotiations, making poor decisions along the way. If you feel rushed or intimidated in a negotiation, slow down, brainstorm, change the environment, and then reconvene.

Not Walking Away

Negotiators often get so caught up in the negotiation process that they forget to assess whether the deal is good for them. Always be ready to walk away and only commit to deals that are better for you than your alternatives away from the table.

> Always explain your reasoning and ask the other party for their reasoning as well.

Negotiating at an Impasse:
Creative Alternatives

Dr. James H. Hennig, author of *Crash Course for Everyday Negotiations*, said his observation of many negotiations leads him to believe that more often than not there are ways over, under, around, or through the obstacles causing the impasse, if at least one of the parties is willing to have an open mind and explore possibilities. Here are Hennig's twenty-five creative alternatives when an impasse occurs. When one or more of the following techniques are applied, the negotiations can often be saved to the benefit of both parties.

1. **Recess.** Often something as simple as taking a break can help you relax, release tension, and cause the creative juices to flow. The length of the break should be appropriate to the circumstance but within reason, the longer the better. Allowing negotiators to sit back for a while, with the pressure off, often enables them to approach the problem from a different perspective.

2. **Recap or summarize.** The process of negotiations is often a detailed and complex one. When an impasse is reached, it often helps to go back and review the progress and the agreements up to that point. It can be encouraging to note how much has already been accomplished in the negotiation.

3. **Employ doomsday tactics.** Although it focuses on the negative rather than the positive, explaining the dire consequences of not reaching an agreement can sometimes shock the other party into a concession or an agreement. In using this tactic to overcome an impasse, consider how it might be presented in a positive way. As an example, it may be your sincere concern for the other party (in addition for yourself) that causes you to point out the dire consequences in the first place. Even when discussing negatives, you can often do it in a way that builds rather than destroys relationships.

4. **Express feelings.** This is a great technique taught by many who understand the importance emotion plays in human behavior. Both parties expressing feelings can often clear the

> Allowing negotiators to sit back for a while often enables them to approach the problem from a different perspective.

air for further progress. Remember, you do not need to agree with or endorse the other party's feelings. Recognizing those feelings, however, can go a long way in both your understanding of the other person and in their feelings toward you.

5. **Introduce another issue.** When an impasse is reached, one of the very best techniques can be to temporarily move to another issue. Move to an issue on which you are likely to get agreement, because this will tend to build the momentum that may have been temporarily lost in reaching the impasse. Momentum plays a major factor in most negotiations. Use it to your advantage.

6. **Seek agreement in principle.** Here is another technique that can help to build momentum. Get agreement on anything you can get agreement on, even if it is only agreement in principle. For instance, you might agree that in the past, both parties have always been able to come to mutually agreeable solutions to their problems. Or you might agree on a mutual deadline time for completing negotiations. You might even agree on an objective procedure to resolve major differences if they occur. All these represent examples of getting agreement in principle to help rebuild the momentum of the negotiation.

7. **Disclose something.** Whether or not to disclose confidential information is always a difficult decision in a negotiation. There are many reasons why certain confidential information should not be disclosed. But when an impasse is reached, many times the disclosure of some portion of the confidential information may lead to a win/win solution. This is particularly true when you feel the other party has demonstrated a true win/win attitude. Your disclosures may also encourage similar disclosures from the other party, particularly when accompanied by a question like, "Do I know everything I should know in regard to this matter?"

8. **Present a hypothetical situation.** Presenting a hypothetical situation such as: "Suppose that . . . " or "What would happen if . . . " or "What would you do if . . . " often stimulates creative thinking by the other party. You can use it to help

> When an impasse is reached, one of the very best techniques can be to temporarily move to another issue.

move their thinking in a direction more favorable to your position by helping them to see situations and circumstances they had not considered before.

9. **Display empathy.** This alternative is particularly effective with open, relationship-oriented negotiators. Expressing empathy, particularly to this type of individual, strengthens relationships and stimulates a win/win environment. Consider this example: "Bill, I think I know what it's like to be in your position. Just last month I was in a situation like this myself when . . . "

10. **Employ the quick close tactic.** One of the most effective alternatives is to have something of value to sweeten the deal when an apparent impasse is reached. A good negotiator will often withhold something of value for that very purpose. See the "Quick Close" as described in the Strategies and Tactics section.

11. **Appeal to an ally.** Who can be your best ally? First, look at the opposing negotiating team. Is there someone who seems easiest to work with or most open to compromise? If so, direct your negotiations to that individual. In other words, seek the path of least resistance through the opposing team. Second, is there anyone on the outside who can influence the other party, such as a mutual friend, business associate, or someone else within or close to the organization? Could they directly or indirectly influence the other party?

12. **Use humor.** Everyone agrees that properly applied humor can go a long way toward releasing tension and loosening up a tight negotiation that has reached an impasse. For example, when the other side suggested that a previously imposed 5 P.M. deadline was Pacific Standard Time because they were from California rather than Central Standard Time (which is where they were negotiating), it brought a laugh from everyone, loosening the tight negotiation and, as a consequence, provided an extra hour of negotiating time. We compromised on Mountain Standard Time, as it was right in between the two sides. The good negotiator uses humor whenever possible to loosen a tight negotiation and to overcome an impasse.

> Expressing empathy, particularly to this type of individual, strengthens relationships and stimulates a win/win environment.

13. **Illustrate.** Reducing facts and figures and agreements and disagreements to writing provides clarification, often making an impasse easier to overcome. The creative use of a flip chart or overhead projector can provide the slight edge in overcoming an impasse. I was once hired to counsel a professional golfer who seemed to not be reaching his natural potential. I asked him to reduce to writing where he wanted to be in one, five, and twenty years. After having great difficulty with this for several weeks, he finally completed the assignment. His comment was, "Writing crystallizes thought, and crystallized thought motivates action." Both crystallized thought and motivated action are what we want in overcoming an impasse in a negotiation.

14. **Consider conditional concession.** An impasse is an appropriate time to consider making a concession, particularly if it can get you something more valuable in return than what you are giving up. As you consider offering a conditional concession—giving something on the condition of getting something in return—remember the concept of relative value. Relative value simply means different items in a negotiation may have different value to the parties involved. If you can concede something with a relatively low value to you that has a high perceived value to the other side, while receiving something in return that has a high value to you and a relatively low value to the other side, you accomplish a true win/win alternative.

    For example, I was recently negotiating a lease for office space that had reached an impasse. I did not want to pay the amount the landlord wanted for the space we needed. I tried a conditional concession to overcome this impasse. I offered to rent a larger suite of offices for a longer period of time if he would make a price concession. The conditional concession worked and was a great deal for both of us. The longer lease was obviously an advantage to him but also was to me because I didn't want to move again in the future as long as we had room to expand as we grow. I can more easily lease the additional offices because I can provide additional

> An impasse is an appropriate time to consider making a concession.

services with my complete office staff and office equipment. Additionally, I can control the length of the sublease so I can plan my expansion without having to move offices. This is a true win/win situation.

15. **Change locations.** A change of scenery can often stimulate creativity. When an impasse is reached, consider changing the location of the negotiation to provide a new and stimulating environment. Different room arrangements, seating positions, lighting, and table shapes and sizes, can often make small but important changes that will help you to overcome an impasse.

16. **Change the shape of the money.** When money is involved in a negotiation, which it practically always is, consider changing the shape of it when an impasse occurs. This could involve changing the payment schedule, the interest rates, the amount of down payment, or smaller payments with a balloon payment at some point in the future. Or you can build variables or options into any of the above. Creativity and relative value are the keys. What can we change about the shape of the money that will provide a win/win situation for both parties?

17. **Change specifications.** A rearrangement of the specifications or the terms of an agreement can often provide a creative alternative at an impasse. In what way might the specifications be altered that could provide an advantage to both parties? How might the terms of the agreement be changed to provide mutual advantage? Be creative. Keep an open mind.

18. **Change the negotiator or team member.** Obviously a new personality to a negotiation can provide a fresh new approach. An excellent alternative at an impasse—changing the negotiator or changing a current team member—can add creativity to overcoming the impasse. The selection of the individual inserted here is highly important and relates to what must be accomplished in overcoming the impasse. Select the individual carefully, taking into account behavioral styles, perceived expertise, and credibility.

> A rearrangement of the specifications or the terms of an agreement can often provide a creative alternative at an impasse.

19. **Provide a guarantee.** Many times an impasse can be overcome by providing some form of assurance or guarantee that certain things will occur. Sometimes a party is reluctant to agree, not because of the particular terms of the agreement but because they lack confidence that certain terms of the agreement may be fulfilled. Eliminating the perceived risk by providing a guarantee can eliminate the impasse.

20. **Bring in an expert.** The added power and prestige an expert can provide is an excellent alternative at an impasse. In addition to the new ideas presented, an expert often provides additional momentum to the negotiation. Consider using an attorney for legal expertise, a CPA for accounting expertise, an engineer or scientist for technical expertise, or a doctor for medical expertise.

21. **Change levels.** Changing your negotiating position up or down a level can be an excellent alternative to an impasse. The details of this alternative are discussed in the Strategies and Tactics section under "Changing Levels."

22. **Refer to a joint study committee.** In major negotiations, one alternative when an impasse occurs is to refer the matter to a joint study committee that can provide additional ideas and options. The use of non-negotiating personnel in this regard, who can explore all possibilities with an open mind, often creates win/win solutions arrived at through no other means.

23. **Use of a mediator or arbitrator.** Bringing in a mutually agreed upon third party to assist and possibly resolve differences is often an excellent tactic when facing an impasse. When the stakes are high and reaching agreement becomes very important for both parties, agreeing to put some of the decision-making power in the hands of a third party can be a wise decision.

24. **Add options.** Creative negotiators often add options when an impasse occurs. The key to creating the right option usually involves an analysis of relative value. What can you provide in the form of an option that would have relatively low cost to you but a very high perceived value to the other party?

> Eliminating the perceived risk by providing a guarantee can eliminate the impasse.

Creative options have been the key to overcoming many obstacles in negotiations.

25. **Postpone.** When all else fails, do not necessarily assume that the negotiation is over. In many cases, it might be better to postpone the negotiation indefinitely rather than to terminate it completely. The passage of time itself may provide solutions to overcome the impasse.

Note: Dr. Hennig's twenty-five creative alternatives are reprinted by permission of the author.

Conclusion

There you have it, a checklist of twenty-five different alternatives when an impasse is reached in a negotiation. The creative negotiator keeps this list handy and is ready to try an alternative that might help his or her team deal with any stall in the negotiation process.

> In many cases, it might be better to postpone the negotiation indefinitely rather than to terminate it completely.

For more information on this topic, visit our Web site at www.businesstown.com

Chapter 22

Putting the Deal Together

In this chapter, you'll learn:

- **Closing the buyer-seller price gap**
- **Asset versus stock transaction**
- **Different deal structures**

Chapter 20

Most sellers start out wanting all cash for the deal. Those in the know will tell you, however, less than 50 percent of the deals are all cash at closing. There is an old axiom that the seller sets the price and the buyer sets the terms. What is evident is that if you demand all cash in the transaction, you'll probably receive a lower price for the company.

Buyers are often capable of paying all cash at closing but are afraid they will lose all their leverage if the business does not turn out to be what was represented. The new owner often wants some hand-holding during the transition period and therefore will structure a consulting agreement over a year or two with the former owner. Terms are perhaps more important for small companies that do not have audited financial statements—particularly if the sale is a "stock" transaction in which the buyer assumes all the assets and liabilities on the balance sheet. Even though an "asset" purchase is a safer method of acquisition for the buyer, the use of terms in the structure is a safeguard for any improprieties or oversights by you.

Closing the Buyer-Seller Price Gap

Often the price gap in the merger and acquisition marketplace is real and not just posturing between buyer and seller. The overriding factor to bridge the gap is whether the principals are truly willing to do a deal and whether their respective advisors are clearly helpful. Here are some specific tactics:

Sell 70 percent of your stock and grant the acquirer a call on the remaining 30 percent: 10 percent each year for three years on a defined formula, such as six times EBIT.

Have the seller retain the real estate in order to reduce the price and rent the facilities. Alternatively, reduce the transaction price so the seller can keep the major machinery and equipment and lease it to the buyer.

Structure royalty on sales rather than an earn-out on gross margins or EBIT.

Charge excessive rent as part of the package price, thus reducing the up-front total.

As the seller, be willing to accept junior capital but arrange with the buyer for senior capital to be paid out first.

Create a subsidiary for the fastest growth part of the business in which buyer and seller share evenly in the piece of the business that takes off.

Second generation sellers can take back preferred stock equivalent to 10 percent of the transaction amount.

Repositioning the Buyer

An investment bank was involved in selling an underperforming company with sales of $30 million. The selling price was originally quoted as book value of $2 million plus assumption of interest-bearing debt of $9 million, making for an $11 million deal. The potential buyers were scared off by the price tag.

Since accounts receivable were factored and insured, it offset the corresponding bank debt. The investment bank restated the balance sheet with the proper explanation, showing a selling price based on a book value of $1 million plus assumption of remaining interest-bearing debt of $4 million, or $5 million total. Bottom line: The buyer's obligation was reduced a whopping $6 million.

In the same example, the investment bank also showed a pro forma opening balance sheet in which a fair market value was placed on the fixed assets, thus significantly improving the book value for the new owner.

> The selling price was originally quoted as book value of $2 million plus assumption of interest-bearing debt of $9 million, making for an $11 million deal.

BALANCE SHEET
($000s)
PRO FORMA OPENING

Line	Assets	Actual	Restated	Fair Market
1	Cash	$0	$0	$0
2	Accounts Receivable	6,000	–	–
3	Inventory	4,000	4,000	4,000
4	Fixed Assets	5,000	5,000	10,000
5	Total Assets	15,000	9,000	14,000
	Total Liabilities and Equity			
6	Accounts Payable	$4,000	$4,000	$4,000
7	Notes Payable	6,000	–	–
8	Long Term Debt	3,000	4,000	4,000
9	Total Liabilities	13,000	8,000	8,000
10	Book Value	2,000	1,000	6,000
11	Total Liab. & Book Value	$15,000	$9,000	$14,000
12	**Proposed Purchase Price**	**$11,000**	**$5,000**	–

Various Deal Structures

While most companies do not factor their receivables, there are other variations to the above example depending on whether the investment bank wants to show a restated balance sheet without real estate, machinery/equipment, or other assets with their corresponding debt, thus reducing the amount of the purchase price.

Case 1

A company with $20 million in sales with an EBIT of $2 million, no long-term debt, and a $3 million book value sold for $9 million. The numbers are evident: 4.5 times EBIT or three times book value. Here is the deal structure.

Buyer's equity at closing	$3 million
Bank debt with cash at closing	$4 million
Notes collateralized by the newly formed buying company	$2 million
Total purchase price	$9 million

The above scenario appears to be a straightforward deal. The transaction, however, is highly leveraged because, relatively speaking, the selling company's hard assets (machinery and other equipment) are modest.

The financial buyer wants to retain the current CEO of the selling company and to have the CEO be motivated and committed to the success of the newly acquired company. One method in achieving this is to require the CEO to buy back 10 percent of the new company's equity for $300,000. Additionally, the buyer offers the seller the option for the CEO or his management team to buy up to 20 percent of the company over a five-year period based on a predetermined formula.

The new corporate owner's objective is to motivate the seller, who remains as the CEO, to grow the company. At the same time the new corporate buyer holds out a carrot: the buyer wants to be sure the CEO does not take any large risks that would cause the business to deteriorate. To encourage the seller

A company with $20 million in sales with an EBIT of $2 million, no long-term debt, and a $3 million book value sold for $9 million.

to keep his nose to the grindstone, the $2 million note is collateralized by the selling company and would be subordinated to the bank note.

Case 2

A small unprofitable medical supply company is at the crossroads of survival. It is backed by venture capital money but investors are not about to hand over more capital. The company has sales of $4 million in which half its sales come from a sophisticated line of ports that are inserted in the body to receive needle injections. The other half of the business is made up of state-of-the-art pumps that are also inserted in the body but that do not yet have regulatory approval. It is the latter product line, however, that has the greatest potential for future growth.

The company is almost out of cash and losing almost $1 million per year. The management decides to sell off the port line of medical products, which will take many years to receive regulatory approval. With the $2 million in cash from the sale, the company devotes its resources to the more proprietary and promising line of vascular pumps.

On the surface, the above transaction appears to be reasonable under the circumstances. In this case, however, the selling company will lose half of its manufacturing volume, which will adversely affect the profitability of its other product line of the pumps. Therefore, the company decided to retain the right to manufacture the ports and to sell these items on an OEM (original equipment manufacturer) basis at cost plus 15 percent for the next two years.

The arrangement allows the seller a chance to build up its volume in the remaining product line without laying off valuable employees, and gives the buyer a chance to set up a manufacturing operation from scratch without rushing the process.

Case 3

The following example was provided by Joseph Myss of Wayzata, Minnesota, and appeared in his pamphlet *Divestiture*

> The selling company will lose half of its manufacturing volume, which will adversely affect the profitability of its other product line.

Strategies for Owners of Private Businesses. The case illustrates the use of an earn-out portion to reconcile the $1 million difference in value between the buyer and seller.

The two parties agreed to use EBIT as the financial benchmark, and they negotiated a minimum EBIT that must be earned, each year, before the earn-out would go into effect. Additionally, the two parties agreed on an amount, in this case 75 percent, that would be paid to the seller above the base EBIT hurdle.

ILLUSTRATION IN MILLIONS

	2003 Actual	2004 Projected	2005 Projected
EBIT	$1,625	$1,780	$2,000
Base EBIT (negotiated)		(1,200)	(1,300)
Excess over Base		580	700
75% of Excess to Sellers		435	525
Cumulative Earn-out Payment		435	960

> The seller should have reasonable control over decisions that can affect the results to be used to measure the earn-out payments.

Interest expense and miscellaneous other non-operating income were excluded from the earn-out formula. Unusual items that were also excluded were sale of non-operating assets, sale and lease back of plant assets, and insurance recoveries past acquisition. The seller should have reasonable control over decisions that can affect the results to be used to measure the earn-out payments.

Case 4

Home Products International (HPI), a $114 million public company based in Chicago, manufacturers consumer space-management products for the housewares and home improvement industries. Some years ago, HPI acquired Tamor Company of Leominster, Massachusetts. Tamor is an injection molding company, principally producing branded storage containers for mass merchandisers such as Wal-Mart. The business is capital intensive and much of the profitability depends on high volume in which the machines are ideally running twenty-four hours a day, seven days a week. HPI bought Tamor for $42.6 million, consisting of:

Cash	$27.8 million
Common Stock	2.4 million
Assumption of Debt	12.4 million
Total Purchase Price	$42.6 million

Tamor's:

Sales	$75.7 million
EBIT	6.3 million
Multiple	6.8 × of EBIT

Two years earlier an undisclosed buyer offered only $14 million for the company based on the following data:

Sales	$53.0 million
EBIT	3.7 million
Multiple	6.0 of EBIT
Equals	22.2 million
Less Debt	(8.2) million
Total Purchase Price	$14.0 million

During the two-year period, the EBIT increased 70 percent. Although the debt also increased more than 50 percent, the seller was able to secure a price three times greater than the undisclosed offer two years ago, although HPI's multiple was somewhat higher (6.8 versus 6.0). The lesson to be learned from the above analysis is the wisdom of the seller waiting to get an acceptable price and perhaps the original prospective buyer's loss by not staying in touch with Tamor's dramatic earnings increase of the two-year period.

What explains Tamor's surge? The company competed directly with Rubbermaid, albeit at lower price points. In previous years, Rubbermaid experienced a turbulent period with its largest customer Wal-Mart, because as resin prices increased dramatically, Rubbermaid was unable to pass on its proposed price increases.

> The lesson to be learned is the wisdom of the seller waiting to get an acceptable price and perhaps the original prospective buyer's loss by not staying in touch with Tamor's dramatic earnings increase of the two-year period.

While it is conjecture on my part, it is likely that much of Tamor's 40 percent sales increase in two years was due to Tamor capitalizing on Rubbermaid's difficulty with Wal-Mart at that time.

Case 5

A consumer products importer/distributor decided to sell the company because its fifty-year-old CEO and part owner was burnt out. The company had flat sales of $10 million, mostly to mass merchants with heavy customer concentration. The company was extraordinarily profitable with $2 million of EBIT after the CEO took out $300,000 for himself. The owners planned to dividend out the $2 million cash and sell the business for four times EBIT of $2 million, or $8 million, cash at closing. Reconstructed book value without the cash was $2 million.

The current CEO was a critical part of the business. He not only designed the products but was responsible for sourcing them in the Far East. Once the business was sold, he was willing to remain as CEO for one year, and for the next four years maintain a consulting agreement for new designs and sourcing to suppliers. Assuming all the customers stayed on board, the $8 million proposed purchase was reasonable, except that such an acquisition, as stated, would create $6 million of goodwill, which for a public company at that time would adversely shelter earnings for the next fifteen years.

A financial buyer was interested but could not justify the cash on the barrel price of $8 million. All potential strategic buyers had fallen by the wayside. In order to meet the selling company's $8 million price, the buyer arrived at the following structure:

- $3 million cash paid to seller for 50 percent ownership interest
- $5 million non-contingent, interest bearing five-year note, subordinate to bank debt and guaranteed by the importer/distributor

The conditions of the above offer were unique:

- The initial 50 percent ownership interest was to be held in escrow as security.
- The remaining 50 percent ownership interest was to be transferred only upon full payment of the note.

> The current CEO was a critical part of the business. He not only designed the products but was responsible for sourcing them in the Far East.

- A corporate governance agreement was to be drawn (a) restricting certain asset sales or other management actions without agreement of all parties; (b) stipulating an ongoing officer/board member role for the outgoing CEO; (c) the right for the former CEO to take over complete management control in the event of default on the loan. Default was defined as non-payment and/or non-compliance with the covenants of senior bank debt or the subordinated note.

Since the seller divided out the $2 million cash and received $3 million cash at closing, the seller started with $5 million cash on day one of the transaction. As an importer/distributor with heavy customer concentration, the seller received a "full price" at four times EBIT, particularly since there was $6 million of goodwill left for the new owner to carry on the balance sheet.

While the seller had downside risk because the remaining $5 million purchase price was not fully guaranteed, the ownership interests were only phased in after certain milestones, and the seller had secured strong debt covenants and a protective governance/management agreement.

On the plus side, the buyer acquired a business with a long history of continual profitability, excellent market position, and reliable cash flow. The buyer paid $3 million cash at closing for a company that had a clean balance sheet with $2 million book value and a $2 million EBIT. Furthermore, the previous owner remained as part of management for the next five years to help ensure the ongoing success of the business. Since the previous owner had a vested interest in the new ownership, he was motivated to ensure the ongoing business was successful.

The above structure was not perfect for either the buyer or seller. But it did enable the seller to receive a full price with reasonable assurances of being paid off in full. The buyer, who planned to use the inventory and receivables to borrow from the bank, was able to acquire a very strong business with a minimum of his own cash and without personally guaranteeing the note.

> Since the previous owner had a vested interest in the new ownership, he was motivated to ensure the ongoing business was successful.

Case 6

In February of 1988, the two owners of a Massachusetts surveying company decided to sell their business. The previous year was the height of a real estate boom in their region. The owners each took out $500,000 from the S corporation.

The potential buyers structured their offer with the two owners remaining as full-time employees at a compensation of $100,000 each. The EBIT figure was therefore $800,000.

The buyers offered to buy 100 percent of the company for $2 million or 2.5 times EBIT plus a non-compete based on a percentage of EBIT. The proposal was as follows:

Acquirer would buy all of the issued and outstanding stock for $2 million of which $1.5 million was to be paid at closing. The balance was to be paid in the form of a five-year note with annual principal repayments of $100,000 and with interest at 2 percent over prime on the outstanding balance.

The sellers would agree not to compete with the business in the future. They would be compensated for this assurance with a cash payment (after each of the first five years of the contract) based upon a percentage of the company's EBIT as follows:

EBIT	%	To Sellers
First	$400,000	0%
Second	$400,000	30%
Over	$800,000	15%

During the first five years after the purchase, the sellers would be responsible for the payments of any contingent liabilities or claims that arose. This responsibility would be limited to the outstanding balance of the note due to them at the time the claim arose.

The buyers offered to buy 100 percent of the company for $2 million or 2.5 times EBIT plus a non-compete based on a percentage of EBIT.

In the end, the sellers refused this offer in lieu of a competing offer, which promised $2 million cash at closing without any additional notes or contingency payments. Ironically, the Massachusetts real estate market plunged and took this highly profitable surveying business into bankruptcy several years later. Obviously, many service businesses are vulnerable to key employees and the regional economy, and it is important to structure an acquisition to account for unexpected events. Of course, the potential buyers who missed out in this deal were mighty glad they did.

Asset Versus Stock Transaction

Very early on in the discussion of selling a particular business, it is imperative that you discuss with the buyer whether the transaction will be an "asset" or "stock" sale. The buyer almost always wants to buy the assets because he can avoid most potential lawsuits from inherent corporate liabilities, plus the buyer can write up the assets for greater depreciation to shelter future earnings.

On the other hand, you will want to sell stock, because as a C corporation there will be only one tax (compared to a double tax for an asset sale). Furthermore, if you have used accelerated depreciation for machinery and equipment, there is a possible depreciation recapture tax for selling the machinery at a higher value than shown on the books.

An asset sale is potentially more time consuming and more costly because there is a legal transfer of each asset, and more difficult because of third party consents from leases, loans, and other such arrangements.

If the transaction is an asset sale, the purchase price is assigned to specific assets at their fair market value (not the depreciated value on the books). The difference between the purchase price and the allocation of the purchase price is goodwill. Under the new tax laws, goodwill can be amortized in fifteen years along with other intangibles such as non-competes and consulting agreements.

> The buyer almost always wants to buy the assets because he can avoid most potential lawsuits from inherent corporate liabilities.

The Stock Versus Asset Quandary

Because it is so important to understand the pros and cons of asset and stock purchase, we are offering the following analysis prepared by PricewaterhouseCoopers, LLP, in its book *Buying and Selling a Business*.

Assets Purchase: Buyer's Position

As with any transaction, there are advantages to either position. What you bring you to the table will determine whether the liabilities, or cons, are relevant factors in your negotiations.

Advantages

- Step-up basis of assets acquired to purchase price, allows higher depreciation/amortization deductions.
- Recapture tax on presale depreciation and investment tax credit paid by seller.
- Buyer can pick and choose assets to buy and liabilities to assume.
- Buyer is generally free of any undisclosed or contingent liabilities.
- Normally results in termination of labor union collective bargaining contracts.
- Employee benefit plans may be maintained or terminated.
- Buyer permitted to change state of incorporation.

Disadvantages

- No carryover of seller corporation's tax attributes (tax basis of assets, earnings and profits, operating and capital loss carry-forwards, accounting methods, accounting periods, installment reporting, or previous sales and employee benefit plan contributions).
- Non-transferable rights or assets (license, franchise, patent) cannot be transferred to buyer.
- Transaction is more complex and costly in terms of transferring specific assets/liabilities (title to each asset transferred and new title recorded; state sales tax may apply).
- Lender's consent may be required to assume liabilities.
- May lose right to use corporation's name.
- Loss of corporation's liability, unemployment, or workers' compensation insurance ratings.

Assets Purchase: Seller's Position

Advantages

- Seller maintains corporate existence.
- Maintains ownership of non-transferable assets or rights (license, franchise, patent).
- Maintains corporate name.

Disadvantages

- Taxation occurs at the corporate level upon liquidation.
- Generates various kinds of gains or losses to the seller based on the classification of each asset as capital or ordinary.
- Transaction may be more complex and costly in terms of transferring specific assets/liabilities (title to each asset transferred and new title records; sales tax may apply).
- Lender's consent required to assume liabilities.

Note: "Asset Purchase: Buyer's Position" and "Asset Purchase: Seller's Position," from *Buying and Selling a Business*, are reprinted by permission of PricewaterhouseCoopers, LLP.

Analysis of Stock, Asset, or Tax-Free Exchange

In the following example, you can clearly see the huge difference in the net proceeds of the sale based on whether it is a stock, asset, or an exchange of stock. It should be noted that this example assumes that the company is a C corporation. If, on the other hand, the company is an S corporation, there is only one tax.

	Stock Sale	Asset Sale	Tax-Free Exchange
Gross sale proceeds	$12,000,000	$12,000,000	$12,000,000
Less corporate income tax	_____	4,200,000	_____
Sale proceeds to selling shareholders	$12,000,000	$7,800,000	$12,000,000
Less selling shareholder income tax (assuming tax cost of $100,000 and 20% tax rate)	2,380,000	1,540,000	_____
After-tax proceeds to selling shareholders:			
Cash:	$9,620,000	6,260,000	–
Securities:	–	–	$12,000,000

Buyers usually want to do an asset transaction because they can pick and choose what assets and liabilities they will assume, can mark up the assets after the acquisition, and are not liable for uncovered liabilities that surface post-closing.

Nevertheless, as a seller with a C corporation, you should be able to convince a buyer to acquire the stock of the company by allowing the buyer's attorney to draft an extensive representation and warranty agreement along with certain escrow accounts.

Conclusion

In the final analysis, if both you and the buyer are significantly motivated to do the deal, there is usually a way to achieve a successful closing, whether it is a stock or asset sale. Of course, both parties will have to be willing to make some concessions to achieve an agreement. One important step to this goal is for you, as the seller, to somehow get into the head of the buyer and understand his concerns. For that, read on.

> Buyers usually want to do an asset transaction because they can pick and choose what assets and liabilities they will assume.

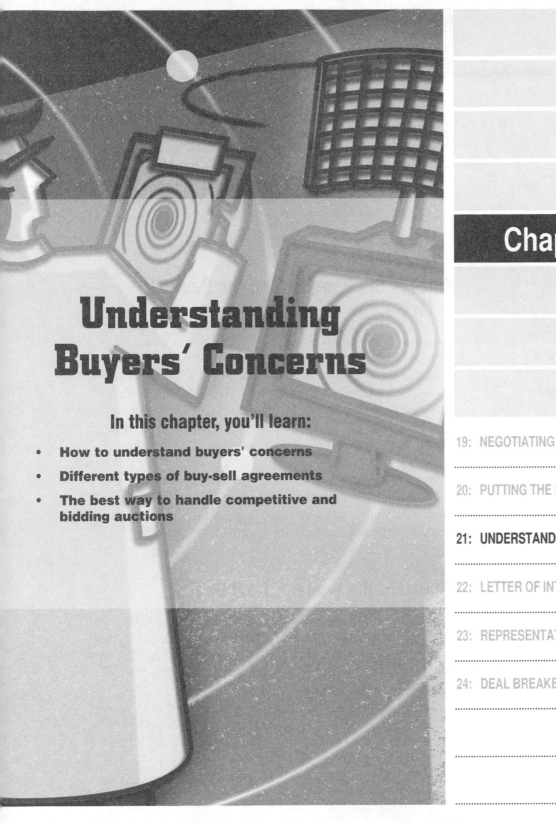

Understanding Buyers' Concerns

In this chapter, you'll learn:

- **How to understand buyers' concerns**
- **Different types of buy-sell agreements**
- **The best way to handle competitive and bidding auctions**

Chapter 21

Business owners who are most successful in selling their company, those who receive the best price and terms, clearly understand the concerns of potential buyers. They are good salespeople because they are able to put themselves in the buyers' shoes and to think like a buyer. By anticipating the buyers' concerns, you will be far better prepared to undertake the difficult process of selling a business. The following are some of the most common concerns.

What Is the Real Reason the Company Is for Sale?

A buyer is usually suspicious as to why the owner is selling the business. Is the stated reason the real reason? What should the buyer do to be sure he or she is not buying a "pig in a poke"—a manufacturer in which the machines and equipment are outdated, the products obsolete, the customers about to defect; the employees about to leave.

To dispel such concerns, a seller has to allow the buyer to talk to a few customers at the due diligence phase after the Letter of Intent is signed. In general, a seller will gain confidence with a buyer if he or she discloses some of the company's deficiencies up front rather than having the buyer identify them during due diligence or exercise his or her rights under the terms of the representation and warranty section of the Purchase and Sale Agreement.

> A seller will gain confidence with a buyer if he or she discloses some of the company's deficiencies up front.

What Are the Owner's Real Goals?

The highest price is not necessarily the winning offer. On the other hand, the seller rarely will announce to the buyer that the highest price is not the most important consideration. As a seller, it is imperative to convey directly or indirectly the various aspects that will influence the buyer's proposal.

For example, you could say: "I would like to retain 10 percent of the company for the next five years so I can participate in its future growth, and I would like to see my son remain with the company. Further, I would like some assurance that the plant will not be closed and moved elsewhere, as the current employees have been so faithful to the company over the past ten years."

Based on this information, a buyer could offer a lower price but include the provisions mentioned above to accommodate you.

Does the Buyer Really Understand the Business?

While a direct competitor may thoroughly understand the business, a financial or synergistic buyer will have certain apprehensions. For example, let's suppose John ran a small regional cracker company that a financial buyer acquires. While the production side of the business is straightforward, the distribution side can be complicated. There are retail sales (supermarkets, convenience stores) and foodservice (restaurants, hotels). Depending on which channel the crackers are being sold to, the company might have salespeople, distributors, or jobbers, or employ direct sales or slotting fees and rebates for incentives.

Because the business could be somewhat foreign to some buyers, John should document the details in a comprehensive selling memorandum and take the time to explain the methodology of doing business in that particular industry segment. In many cases, sellers do not want to take the time to discuss such matters unless the buyer is fully knowledgeable about all the nuances of the industry.

Who Else Is Trying to Buy the Business?

Naturally, a potential buyer is concerned with who the competition is, or if there is any. Certainly, you want interested buyers to realize who else is interested in acquiring the company, although rarely are the others identified by name. Sometimes you may want to try to entice buyers to offer a full price by mentioning that a *Fortune* 500 company and an overseas buyer, for example, have expressed interest. The presence of other buyers is often the leverage you can use to either speed up the selling process or to increase the perceived value.

Why Families Should Go Legal

It is common among family companies to have buy-sell agreements to help ensure that control remains within the family. These legal documents also cut back on future family disputes and provide owners with an exit strategy if they choose to leave.

When done properly, buy-sell agreements spell out a fair process that protects the interests of the departing owners, the owners staying behind, and the business itself.

There are three types of buy-sell agreements:

1. With *cross-purchase agreements*, all the shareholders agree that one or more of the other owners will buy the departing shareholder's interest.
2. With *under redemption agreements*, the company itself buys back the shares.
3. With *hybrid agreements*, it allows some shares to be purchased by the company and the rest by the remaining shareholders.

Will the Business Continue as Purported?

Perhaps there is no other concern for the buyer as important as whether the company's future will continue on the same path. Will sales and earnings stay at least as high as past levels or has the industry and this company crested? Imagine buying a retail lumber store chain in Massachusetts a dozen years ago, just as Home Depot established its first store in Springfield. It would have taken only a few years before other Home Depot outlets clobbered the small regional lumber stores.

Buyers worry that the owner/CEO is "the business" in terms of new products and services, selling relationships, and employee faithfulness. The buyer might be concerned that there is not sufficient product diversity, that the critical source of supply is limited, that the intangible assets are not that valuable, and that the market is cyclical. In other words, will the business perform as advertised?

What Is the Real Value of the Company?

Something else that keeps the buyer up at night is understanding the real value of the company. You may be basing the value of your company on a multiple of next year's EBIT. The buyer may be accustomed to using an average of several years' earnings or the last twelve months. The buyer may even be using EBITDA-CAPX, which refers to earnings before interest depreciation and amortization less capital expenditure.

If you do not have audited financials, the buyer often will value the company substantially less because of the uncertainty of up-to-date inventory, receivables, and other matters. The buyer will be concerned that you have purposely tried to spike the earnings in the past year by reducing advertising, promotion, research and development, or maintenance. Or maybe you, the seller, have included too many add-backs to bolster reconstructed earnings.

Further, if the buyer acquires the assets of the company, all the contracts with the employees, customers, and vendors will have to be rewritten because they cannot just be assumed. Conversely, if the

---

Going Once, Going Twice . . .

To encourage competitive bidding is usually a sound approach, but keep in mind that if an auction is implemented it sometimes backfires. An auction occurs when a seller or his intermediary orchestrates the selling process by encouraging buyers to bid and re-bid until the highest and best offer is received. The basis for the winning bid is the highest price and the best terms. The reason an auction could backfire is that other considerations—should most of the employees be fired? must the plant be relocated?—are not relevant.

If you feel these types of considerations are important, do not enter into an auction.

buyer acquires the stock of the company, he or she will be concerned with the unknown liabilities to be assumed from former products and services and environmental situations, as well as from covenants assumed on bank notes and leases.

You, therefore, should be empathetic with the buyer's concerns on the valuation issues and either have his or her advisors address those concerns or do so yourself.

Why Is the Company Not Represented by an I-Banker?

In the middle market, owners of companies who decide to sell their business most often retain an investment banker to represent them in order to obtain the best deal. If you do not retain an investment banker, the potential buyer will wonder: Why not? Is your company really for sale? Are you just trying to get an indication of value from the marketplace? Unless you are properly advised, will a deal ever be consummated?

I have had buyers tell me that they wanted the seller to be professionally represented because then there was a far greater likelihood of a deal being completed. If an investment banker is involved, a buyer can expect to receive a complete selling memorandum, up-to-date financials on a monthly basis, a creation of a war room to check all pertinent documents, and a professional who knows the deal process.

> Owners of companies who decide to sell their business most often retain an investment banker to represent them.

I Am a Foreign Buyer

Naturally, any buyer from a foreign country will have apprehensions regarding the gap in culture, language, nuances, customers, and protocols. Aside from these "soft" issues, the "hard" issues of accounting, tax, and related legislation require a buyer to receive professional advice.

For example, it is customary in Italy for private middle-market companies to have two sets of accounting books, sometimes even three sets. In Germany and France, it is customary to award severance for laid-off employees, one month for every one year of employment or one year for twelve years of service. Having a sense of a foreign buyer's background and culture will help when it comes to negotiating terms of the deal.

Conclusion

In summary, you should understand a buyer's concerns because doing so will help enormously to expedite the sale. Once you understand such issues, you are one step closer to crafting a win/win sale.

> Once you understand such issues, you are one step closer to crafting a win/win sale.

For more information on this topic, visit our Web site at www.businesstown.com

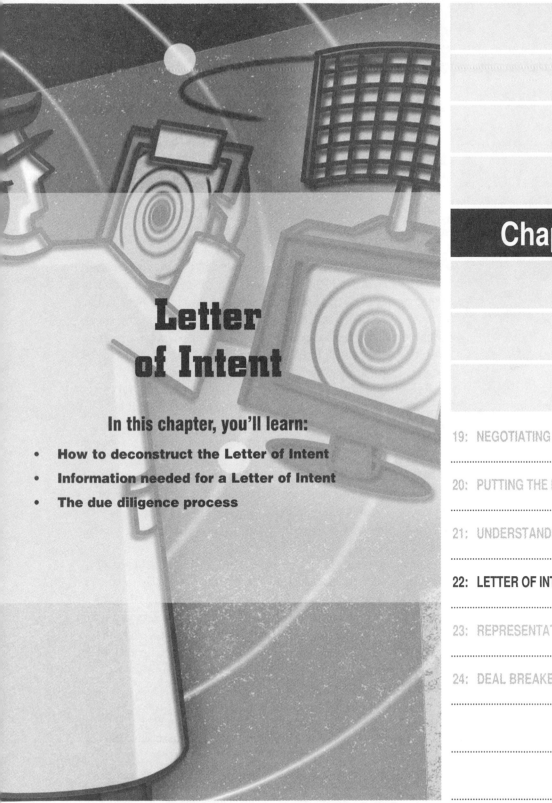

Letter
of Intent

In this chapter, you'll learn:

- **How to deconstruct the Letter of Intent**
- **Information needed for a Letter of Intent**
- **The due diligence process**

Chapter 22

T he Letter of Intent (LOI) is a pre-contractual written instrument prepared by the buyer for the seller, which is usually the preliminary understanding of both parties. Other names used for LOI are Memorandum of Understanding and Agreement in Principal. The LOI precedes the Acquisition Agreement, better known as the Purchase and Sale Agreement. It is a non-binding agreement subject to the buyer obtaining satisfactory financing and subject to satisfactory due diligence by both parties.

This is how the LOI has been defined by Stanley Foster Reed, author of *The Art of M&A*: "A Letter of Intent is a pre-contractual written instrument which defines the respective preliminary understandings of the parties about to engage in contractual negotiations. In most cases, such a letter is not intended to have a binding effect except for certain limited provisions. The Letter of Intent crystallizes in writing what has, up to that point, been oral negotiations between the parties about the basic terms of the transaction. While the Letter of Intent is usually non-binding, it does create a moral commitment and allows the buyer to proceed with the extensive due diligence process with a feeling of confidence. Conversely, the seller is required to withdraw the company from the marketplace and not discuss the potential sale with anyone else."

Letters of Intent are written after the two parties have had a serious discussion on the price, terms, conditions, and time period of the proposed transaction. In my experience buyers will usually submit a LOI after they feel they understand the parameters of what a seller will accept.

In many cases, the buyer uses the LOI as the initial basis of negotiating. If there is reason to believe that the two parties are fairly close to agreement, the buyer will draft a second LOI. If the buyer is experienced or is working with an experienced intermediary, it may not be necessary to involve a lawyer at this time. It should be noted, however, that lawyers resent being pulled into the deal after the LOI, and if it is necessary to make a material change in the future, it becomes very difficult to do so.

The LOI is at the heart of the transaction and reveals key issues early on in the process. Before you, as the seller, sign the LOI, I urge you to solicit a second or third opinion from a transaction attorney,

> Other names used for LOI are Memorandum of Understanding and Agreement in Principal.

a competent intermediary, or a corporate appraiser. A few hours spent with these professionals at approximately $200 to $300 per hour would be well worth the expense. Although their advice should be taken seriously, ultimately you have to make the decision.

Deconstructing the Letter of Intent

The elements of the Letter of Intent are as follows:

- The price of the company
- The form of purchase: is it a stock or asset sale? What is being purchased and what is not?
- The structure: cash, notes, stock, non-compete or consulting agreements, contingencies?
- Management contracts: for whom, duration, and incentives
- Closing costs and the responsibilities of the buyer and seller, such as environmental due diligence and title searches
- Representations and Warranties: boilerplate legal statements
- Brokerage fees: who pays and how much
- Timing for completion: drop-dead date for due diligence and financing period as to how long before money is exchanged and final closing takes place
- Insurance: proof of insurability; what happens with policies?
- Disposition of earnings before closing and viability of non-ordinary expenditures before closing (conduct of business)
- Access to books and records, key customers, and key employees prior to closing
- Disclosure of any outstanding non-compete agreements or obligations with third parties
- Stipulation of confidentiality of buyer (a breach could cause the seller to sue the buyer): The buyer promises not to disclose information about the seller to outsiders and to not disclose that negotiations are underway.
- Seller will take the company off the market for a designated period of time of forty-five to sixty days (a breach could cause the buyer to sue the seller).

> What is being purchased and what is not?

Data Needed Before Reaching a Letter of Intent

Let us assume that the buyer has visited you two or three times; he or she has received three years of financials, understands your compensation and add-backs, and is now ready to make an offer. Based on all the information at hand and on the buyer's best judgment, he or she tells you that they are prepared to draft a Letter of Intent with a purchase price of $5 million of which $3 million would be paid at closing. Additionally, he or she states their intention of making an asset purchase or stock purchase.

If you indicate you are close enough to have the buyer draft a Letter of Intent, then the following items will probably be requested of you:

- Annual financial statements with footnotes for last five years
- Listing of shareholders and key managers showing name, age, shares owned, current position, years of service, annual salary, fringe benefits, last raise, and breakdown of bonuses between discretionary and formula basis
- List of all contractual obligations
- List of top twenty customers, substituting letters for actual names followed by annual sales for last three years
- Description of bonus or incentive system
- List of accounts receivable at signing
- Add-backs or any earning adjustments that probably would not be incurred under new ownership
- Real estate, machinery, and equipment appraisals (if any)
- Breakdown of inventory between raw, finished, and work in process (Banks do not lend against the latter.)
- Amount and description of capital expenditures for last five years and estimate of future needs
- If a stock purchase, then a copy of loan documents
- If a stock purchase, then listing of life insurance policies showing insured, face value, any cash surrender value, and annual premium

An Embarrassment of Riches

There are times when a seller may be looking at more than one Letter of Intent. When a business broker holds a controlled auction, select potential purchasers are invited to submit letters of intent on a specified date.

The seller then has the opportunity to consider all the letters at the same time before deciding on the most suitable.

In an auction situation, the initial offers are usually the best, and the seller is encouraged to accept one of the offers as presented. That one letter is the one that is then signed by the seller.

Once the LOI Has Been Delivered

The next step is for the buyer to deliver the Letter of Intent, preferably in person to you, the seller, and to explain each item point by point. There are now a number of issues you will have to be aware of, including price, terms, the chemistry with the buyer, non-financial issues, and how fast the buyer can close.

Usually, when the buyer and seller strike a deal, the quicker the buyer can secure the financing, complete the due diligence, and draft the Purchase and Sale Agreement, the less chance both parties will change their mind. After the Letter of Intent is signed, an expeditious closing will take place between sixty and ninety days, assuming there are no major glitches such as environmental issues. It will be a time-consuming job to bring the deal to a successful close.

When the Letter of Intent is delivered, neither party wants to lose momentum. Allow plenty of time for discussion. Expect to come to an agreement on the non-binding Letter of Intent by at least the second meeting.

You should predetermine your negotiation strategy. Before you begin negotiating the LOI, you should know your lowest price (although you may not play it), identify key issues to both you and the buyer, and anticipate the responses of the buyer. You should also determine before the meeting whether you or your advisor will be the major spokesperson. Perhaps if there are some negative comments about the buyer that need to be expressed, they should be mentioned by your advisor (bad guy) but not you (good guy). Such negatives could include previous aborted deals or a perceived lack of capital for acquisitions. Such comments would show the buyer you have a good understanding of the merger and acquisition business. Furthermore, you can tell the buyer you cannot sell the business for less because you have other potential buyers who have expressed interest in purchasing the company.

The signing of the Letter of Intent triggers the buyer's commencement of the due diligence process and his ability to secure the necessary financing. You will want to check out the buyer to know whether he or she is creditworthy and whether the buyer is committed to completing the deal. An individual's credentials should be examined more closely than if the buyer is a corporation.

> The signing of the Letter of Intent triggers the buyer's commencement of the due diligence process and his ability to secure the necessary financing.

A buyer will probably verify his or her financial strength by presenting detailed financial statements and emphasize their liquid assets. As a seller, you should request that the buyer submit a list of potential lenders or investors for this proposed acquisition. Aside from the buyer's financial posture, you will want to know about his or her personal characteristics, so take time to meet with the buyer socially. You want to maximize the likelihood of a successful sale.

Make no mistake, this is likely a do-or-die period. According to the Geneva Company, a nationwide intermediary, 50 percent of all deals fail at the Letter of Intent stage. Another 25 percent of all deals fail at the due diligence stage, and 15 percent of all deals fail at the documentation stage. Only 10 percent of all potential deals make it all the way to closing.

> As a seller, you should request that the buyer submit a list of potential lenders or investors for this proposed acquisition.

The Critical Ingredients

The critical ingredients in the Letter of Intent include the following:

1. The proposed purchase price
2. What the down payment would be
3. The size, length, and interest rate of a note and how it would be secured
4. Other considerations affecting the price, such as partial earn-out based on a predetermined formula
5. A list of contingencies

The contingencies would include the arrangements under which you, the seller, would stay on. If you leave, then an agreement on the length and terms of any training period as well as a non-compete agreement should be addressed. Other contingencies that will probably be requested by the buyer include: a review of the company's financial records, an examination of insurance policies, the availability of vendor and customer contracts, and assignment of the lease.

It is customary for agents who broker small companies with sales of less than $1 million to ask the buyer for a good-faith deposit of $5,000 to $10,000, but this is not common for middle-market transactions.

The cost for due diligence is the burden of the buyer. Depending on the complexity of the due diligence, it can cost the buyer of a

Checklist of Items in Letter of Intent

This is what you will see when you receive a Letter of Intent:

1. Description of the buying organization, such as place of business and owners.
2. Statement of price, structure, contingencies, and exactly what is being purchased.
3. Description of any notes: their interest rate, term, amortization provisions, whether or not they are secured or unsecured, negotiable or non-negotiable: Will the buyer have the "right to offset" part of the note if the seller does not meet certain conditions in the Purchase and Sale Agreement?
4. Specification of management contracts: for whom, duration, and what the incentives are.
5. Explanation of closing costs, including intermediaries fees as to who pays what.
6. A statement that representations and warranties will be a part of the Purchase and Sale Agreement.
7. Description of profit-sharing arrangements.
8. A list of contingencies that have to be resolved in order for the transaction to be completed (environmental studies, title transfers).
9. Planned changes to be made, such as management and continuity items (will the plant be relocated?).
10. Estimated date of closing.
11. Transferability of insurance.
12. Reconciliation of debts or collections with shareholders.
13. Continuity of business until closing date.
14. Access to books and records.
15. Description of consulting and non-compete agreements.
16. The adherence to confidentiality by both parties and the understanding that the Letter of Intent is non-binding and that the seller will take the company off the market for a specified period of time.
17. A consideration of whether the parent company (if there is one) should also sign the Letter of Intent and/or if the guarantors of the selling company's obligations (if there are any) should also sign the document.
18. Whether to create an escrow account to handle post-closing adjustments to the purchase price to reflect changes in inventory, final audited financials, or collections of accounts receivable to offset seller's contractual claims.

middle-market company between $10,000 and $100,000. If the seller backs out of the deal for any number of reasons including "seller's remorse," the buyer has no recourse unless he has a so-called breakup fee written into the LOI. While the latter is desirable for the buyer, it is very hard to persuade the seller to comply.

The success or failure of completing the transaction hinges on the LOI. Upon signing the agreement, both parties are morally but not legally committed to do their utmost to complete the transaction. The outcome depends on the results of the due diligence, the ability to put the deal back on track if it is temporarily derailed, and attention to detail and speed without loss of momentum.

The important issue goal is the signing of the Purchase and Sale Agreement after the due diligence has been completed. The buyer's greatest fear is not knowing everything about your company; that due diligence did not uncover everything. And your fear is that information will leak out—that your employees, customers, and suppliers will hear about the deal prematurely—or the buyer really does not have enough money after all.

> The buyer's greatest fear is not knowing everything about your company.

Conclusion

Because the LOI is a non-binding agreement, if so stated, the buyer has the comfort level of knowing he or she can back out. The chances are slight, however, that either the buyer or seller can materially change the price and terms of the deal after both parties have entered into the LOI.

One of the biggest concerns you may have is whether the buyer has the financial resources to complete the transaction and to have the reserves in case the business needs another infusion of capital. As a seller, you are entitled to receive financial information from the buyer.

David Broadwin, transaction attorney for Foley, Hoag & Eliot in Boston, says: "You should devote careful attention to LOI [Letters of Intent] not only because they memorialize the terms of a proposed transaction and give the principals a feeling that they have reached an understanding, but also because they exert a profound influence on the definitive documentation of the transaction."

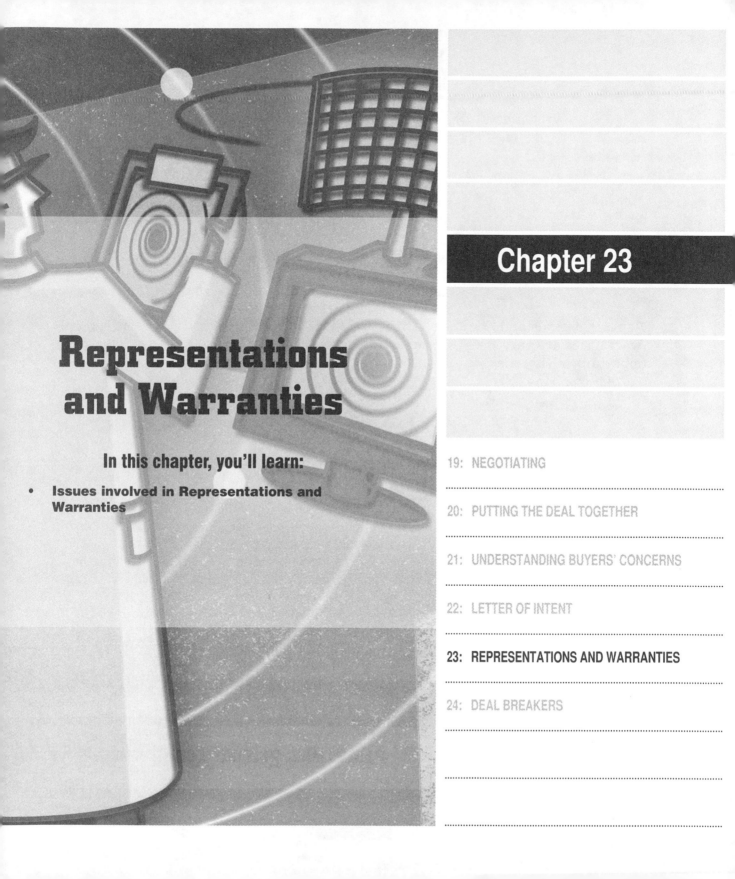

Representations and Warranties

In this chapter, you'll learn:

- **Issues involved in Representations and Warranties**

Chapter 23

The representations and warranties in the Purchase and Sale Agreement take effect the date of signing. According to Stanley Foster Reed, author of *The Art of M&A—A Merger Acquisition Buyout Guide*: "These conditions are intended to disclose all material legal, and many material financial, aspects of the business to the buyer. The seller also gives assurances that the transaction itself will not have adverse effects upon the property to be conveyed. The buyer should be aware that lenders providing acquisition financing will require the buyer to make extensive representations and warranties about the target as a condition to funding."

Exhibits are an integral part of the representations and warranties. Examples used by Stanley Reed are as follows:

> No undisclosed liabilities of the target company except as set forth on Exhibit A.

> No litigation that might have an adverse effect on the target except as set forth on Exhibit B.

Representations and warranties are very important in the sale of a company. According to Reed, "A buyer or seller will be able to back out of the agreement if it discovers that the representations or warranties of the other party are untrue to any material extent." The words "no material adverse change" or "not material to the transaction" are the key phrases. In fact, you may insist on inserting the word "material" when referring to liabilities or litigation. While "material" can be construed as ambiguous, the parties can set a dollar threshold that defines it in particular circumstances.

The Important Elements

In representations and warranties, the important issues to focus on are financial statements, litigation, undisclosed liabilities, and taxes. Regarding the latter, for example, if the sale of the company involves

---

Representations and warranties are very important in the sale of a company.

---

a stock transaction, the following representations and warranties would be appropriate:

- Seller has filed all required tax returns.
- Seller has paid all the taxes due.
- Adequate tax reserves are reflected in the balance sheet.

An explanation of the basket provision is also used to protect you, the seller, by indemnifying you for damages only up to a certain amount. Furthermore, there is usually a cutoff date by which the buyer can seek claims from the seller; three years is the outside limit.

One way to facilitate the buyer's claims is to allow him or her to off-set these amounts from the note due to you. Another method is to set up an escrow account equivalent to 5 to 10 percent of the purchase price.

The Purchase and Sale Agreement defines the parameters of both the purchaser's and seller's representations and warranties. The heaviest negotiating near the closing date usually involves the representations and warranties as well as the indemnifications. Also, your representations and warranties normally account for the largest part of the Purchase and Sale Agreement. The investigation follows the execution of the Purchase and Sale Agreement and is obviously before the closing. If an adverse material fact surfaces after the closing, then you will have to compensate the purchaser based on a breach of representation.

The Key "Reps and Warranties"

The following seller's representations and warranties are the most important:

Financial statements. A closing audit is imperative to verify the authenticity of all the items, particularly inventory, receivables, and payables. Then a post-closing adjustment is factored into the final floating payoff at closing.

Assets. The buyer wants to be sure he is gaining full title to the assets, particularly as it pertains to items such as intellectual

Seeking R&W Coverage

With the growth in the number of mergers and acquisitions, there has been considerable interest in representation and warranties liability insurance policies. Offered by a number of insurance companies, such policies protect companies against certain undiscovered liabilities associated with buy/sell transactions. Sellers are protected from financial loss resulting from a lawsuit triggered by a breach of one or more insured representations or warranties.

Such liability insurance policies can be used as alternatives to a large escrow. They can also be used to work around contentious negotiations over indemnification and survival period of representations and warranties.

property and patents. Also, the buyer wants assurances that the machinery and equipment are in good working order.

Taxes. Not only is it critical to verify your tax liability if it is a stock purchase but in the case of an asset purchase, you want to be sure there are no liens on assets due to failure to pay taxes.

Employee relations. Employee contracts and employee benefits are important even if it is an asset sale because if a new owner takes away knowingly or unknowingly an employee's privilege, then he or she will walk into a hornet's nest.

Environmental. Many transactions in today's merger and acquisition business are being negated because of environmental liabilities. Just because the buyer leases the premises instead of buying the property does not mean that as a tenant you would not be held responsible in part for the contamination caused before your arrival.

Pending and potential litigation. This becomes a bigger issue with a consumer product company just by existing in our litigious society. You will want to place a time period or cap on his or her total responsibility. Usually, the buyer ends up sharing some of the risk for previously made products.

Authorization. To sell the company from stockholders, directors, or third parties such as the bank you will require authorization. You will be expected to ensure to the buyer that: all liabilities are represented; all contracts are disclosed; all wages, taxes, and insurance are current; and all bonus plans are disclosed.

While most of the burden for representations and warranties is on you, the buyer may be required to warrant that the acquisition does not violate their loan agreements or, if stock is to be used, that it is properly authorized. Obviously, if the transaction is a stock sale in

> To sell the company from stockholders, directors, or third parties such as the bank you will require authorization.

which the buyer assumes all the assets and all the liabilities, the representations and warranties are more lengthy and complex. Often the buyer is only willing to undertake a stock transaction based on the tightness and thoroughness of the representations and warranties.

For you, the seller, the important issue is which representations and warranties survive the closing and which ones cease. Those that customarily cease at closing include warranties on equipment and guarantees on licenses. Those that often survive the closing include matters of litigation.

Conclusion

The following advice of Nelson Gifford is an apt way to end this chapter. As former CEO of the Dennison Manufacturing Company, Gifford was involved in more than thirty-five transactions. He says that from the buyer's point of view, "the critical aspect of negotiations is what is stated in the representations and warranties such that the document reflects the following:

Everything you know, you told us.

Everything you told us is true.

Everything you didn't know, you should have known."

> The important issue is which representations and warranties survive the closing and which ones cease.

For more information on this topic, visit our Web site at www.businesstown.com

Deal Breakers

In this chapter, you'll learn:

- About elements that could cause your deal to break down
- How to save a deal from undue diligence
- Financial concerns that could sabotage a deal

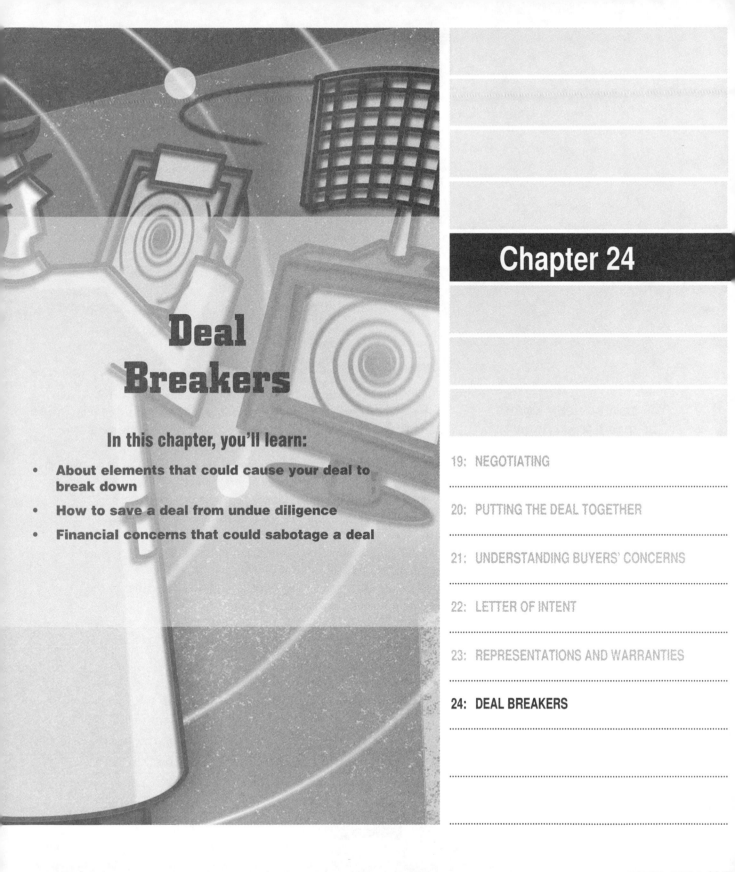

Chapter 24

For a variety of reasons, about 50 percent of the deals that reach the Letter of Intent stage fail to result in actual transactions. Some experienced investment bankers figure that deals often fall apart three to four times before closing. Robert Shee, an investment banker with Robertson & Foley of Charlotte, North Carolina, facetiously states: "A deal only starts once it has died."

Often, buyers and sellers are so excited about the prospect of a transaction because of their verbal agreement that they do not begin to address all the complications and ramifications of a deal. The following items are common deal breakers after a verbal understanding has been reached or after a Letter of Intent has been consummated.

Advisors Who Let You Down

In Chapter 10, I emphasized the importance of utilizing numerous advisors. While I stick with that statement, you should be aware that if various advisors—such as an attorney, accountant, or investment banker—have sharply different advice, the deal could blow up as a result of unmitigated confusion. History reminds us that General Eisenhower was advised differently before committing the Allies to the invasion of Normandy. Ultimately, Ike made his own decision, just as the owner of a company must assess the information and make his own call. You have to use your best judgment based on facts and intuition, and ultimately make the final decision regardless of whether you overrule your business advisors.

> You have to use your best judgment based on facts and intuition.

Another example of a loss of control of the deal, either to the buyer or to one of the advisors, is a result of the seller, you, not being accustomed to the selling process. Out of resentment or frustration, the seller may pick up his or her marbles and go home.

Due Diligence Uncovers a Skeleton

An undisclosed material fact surfacing at the due diligence stage or just prior to closing that causes either the buyer to lose confidence in you or you in the buyer will usually result in a deal breaker. Often, selling companies have some warts, items that are far less than perfect: warranty problems, a pending lawsuit, an environmental spill near the plant. An experienced buyer will usually be able to work around such issues but for an inexperienced buyer they may be deal breakers.

Due diligence usually covers financial, legal, operational, marketing, and investigational matters. Operational due diligence could include an assessment of machinery and equipment as well as the plant. If such items are archaic, a buyer could feel the cost of replacement would be too expensive.

Many acquirers use a multiple of EBIT or EBITDA when in fact they should use EBITDA–CAPX. In other words, if an acquirer has to buy all new equipment to replace the century-old machinery, that has to be considered in the price, and the issue could very well be a deal breaker.

Market due diligence will reveal whether there is very intense customer concentration and, more importantly, whether there is a likelihood of potential loss of these key customers. These items too can be deal breakers.

Financial Concerns Resurface

One of the major reasons for deal breakers is the sudden downturn of sales and earnings just prior to closing. Either you refuse to renegotiate the price accordingly or, more important, the buyer doubts the validity of the company to sustain the business as set forth in the projections.

Often, the seller fails to compute what will be realized after taxes, debt repayments, and closing costs are accounted or until the eleventh hour of the transaction. For example, a C corporation figures out the amount of the double capital gains taxes in an "asset" sale and tries unsuccessfully at the last moment to convince the buyer to do a "stock" sale that would be a single capital gains tax. From the buyer's perspective, he or she may be undercapitalized and just before closing, the buyer is unable to raise the necessary cash to do the deal.

In order to avoid the deal breaker because of financial concerns, namely the sudden downturn in sales, earnings, and backlog, place

Saving a Deal from Undue Diligence

There are a number of ways to avoid killing a deal as a result of due diligence. The most effective way is to divulge all the company's warts up-front and get them on the table early on. Of course, you should also have explanations as to why or how the warts can be addressed and overcome.

For example, say your company has excessive customer concentration, a major concern for buyers. You should be able to either explain that this situation has successfully endured for the past five years or that you have successfully addressed this situation by substantially reducing your company's dependence on these customers over the past year.

heavy responsibility on the investment banker to handle the buyers so that you do not become distracted from running the business. Additionally, provide incentives to top managers to make the extra effort to increase productivity by offering them phantom stock redeemable upon the final sale of the company.

Don't let up just because you think the sale is imminent. Be sure you and your accountant have properly figured out what you will net out from the deal after taxes and closing costs so there won't be any last-minute surprises. And, finally, do a thorough checkup on the buyer to be sure he or she has the financial capacity to fund the transaction.

The Intangibles Become Tangible

If the chemistry between you and the buyer was never really established, or when the deal runs into roadblocks for a number of reasons, there is no personal relationship to bridge the differences and get the deal back on track. This lack of relationship can be a deal breaker.

Seller's remorse happens more often than you might expect. It is like a bride or groom backing out of marriage a day before the wedding. In this case, you realize that your life's work, the company, is too important and you cannot part with it.

Alternatively, the deal can lag and either you or the buyer lose trust or patience, or confidentiality has been breached and either party walks away from the deal.

In order to avoid the deal breaker because of such intangibles, be sure you make the time to get together with the principals of the acquirer over a relaxed dinner or on the golf course. Involve your spouse or a good friend in the selling process so that if you need emotional and psychological support to complete the deal, you have your closest confidant right beside you.

Negotiations Go Stale

Either party being inflexible in the negotiating process can result in a deal being broken. Maybe you want all-cash at closing or all notes

> Lack of relationship can be a deal breaker.

and consulting agreements collateralized, while the buyer wants a hefty escrow account or an overbearing list of "reps and warranties." If neither you nor the buyer is willing to give in or compromise, the deal is cooked.

Another deal breaker, particularly for private equity groups, can be management wanting to retire soon after the transaction is completed. Occasionally, the CEO has negotiated the deal only to find out the company directors are not in agreement with the price, terms, and conditions, or the CEO does not have proper approval from the stockholders.

Finally, some buyers will walk away from a transaction because they have been simultaneously negotiating with another seller, or suddenly their publicly traded stock has tanked.

In order to avoid the deal breaker because of negotiation, be sure that your advisors—transaction attorney, accountant, investment banker—have properly prepared both you and the company to complete the transaction. Continually communicate with the buyer before the heavy negotiating begins to be sure that most of the matters have already been discussed and are more or less resolved. A skilled negotiator who focuses on the big picture will help you successfully close the deal.

Conclusion

You are so close to cashing out, you can almost taste it. But there is still a 50 percent chance that the deal will go down the tubes. Seriously consider the points made in this chapter. If your favored option—a full sale of your company—cannot be realized, study the advice offered in the following section concerning alternatives to outright sales.

> Continually communicate with the buyer before the heavy negotiating begins.

For more information on this topic, visit our Web site at www.businesstown.com

Alternatives to Outright Sale

Summary of Part VI

- Facts about management buyouts

- What Employee Stock Ownership Plans are

- Advantages to leverage re-caps

- How selling parts of a company can help you

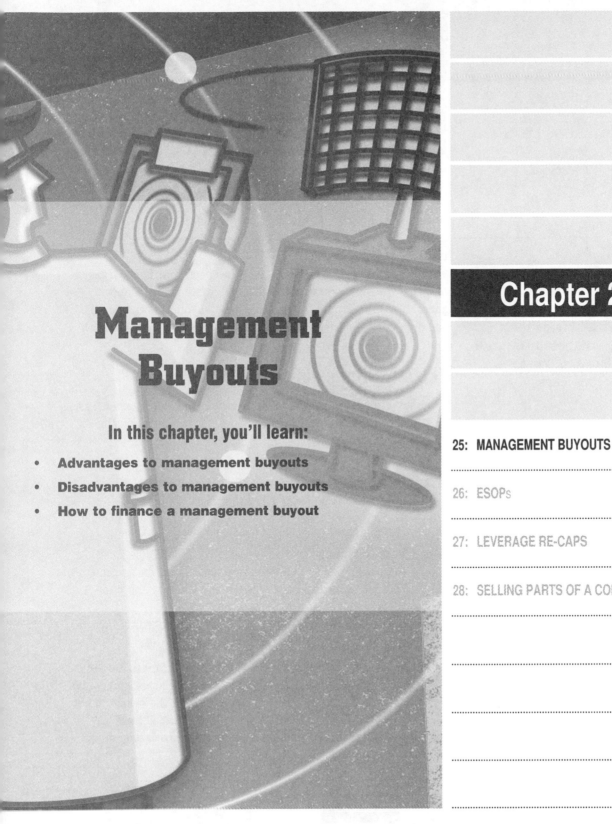

Management Buyouts

In this chapter, you'll learn:

- Advantages to management buyouts
- Disadvantages to management buyouts
- How to finance a management buyout

Chapter 25

Suppose that you have reached retirement age and you have no heir apparent. While you could hire a CEO to run the company in your retirement, you want to cash out now to alleviate your financial worries.

You ponder your choices and reflect on the disadvantages of each type of buyer. A competitor is apt to close your facility and consolidate it with theirs. A strategic buyer is likely to replace your management with theirs. A financial buyer most likely will resell the company in five to seven years.

You rationalize that the company has been your family legacy for many years and you want to see a better fate than the above alternatives. The solution is a management buyout. In other words, you decide to sell your company to management.

The Advantages of an MBO

In addition to selecting a management buyout, commonly known as an MBO, for the reasons mentioned above, other motivations may include the following:

- You have a feeling of responsibility and compassion for the management team such that if a reasonable price can be negotiated, you decide to sell to them.
- There is a greater chance your business will continue intact without operational and cultural changes as a result of a management buyout.
- A quick transaction can be consummated with management because virtually no due diligence is necessary and often there are no competing offers.
- A management buyout obviates your possible fear of breaching confidentiality.

With all these advantages, however, it is important to note that a management buyout usually is initiated by management and not by the owner. The threat, implied or not, is that if you the owner do not cooperate with them and negotiate a fair deal, they will leave the company and place you in an untenable position to sell to another company. It is a squeeze play.

> A financial buyer most likely will resell the company in five to seven years.

Disadvantages of an MBO

It is unlikely that you will get the best price or an all-cash transaction by selling to management. Most MBOs are completed without competitive bidding from numerous potential buyers. Furthermore, management expects and usually receives a favorable price. Not only is management in a highly favorable position to negotiate but they also know about the company's warts and where the bodies are buried.

MBOs are often substantially leveraged because management is usually undercapitalized. The leverage comes from bank debt but also from the management officials structuring an offer with their own notes payable to you, the seller.

If you own a public company, it is necessary to have a Fairness Opinion by a qualified corporate appraiser to justify the valuation of a fair price because an MBO is an inside deal often without competing offers. A Fairness Opinion can cost between $25,000 and $50,000 for companies with sales under $30 million, and much more for larger companies. If your company is private but has numerous stockholders, a Fairness Opinion may be necessary to reduce the possibility of a stockholder lawsuit even if the stockholders are in the minority.

A final disadvantage of an MBO is the possibility that the head of the new company will not be a good CEO. Since you will probably be holding a substantial amount of the purchase price in notes from the buyer, you will not want to take the risk of the company's financial future if the new CEO is perceived to be unqualified.

An Example of an MBO

With Polaroid fighting for its corporate life and deep in debt, it decided to sell its Identification Card (ID) business with revenue of about $100 million. The unit, known as ID Systems, supplies driver's licenses to thirty-six states and other cards to a growing number of foreign governments. According to the *Boston Globe*: "Polaroid faces growing competition from the second-largest player in the industry, Visage, which serves 12 states. The other major competitor is Britain's De La Rue Group PLC. Another possibility is a buyout of the division by its senior executives, a solution some see as best for

The Making of an MBO Warrior

According to consultants L. William Teweles & Co., the following is a profile of a successful management buyout executive:

He has a proven track record in a large company or major division as chief executive officer, president, or general manager, with bottom-line responsibility.

He knows the target company is available for acquisition.

He has in-depth knowledge of the industry in which the acquisition is to be made.

He can assemble a top management team to operate the acquired company.

He has a burning desire to build a successful, world-class enterprise.

the unit itself. For ID Systems, a management buyout might raise fewer antitrust concerns than would a sale to Visage, since the two companies account for almost all of the 50 million U.S. driver's licenses issued each year."

A few days after the article appeared, Polaroid announced that it had agreed to sell the ID Systems to management. Financing sources were not identified but clearly one of the major private equity groups was involved. Subsequently, Polaroid entered Chapter 11, and the court disavowed the MBO as being financially unfavorable to Polaroid's creditors.

Financing the MBO

One of the most important components of a MBO is how it will be financed. The following example is just one scenario.

Our sample selling company is a heavy equipment manufacturer with extensive machinery and equipment, inventory, and accounts receivable, all of which can be highly leveraged (capable of bank borrowing). Additionally, the selling company has no bank debt. Let's say the purchase price is $6 million with the structure as follows:

Management's equity	$1 million
Bank debt	$3 million
Management's note to seller	$2 million
Total	$6 million

This deal is found to be too large for managers to finance themselves so they engage a private equity group to provide most of the equity. Management puts up a small amount of the equity and is willing to initially own a minority position of the new company. Over the next five to ten years, however, management has the ability to completely buy out the private equity group in the form of an earn-out.

Conclusion

MBOs are useful when the owner wants to transfer ownership to key managers either because he is altruistic or because the threat of their departure would cripple the company.

MBO-Friendly Industries

Not all industries are well suited to management buyouts. The best candidates are established and mature industries in which substantial cash flow does not need to be plowed back into research and development and rapid expansion.

The industry should be relatively unaffected by recessions so a steady cash flow is available to service debt requirements. A cyclical industry will make the new managers grow old quickly.

And the industry should not be subject to rapid technological or consumer obsolescence. The high-technology industry, for example, is marked by rapid technological obsolescence and must be continually stoked with capital to generate new products.

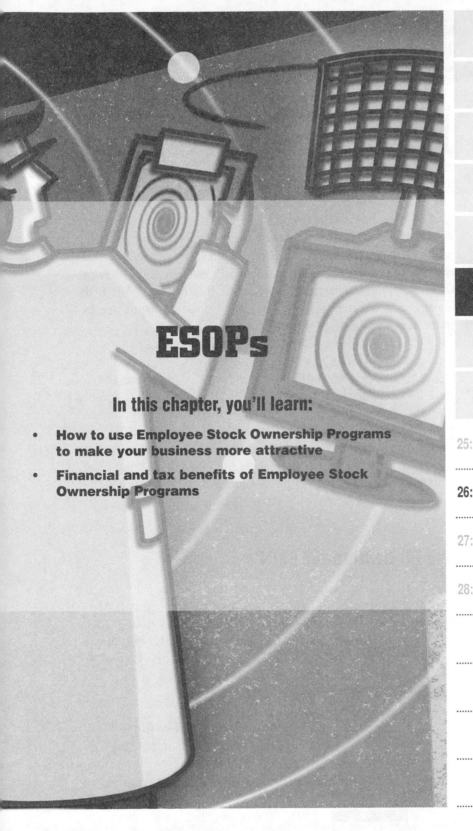

ESOPs

In this chapter, you'll learn:

- **How to use Employee Stock Ownership Programs to make your business more attractive**

- **Financial and tax benefits of Employee Stock Ownership Programs**

Chapter 26

mployee Stock Ownership Plans (ESOPs) are viable alternatives to an outright sale. An ESOP is an employee benefit program that is designed to invest primarily in the stock of the employer corporation and to provide employees with an ownership interest in the company in which they work.

One of the foremost authorities and advisors for ESOPs is Atlantic Management Company (AMC) of Portsmouth, New Hampshire. AMC believes ESOPs are one of the best-kept secrets in business today because most owners still haven't heard about the valuable associated financial and tax benefits. One reason ESOPs receive so little attention is that they appear to be more complex than they really are. An ESOP is simply a "qualified employee benefit plan," similar in some respects to the more familiar profit-sharing plan.

According to Scott Rodrick, author of the booklet *An Introduction to ESOPs*, "In the U.S. today, over eight million employees, or about 6 percent of the non-government U.S. workforce, own stock in the companies through an ESOP. The over 11,000 companies with ESOPs range from the local machine shop to United Airlines and from small insurance agencies to McDonald's. Companies set up ESOPs for a variety of reasons, including buying out existing owners, borrowing money to acquire new assets, and providing a reward system that fits today's participative management styles. These and other applications receive substantial tax benefits."

> One reason ESOPs receive so little attention is that they appear to be more complex than they really are.

The Motivation for ESOPs

Most ESOPs transfer ownership over a period of years, usually in three stages such that 100-percent employee ownership may not be achieved for around ten years. Since employees are borrowing money to buy out their owner, they have to incur the bank debt in stages in order to adequately pay down the debt from normal cash flow.

There are basically four motivating points for the owner to implement an ESOP:

1. **To overcome the difficulties in selling service firms.**
   Service firms represent approximately 70 percent of all

businesses in the United States, manufacturers represent about 20 percent, and the balance is made up of farming, fishing, mining, and similar enterprises. Despite this, service firms are not as saleable as manufacturers. The reason, of course, is that the major asset of most service firms are the employees and yet there is very little assurance that employees will remain with the company after the company is sold.

Unless it is a very large service company, most owners have to be willing to sell their service firm with future payments conditioned as retention of sales, customers, employees, or all three.

If the above factors are so critical in selling, why not just sell the company to employees in order for the owner to realize a liquidity event? Or, if there are two 50-percent owners and one wants to retire while the other owner wants to continue, an ESOP arrangement could nicely buy out the other 50-percent owner.

2. **To reward the employees.** Some employers appreciate that over the years, the employees have been largely responsible for the success of the company, so why not reward them by giving the employees the opportunity to own the company? While the employer's motives are altruistic, Scott Rodrick points out the benefits for the company of rewarding the employees. "Participation management in which rank-and-file employees participate in decisions affecting their jobs through such means as work teams, total quality management, or employee task forces has only a small positive effect. However, companies that combine employee ownership (as through an ESOP) and participative management tend to show substantial gains in performance, growing 6 percent to 11 percent per year faster than would otherwise be expected."

The employee receives his distribution after leaving the company. When a participant retires, becomes disabled, or dies, the ESOP must begin to distribute vested benefits during the plan following the event.

3. **To gain tax benefits.** While tax incentives were the original driving motivation for owners to implement ESOPs, the

When the IRS Is on Your Side

Setting up an ESOP can be an expensive proposition, costing at least $25,000 or more in legal and valuation fees, plan administration costs, and loan commitment expenses. On the other hand, there are sweet tax incentives to borrowing through an ESOP. Contributions to the purchase of an ESOP are tax deductible, which means that for a leveraged ESOP the principle and interest can, in effect, be deducted from taxes. Also, dividends received by employees on ESOP stock or used to repay an ESOP loan, are tax deductible.

It is not often that the Internal Revenue Service is on your side, so it might be wise to take advantage.

other reasons mentioned in this section are of equal or greater importance. For an owner, an ESOP uses tax-deductible corporate earnings to buy shares from owners who wish to sell while deferring taxation on capital gains from the sale.

For employees, when an ESOP is implemented, those who participate in it have an ownership position that is also not taxed until they receive distributions. Owning stock through the ESOP allows participants to share in the growth of their company, just as stock ownership did for the original owners.

4. **To take some money off the table.** By selling part of the owner's interest, the owner can gradually ease out of the company while maintaining management responsibilities.

Rules of Thumb

The number of companies that are full ESOPs are a minority; however, this category is becoming increasingly popular. A candidate for an ESOP should be a company with steady and healthy profits with relatively little bank debt. The company should have minimum sales of around $2.5 to $3 million and an annual payroll of about $1 million. Your payroll must be adequate if you want to buy out an owner's interest in a company through a leveraged ESOP; otherwise, it could be impractical if your covered payroll is too small relative to the value of the owner's interest. It is a portion of the employee's payroll that is used to pay off the debt that funded the owner's equity.

Another rule of thumb is that most ESOPs start with an ownership transfer to employees equivalent to 30 to 50 percent of the entire ownership so as to avoid making it too onerous to pay down the incurred debt. The second payment of the employee ownership may be another 30 percent ownership after three to six years with the final payment exercised in the seventh to tenth year.

Lastly, your corporate culture must be suited to, or adaptable to, employee ownership, according to Scott Rodrick. In his booklet

Take Back the Note

If your employees do not have the cash on hand to go through with a non-leveraged ESOP, they can still proceed by borrowing money in what is known as a leveraged ESOP.

In this model, the ESOP borrows from a bank to buy your shares of the company. The company itself guarantees repayment. In the meantime, the stock is held in a "suspense account" and is released as the loan is repaid.

If a lending institution will not finance the entire ESOP, you, as the seller, can take back a note in exchange for stock.

An Introduction to ESOPs, he writes: "If the managers or now management employees in your company are not and will not be comfortable with the concept of employee ownership, an ESOP is not likely to work. For example, if managers refuse to treat subordinates as co-owners who have something to say about how their jobs are performed, the employee owners may feel cynical about the plan."

Conclusion

Since ESOPs can be complex for some business owners, it is important that they seek advice from ESOP professionals, especially those who are involved in about ten ESOPs per year.

> Since ESOPs can be complex for some business owners, it is important that they seek advice from ESOP professionals.

For more information on this topic, visit our Web site at www.businesstown.com

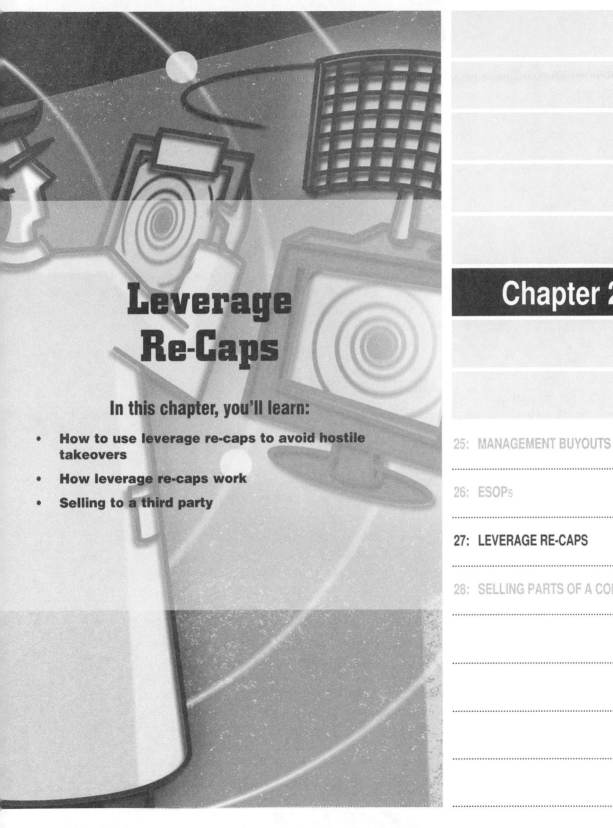

Leverage Re-Caps

In this chapter, you'll learn:

- **How to use leverage re-caps to avoid hostile takeovers**
- **How leverage re-caps work**
- **Selling to a third party**

A leverage re-cap is the jargon for the word "re-capitalization," which means a revision of the capital structure. According to Webster's dictionary, capital structure is "the makeup of the capitalization of a business in terms of the amounts and kinds of equity and debt securities of a business, together with its surplus and reserves." Patrick Gaughan in his book *Mergers, Acquisitions, and Corporate Restructurings*, offers his own definition: "A re-capitalization plan often involves paying a superdividend to stockholders, which is usually financed through assumption of considerable debt. For this reason, these plans are sometimes known as leveraged re-capitalizations. When a company is re-capitalized, it substitutes most of its equity for debt while paying stockholders a large dividend."

> When a company is re-capitalized, it substitutes most of its equity for debt while paying stockholders a large dividend.

Selling to a Third Party

Leverage re-caps are an alternative to selling the company outright. While most of this book focuses on selling to a third party, there are potential problems selling to a third party, namely:

- The alienation of junior management
- The complete removal of the owners from active management soon after the purchase (some owners wish to sell the company to liquefy their investment, but remain with the business)
- A failed sale under new management resulting in negative repercussions with suppliers, customers, and employees

According to John Slater, managing partner of Slater & Company of Memphis, Tennessee, L.P., a professional investment banking firm, re-capitalizations require sufficient company assets and income to support leveraging the company to its maximum level in order to distribute the proceeds to the equity holders. "In a re-capitalization," he says, "corporate owners can receive substantial cash for their ownership interest and yet still retain a leadership role in operations during a carefully planned ownership transition. Transfer of equity can take place over time as the new management 'earns' its ownership. So long as bank debt is limited to a level which supports an asset-based loan on a non-recourse basis, the owner can accomplish the transition without taking on any personal liability."

Slater structured a leverage re-cap for a successful privately held company in which 80 percent of the stock was owned by the founder and 20 percent by the firm's president who had been there many years. The best option was for the corporation to redeem approximately 75 percent of the founder's stock, which had the effect of shifting ownership from 80/20 to 51/49, with the president moving from the minority to the majority position. This redemption was required to assure that the transaction would be treated as a sale subject to capital gain rates rather than a dividend taxable to ordinary income tax rates.

Asking the Tough Re-Cap Questions

To better understand the risks of a leveraged re-capitalization, a solvency analysis should be performed, say Rick Braun and Dan Smith, managing directors of Willamette Capital, Inc., in McLean, Virginia. A solvency analysis compares a company's projected post-transaction cash flows to its obligations, such as the need to make capital expenditures and pay interest and principal on debt.

According to Braun and Smith, a solvency analysis asks the following questions:

1. Does the fair market value of a company's assets exceed its stated and contingent liabilities?
2. Does the company have adequate capital to conduct its business as anticipated?
3. Will the company have sufficient cash flows to support operations and still pay debts and other obligations as they become due?

The company's projections should be subjected to "sensitivity analysis" to determine at what point the answer to one or more of these questions is "no." Braun and Smith write: "For instance, suppose the company's projections show a 10 percent annual increase in revenues. If growth is cut to 5 percent instead, can the company still meet all of its projected obligations including the repayment of debt? If not, what is the likelihood that the company will fail to achieve its projected growth rate and fall short of its obligations?"

Slater's transaction looked like this:

BALANCE SHEET

$000s	Pre-Closing	Closing Adjustments	As Adjusted
Current Assets	6,500		6,500
Net Fixed Assets	1,600		1,600
Other Assets	375		375
Total Assets	**8,475**		**8,475**
Current Liabilities	3,250		3,250
Long-term Liabilities	950	3,875	4,825
Net Equity	4,275	(3,875)	400
Total Liability & Equity	**8,475**		**8,475**

The re-capitalization took the form indicated above, borrowing the funds using corporate assets as collateral to redeem stock from its founders.

SUMMARY HISTORICAL FINANCIAL STATEMENTS

$000s	Year 2	Year 1	Year 0
Net Sales	29,000	37,300	37,000
Gross Margin	7,450	6,950	7,100
Operating Profit	1,175	375	972
Net Income	560	180	582
Total Assets	**10,763**	**9,355**	**8,475**
Funded Debt	3,559	2,752	950
Book Equity	3,693	3,683	4,275

The summary financial statements show the cash flow generated prior to the re-capitalization that prepared the company for the transition. The parties completed the second phase of the buyout in five years to coincide with the founder's desired retirement date.

John Slater points out that many businesses have several key employees in their late thirties and mid-forties who are capable of running the firm and interested in doing so. Yet these individuals have no capital of their own. For their part, the owners would like to pass on the operation and ownership of the business to the

> Many businesses have several key employees in their late thirties and mid-forties who are capable of running the firm and interested in doing so.

managers so long as the sale does not create extra costs or risks to them. In such a scenario, the leverage re-cap is a viable alternative to selling the company to a third party.

Re-Caps as Anti-Takeover Defense

In the late 1980s, re-caps became a popular defense against takeovers for public companies. That is because a re-capitalization plan allows a corporation to act as its own white knight. The large increase in the company's debt makes the firm less attractive to bidders.

Of course, some companies may be limited from using the re-capitalization defense by restrictive covenants in prior debt agreements. The corporation enters into these legal agreements when it borrows from a bank or from investors through the issuance of corporate bonds. Such agreements limit the firm's future options in order to provide greater assurance for the lenders that the debt will be repaid.

The Re-Cap Kings

One private equity group, FCP Investors, Inc., of Tampa, Florida, specializes in leverage re-caps. In fact, utilizing re-caps has become FCP's competitive advantage because when cash is the only consideration, they rarely are the high bidder. But when management's participation in the equity ownership is a factor, FCP is hard to beat.

FCP is generous with equity for its management teams and the strategy has paid off. The large equity participations for FCP's management partners often closes the price gap and wins deals for the firm. With equity participation as its cornerstone, FCP has been most effective in structuring re-capitalizations. As much as 80 percent of the group's transactions have been re-capitalizations in which the sellers partner with FCP. This structure has three primary components: an all-cash price for the company; large equity participations for the owner/operators who continue to run the company; and access to non-dilutive equity from FCP to help the company grow.

This structure is unique in that the owners have taken cash out of their business without giving up operating control. Unlike many other groups, FCP structures its re-caps so that additional add-on equity from the fund does not dilute management's common ownership or require additional equity investments from the management team.

Conclusion

Leverage re-caps are an interesting alternative to a third party sale if the owners want to take some money off the table for liquidity reasons during a time in the market that corporate valuations are depressed. In other words, the owners do not want to sell their entire business at a perceived undervalued price, yet they need or want to take out a considerable amount of cash from the company. Later, when the market stabilizes and valuations increase, the entire company is sold at a higher price.

> Leverage re-caps are an interesting alternative to a third party sale if the owners want to take some money off the table.

For more information on this topic, visit our Web site at www.businesstown.com

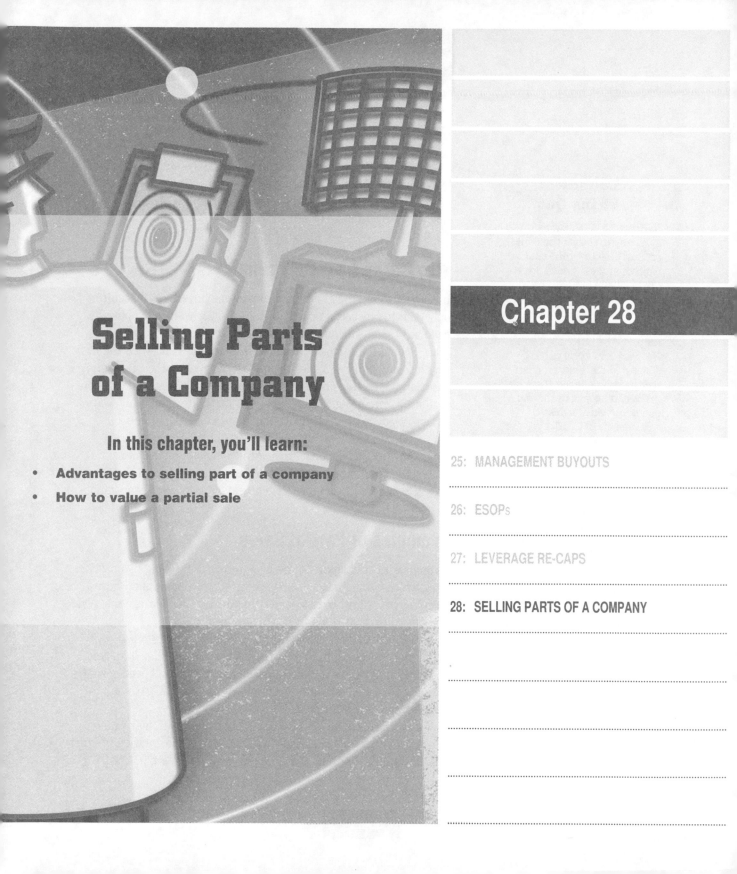

Selling Parts of a Company

In this chapter, you'll learn:

- Advantages to selling part of a company
- How to value a partial sale

Chapter 28

Yet another alternative to an outright sale is to sell the company in parts or sell it as a product line without the normal infrastructure of an ongoing business. Owners sell parts of businesses for different reasons and this chapter addresses those issues. (To simplify matters, we are not referring to the sale of subsidiaries or divisions.)

Why Carve Up a Company?

It is easier to sell the entire company to one buyer. But if acquirers only want to buy certain parts, then as a seller your only option may be to sell the business in pieces or else face a serious reduction in price. Selling the company in pieces is more prevalent when the business is losing money. In such a situation, frequently the valuation is based on book value or a slight premium to book value. Chances are that in this circumstance, acquirers are like vultures and will swarm around, ready to pick off the desirable pieces.

A second motivation to sell off parts of the company is to reduce the debt load, particularly if the debt is burdensome.

A third motivation leading some owners to sell part of their business is to either focus on their core operation or to simplify operations.

Examples of Partial Sales

As an investment banker, I have been involved in selling two product lines, which is the same as selling parts of a company; and I have been involved with two companies that did not sell because the owners refused to divide their business into pieces.

In the summer of 2001, GenRad Company, of Littleton, Massachusetts, announced it would sell their business to Teradyne Corporation. Prior to this announcement, GenRad had been selling off non-core businesses in order to raise much needed cash and to focus on their base business.

I represented the buyer who in conjunction with a private equity group acquired GenRad's $10 million instrumentation product line. The transaction was a win/win deal for both parties, but there was an interesting hiccup a year after the closing. Since GenRad sold a product line and not a subsidiary or a division, the financials of this $10 million entity, including gross margins and general and administrative expenses, were not precisely documented.

Fast forward to a year after the closing when the new owner of the instrumentation product line noticed that gross margins were not 45 percent but rather 35 percent, a huge difference. The buyer and seller resolved this issue by the buyer cancelling their $1 million note to the seller as a retroactive price settlement.

The following are examples of businesses that should have considered selling pieces of their operations in parts but ultimately failed in their efforts.

Office Product Company #1

This company had sales of approximately $20 million, producing two distinctly different product lines for retail chains. One was a branded calendar/organizer similar to the well-known product Daytimers. The other was a line of Casio calculators under the company's own brand.

After going to market for several months, the investment banker created considerable interest but potential buyers wanted either just the paper product line or the electronic product line but not both. From the buyer's perspective, the two product lines were incompatible.

Office Product Company #2

This company also had sales of approximately $20 million, producing a wide range of clipboards both in wood and metal. Unlike the previous example, this was a single product line; however, their distribution network was split between mass merchandisers/retail chains and schools/municipalities.

Again, after several months, the investment banker created considerable interest but the potential buyers were principally interested in just the part selling to the mass merchandisers. From the buyer's perspective, they were not interested in the sales to schools/municipalities because their business did not sell into those markets.

> After going to market for several months, the investment banker created considerable interest but potential buyers wanted either just the paper product line or the electronic product line.

Valuing the Sale for Part of the Company

If you sell part of a company with its infrastructure—employees, plant/office, assets—then the company should be worth more than if you just sell a product line without the infrastructure of the company. And if you sell the majority of the company to one buyer and the minority to another buyer, most of the infrastructure would be allocated to the majority portion of the company.

Valuing the sale of a product line is different from valuing the sale of a company. In the case of a product line, you should not be concerned with the sales, general, and administrative (SG&A) expenses but rather with only the sales and the gross profit of the product line. The buyer will have their own SG&A so the buyer is not going to focus on these expenses.

In determining some sort of multiple for valuing a product line, I suggest a multiple of one or two times "gross profit" compared to a five or six times EBIT for the entire company. Let's use the following examples:

			Multiple	*Value*
Sales	*$10 million*			
Gross Profit	4 million	x	1	= $4.0 million
EBIT	1.5 million	x	5.5	= $8.25 million
Sales	*$10 million*			
Gross Profit	5 million	x	1.25	= $6.25 million
EBIT	2 million	x	6.00	= $12.00 million

The above scenarios show that if you sell the entire company with the infrastructure, it should be worth around twice the value of the product line without the infrastructure. In the case of consumer products, the retention of the product name is critical because it represents the goodwill.

Conclusion

Selling parts of a company is a viable option, particularly if it is done in conjunction with selling the balance of the company that contains the infrastructure.

> Valuing the sale of a product line is different from valuing the sale of a company.

Closing

Summary of Part VII

- Legal and tax issues involved in selling your business
- Disclosure questions you may be asked
- Possible problems during change of control
- Red flags to look for before closing
- Preparing for closing

Legal and Tax Issues

In this chapter, you'll learn:

- **How to understand basic tax and legal issues**
- **What disclosure is**

Chapter 29

While you will likely have knowledgeable advisors to help you navigate the legal and tax shoals of selling a business, it would be wise to be familiar with some of the basic issues at play.

Asset and Stock Transactions

Inevitably, you and the buyer are confronted with how the transaction should be structured, and the tax implications arising from your decision. On the one hand, the buyer wants an asset purchase in order to step up the value of the inventory, plant, and equipment for future large depreciation deductions. As the seller, you want a stock sale to mitigate the capital gains tax and to avoid the recapture tax. The latter results when the capital gain of the business exceeds the depreciation already taken. The end result frequently is a significant amount of income that you must recognize.

If the decision to purchase the business is an asset deal, the various components of the business should be broken down: land, buildings, equipment, inventory, patents, and goodwill. The buyer obviously wants the least amount of goodwill on the books because it is considered a soft asset. Also, the buyer will want a lower value placed on land compared to buildings because it is not a depreciable item.

On the other hand, sellers of a C corporation are not only faced with a double tax by selling the assets instead of the stock but are also faced with the possible recapture of some depreciation previously taken on the equipment of the corporation. For companies with heavy capital equipment, such as plastic injection molders, the depreciation recapture may be substantial. It will also be taxable at the maximum rate of the corporation, and will ultimately erode the new purchase price available to the seller.

Covenants: Consulting and Non-Compete Agreements

Aside from the buyer's basic motive of employing key personnel part time and preventing them from competing, buyers have a tax reason

Getting the Most Out of an Earn-Out

What should you do in an earn-out situation to maximize your eventual payout? Lawyer Sarah Richmond of Lucash, Gesmer & Updegrove, LLP, advises sellers to accept an earn-out only when one or more of the selling shareholders will stay on with the buyer and exercise control over development and marketing of the acquired assets:

"Make sure the earn-out formula directly tracks the performance of the assets acquired in the sale, rather than the seller's overall business," she says. "Evaluate the timing of the earn-out, as well as the milestones and the likelihood of achieving them. Make sure the buyer commits to a large enough marketing and hiring budget for the entire earn-out period. Maintain as much control as possible over whether the earn-out is reached: Paying attention to these details before the sale is finalized is the best way to do that."

for structuring these terms into the Purchase and Sale Agreement. Payments made by a buyer to a seller for these covenants are deductible by the buyer as a regular expense in the year that payments are made. Conversely, payments received by you for these covenants are taxable as ordinary income instead of being taxed at the lower capital gains tax rate.

Furthermore, a $1 million non-compete agreement in which $333,333 is paid at the end of each year for three years has a total present value of $828,951 using a 10 percent discount rate. One advantage for you is that the tax payments are spaced over a three-year period.

While in many cases the buyer wants the covenants for genuine reasons, the buyer also intends to use the covenants to pay you over time and to allocate the purchase price to intangible assets, thus mitigating the goodwill on the balance sheet of the new company. These covenants are, however, more advantageous to the buyer than you because they will generate ordinary deductions to the buyer but ordinary income to you. Of course, the tax on income is higher than the tax on capital gains.

To the extent that the overall purchase price can be reduced by allocating payments to covenants with you, there will be that much less residue of purchase price to be allocated to goodwill.

> While in many cases the buyer wants the covenants for genuine reasons, the buyer also intends to use the covenants to pay you over time and to allocate the purchase price to intangible assets.

Security on Your Notes

Most transactions are structured so that there are three or four components:

- Cash at closing
- Seller's notes
- Covenants: consulting and non-compete agreements
- Perhaps a partial earn-out

The issue of how the buyer will secure the notes always seems to be a negotiated item. Usually, the buyer has pledged the key assets to his bank for the acquisition financing and his normal credit lines. If the bank only requires collateral from the accounts receivable and inventory, then you can take a first position on the machinery and equipment and a second position to the bank's collateral.

On smaller transactions, it is common for the buyer to personally sign for the notes and perhaps offer a lien on a summer home or other asset. If there are two individuals buying a business, your lawyer will probably want the buyers to personally sign a "joint and several" agreement, which means if one partner fails to live up to his commitment, the other partner is responsible for all his partner's shortfall. Buyers will want to avoid such agreements.

Tax-Deferred Transactions

The installment sale by definition is when at least one payment is to be received after the close of the taxable year in which the sale occurs. In other words, the recognition of the capital gain is postponed. If structured properly, both you and the buyer benefit. In your case, the taxes are deferred; in the case of the buyer, the payments are also deferred.

From a seller's perspective, the deferred payment may be exchanged for a promissory note by a third party or standby letter of credit; however, installment obligations secured by cash or certificates of deposit of U.S. Treasury instruments do not qualify.

Disclosure

As part of a buyer's due diligence on the selling company during the Purchase and Sale Agreement stage, the buyer will obviously inspect the business and its financial and other records. The buyer's attorney will undoubtedly submit a disclosure questionnaire such as the example included here. If you respond "yes" to any of these questions, then an explanation is required on the addendum. It should be noted that there are also other sections of the disclosure statement, such as regulation and legal considerations.

A Ballooning Tax Rate

C corporations are a tax nightmare for the seller if assets are sold, says James Laab, president of the Business Sale Center. Laab says that if you are selling a C corporation, for all practical purposes you must sell the stock, not the assets. If you sell the assets, the corporation will have to pay tax on the sale, then you will personally pay tax again on the after-tax amount you remove from the corporation.

Laab offers the following example. "Let's use a combined state and federal tax rate of 40 percent for the corporation and individual. For each $1,000 in assets sold, the corporation pays $400 in taxes and keeps $600. Then the corporation pays you $600, but you must pay $240 in taxes. You are left with $360, so the total tax rate is 64 percent."

Disclosure Questionnaire Examples

1. Are you aware of any circumstances in the industry or market area that may adversely affect future profitability of the business?
2. Are there any revenues or expenses of the business that are not clearly reflected in its financial statements?
3. Is the business in default of any of its financial or contractual obligations?
4. Has the business or any of its owners been the subject of any bankruptcy filing, assignment for benefit of creditors, or insolvency proceeding of any kind during the last five years, or consulted with any attorney or advisor regarding such proceedings?
5. Are there any individual customers who account for more than 10 percent of annual gross sales? If yes, list each by name and indicate the approximate percentage of annual gross sales and any relationship to the business or its owners.
6. Are there any commitments to employees or independent contractors regarding future compensation increases?
7. Are there suppliers who have a personal or special relationship with the business or its owners? If yes, list each such supplier, the nature of the relationship, and the approximate amount of annual purchase.
8. Are any of the employees or independent contractors related to any of the owners of the business, or one another? If yes, list them by name and describe their relationship.
9. Have you had or do you anticipate any disputes with the landlord or problems with the premises the business occupies?
10. Are there any terms or conditions of the premises lease with which the business or the landlord is not in full compliance?
11. Have there been any deaths, violent crimes, or other criminal activity on the premises within the last three years?
12. Are you aware of any substances, materials, or products on or near the premises which may be an environmental hazard such as, but not limited to, asbestos, formaldehyde, radon

> Are there any commitments to employees or independent contractors regarding future compensation increases?

gas, paint solvents, fuel, medical waste, surface or underground storage tanks, or contaminated soil or water?

13. Is there any equipment used in the business that it does not own?

14. Is there any equipment used in the business that is not in good or operable condition, or for which maintenance has been deferred?

15. Does the business have a franchise, distributorship, or licensing agreement? If yes, please provide a copy of each.

Conclusion

As intimidating as a due diligence questionnaire can be, honest disclosure is in the interest of the seller in order to avoid legal repercussions later on. And taxes can have such a large impact on the final deal that it is worth devoting considerable resources to find the best approach.

> As intimidating as a due diligence questionnaire can be, honest disclosure is in the interest of the seller in order to avoid legal repercussions later on.

For more information on this topic, visit our Web site at www.businesstown.com

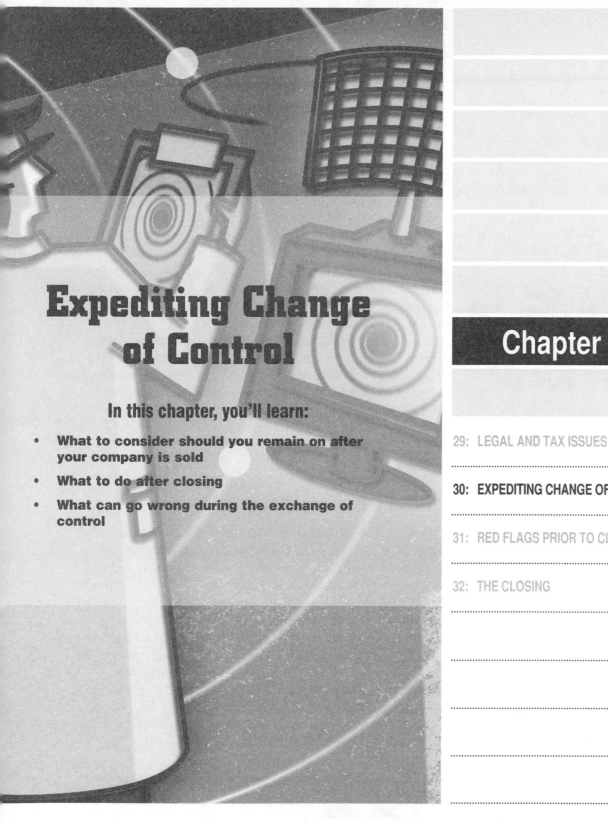

Expediting Change of Control

In this chapter, you'll learn:

- What to consider should you remain on after your company is sold

- What to do after closing

- What can go wrong during the exchange of control

Chapter 30

During the Second World War when Churchill, Roosevelt, and Stalin met to discuss their war plans, they also discussed the disposition of Germany after their victory. It may seem somewhat presumptuous for the Big Three to plan for post-World War II when the outcome was still in doubt. While Roosevelt's compromises with Russia may have left a lot to be desired, the point is that the leaders had enough foresight to look into an uncertain future.

As a seller of a company, it is to your benefit to plan the change of control so that it can be expedited properly. Picture yourself going through the final stages of the merger and acquisition process. Everything seems to be happening so quickly. As you concentrate on running your business on all eight cylinders to avoid a slowdown at the end, you are also negotiating with several buyers demanding your keenest concentration. You are working with the investment banker, attorney, accountant, board of directors, and perhaps other advisors. The entire episode requires plenty of decisions, both large and small, all of which create excitement, anxiety, and emotion. In this environment, you want to expedite a smooth transition, so you ask your advisor to point out the critical considerations. This is what the advisor will tell you.

> As a seller of a company, it is to your benefit to plan the change of control so that it can be expedited properly.

Critical Considerations

If you are to remain as CEO with the company for a few years, what autonomy will you have with the parent company and what sort of direction will you be able to provide, or will you be inundated with filing reports? Checking with other CEOs who sold their company to the potential acquirer is highly recommended as well as personally visiting the acquirer's management team at their facilities.

If your acquirer plans to move the company's operation more than fifty miles away, who will pay for the employee severances: you or the acquirer? What amount of severance is fair: an average of $10,000 or $30,000 per employee?

If you are expected to set up an escrow account for the benefit of the buyer, who pays for the trustee's fees and do you receive the interest from this account?

The buyer will want to peg the closing price (up or down) to a specific figure for net worth and working capital. Will you agree to the figure for the last month prior to the date of the Purchase and Sale Agreement or the one based on an average of numerous months?

If your management team is remaining, what sort of employment agreements can you negotiate for them?

The Need for Security

If the buyer has a note with you as the seller, how is it secured? Many private equity groups are known to secure the note with the company you just sold them. In other words, in this case you are indirectly securing the note yourself. Usually, the seller asks the parent company to secure the note. But you do not want to wait until the eleventh hour of putting the deal together only to find that the security for the note is unacceptable.

About twenty years ago, I sold a sporting goods store to a buyer who had to really stretch to do the deal financially. Of course, the buyer used the bank to finance most of the acquisition price and had a relatively small note with me for the balance. My attorney wisely insisted that the buyer secure my note, because we did not want to take a second position behind the bank. In looking around for some other collateral aside from the business, we persuaded the seller to give me a second mortgage on his summer cottage that was located in another state. Several years later, the buyer ran the business into the ground, could not pay his financial obligations, and declared bankruptcy. Thanks to my attorney, I collected 100 percent of my note by enforcing our collateral agreement.

> Usually, the seller asks the parent company to secure the note.

Stock Answers

A "stock" sale is much easier to close than an "asset" sale, because the former is a turnkey transaction. Most contracts including leases are not transferable, therefore in an asset sale the buyer will want to have these contracts subject to transfer at the time of closing. Aside from the bother of putting these contract transfers in place, the buyer can always back out of the deal up to the very last minute, thus jeopardizing your future relationships with the recipients of the contracts.

Future Relationships

Perhaps the most sensitive issue in expediting the change of ownership is the buyer's insistence of talking to a few key customers or vendors prior to the closing. If there is customer or vendor concentration, the buyer wants assurance from some person in authority that these critical relationships will continue in the same manner once the new owner takes over. You, the seller, will be concerned that if the deal doesn't close these key relationships will be in jeopardy because of your uncertainty. Obviously, there is no easy answer and each situation has to be determined on a case-by-case basis. I would suggest, however, that when you are negotiating with several buyers, that at that time, you ask them to explicitly tell you of their due diligence requirements. You may select one buyer over the other depending on their specific response.

When you are negotiating with the buyer, you should urge the buyer to continue to use your bank, which will probably want to keep this account. Doing business favors, such as giving this recommendation, can help you in the future. Furthermore, your bank is familiar with your account and their understanding of the business should help in establishing the new relationship quicker than another bank.

Expediting Change Post-Closing

The deal is done and you have completed the closing. Now what do you do? You help the new owner because chances are that you have some vested interest in the new entity, and it is in your best interest that the new owner succeeds. For example:

- There may be an escrow account due you.
- The buyer may have given you a note.
- You may be the landlord, and the buyer the tenant.
- Your name remains on the company letterhead, and your personal reputation continues to be associated with the business.
- Your former employees depend on you to have made the right decision in selling to the particular buyer, thus preserving their jobs.

Make a Dry Run

Even though you have an experienced transactions attorney, do not assume everything will go smoothly at the closing. In fact, you may want to have a trial closing several days prior to the actual closing. A trial closing will allow you to ensure that your bank will release all their liens on your company so that you can deliver a clean title to the buyer, and that the buyer has the funds properly in hand to pay you at closing. It is disheartening to sign all the paperwork at the closing only to be told that the buyer's check will be deposited in your bank account several days later.

As the seller, you may have been retained on the company payroll or you may be receiving compensation from non-compete or consulting agreements. So, for all the reasons mentioned and perhaps more, you should help the buyer succeed after buying your company. There are a number of ways to achieve positive results.

First, address all your employees in conjunction with the new owner. Explain the positive reasons for the decision and how the employees will benefit over the long term. If the buyer plans to lay off employees because of one reason or another, tell them up front that some cutbacks will be done within days. Be honest with the employees. They will want to ask some questions regarding benefits and job security. Urge the new owner to be prepared to address these issues, not only for the employees but to help you save face.

Next, you should visit or telephone your top customers and vendors, along with the new owner or CEO, to build trust, create goodwill, and allay possible apprehensions.

Mail announcement letters to all stakeholders of the company, preferably under your name and the new owner's. Press releases

Go into the Deal with Cap and Basket

Once a business changes hands, one nagging worry of both buyers and sellers is the possibility of unexpected nickel and dime expenses, such as bills that are not included on the list of liabilities or a customer returning a shipment of defective products. A cap and basket sets ground rules to avoid such problems, says James Laab, president of the Business Sale Center.

As Laab explains it, each time a small, unexpected expense occurs, the buyer puts it into a "basket," which has a predetermined limit (say $10,000, for example). "Until the amount of liabilities in the basket reaches $10,000, the buyer is responsible for them," Laab says. "If and when the basket is full (it reaches $10,000) the buyer can pass liabilities over and above $10,000 to the seller. It's similar to a deductible on an insurance policy. The buyer knows up front they are assuming a certain level of risk, and the seller knows they won't be bothered with minor oversights that are bound to happen in a sale."

A cap is a limit on total liability to the seller, set at a mutually agreed level, but is often in the hundreds of thousands of dollars. "It comes into play in stock sales where the buyer assumes unknown future liabilities, such as lawsuits that exceed insurance coverage," says Laab. "The seller may be required to pay back some portion of the sale proceeds in this extremely unlikely event, but the seller's maximum liability is limited."

should be mailed to the various trade publications announcing the transaction. And if there are forthcoming trade shows for the company, consider attending to show solidarity and support.

What Can Go Wrong in Exchange for Control

Nirvana is selling your company for the top price with the best terms at the right time to the most desirable buyer. Of course, such an occurrence would be nearly impossible. So what can go wrong?

> Depending on the situation, selling the business might be the correct decision.

You can sell your company too soon before it has reached its full potential, thus leaving considerable money on the table. We discussed earlier, however, that selling a business for monetary gain is generally not the primary motivation for selling a company. Nevertheless, some people sell their business prematurely because they lack the necessary working capital or financial resources to remain competitive. Alternatively, they could have re-capitalized the company or sold stock in order to raise the necessary funds.

Instead of merging with another company and retaining some equity interest in the combined entity, the owner sells the company. Depending on the situation, selling the business might be the correct decision; however, the two founders of Cisco Systems sold the company when sales were only around $2 million and now fifteen years later sales are $20 billion. Not all business owners want or have the ability to significantly grow the business.

You can sell your company too late after it has past its full potential, thus missing the opportunity to cash-out at the top of the market. Selling a company, if you own it principally for financial reasons, should be treated like owning securities; that is, buy low, sell high. Aside from not maximizing your investment by selling too late, some people sell too late for personal reasons.

I have a friend who owned a tourist lodge in Alberta, Canada. He worked most of his life at this lodge to retire the company's debt and to improve the lodge so it would reap an attractive price when it was ready to be sold. When he reached seventy-five years old, he sold the lodge for $4 million and retired to his new home to live out his life in peace. Two years after he sold the company, his wife died. Compounding the hurt was the loss of his son in a tragic accident. Now, he was faced with living alone the rest of his life only to wonder why he didn't sell the business ten years early so he could have spent his twilight years with his beloved wife, a person he often neglected during his years of hard work.

You can sell your business to the wrong company and/or person. In my earlier life, I sold two of my operating companies; one was a wonderful experience in expediting change post-closing, and the other was very discomforting. In the latter case, I sold a sporting goods store that had a wonderful reputation with our customers and the community. Soon after, the new owner developed a reputation of being rude to the customers and not paying one of my former suppliers a large invoice. Both incidents were not only personally embarrassing but disheartening because of all the effort I exerted to create goodwill among the customers.

While it did not happen to me, there are numerous stories about how buyers have stiffed the seller on all sorts of obligations, including non-compete/consulting agreements, notes, and earn-out arrangements. Earn-outs, historically, have been subject to many disputes; therefore, a royalty on sales is a more definitive benchmark to measure increased performance. As a seller, you owe it to yourself to thoroughly check out the buyer's reputation and the company's previous record on acquisitions.

> You owe it to yourself to thoroughly check out the buyer's reputation and the company's previous record on acquisitions.

Conclusion

Many sellers feel the deal is done when they sign the Letter of Intent or when the Purchase and Sale Agreement is prepared. The ultimate success of the transaction is often dependent on properly expediting change of control pre- and post-closing.

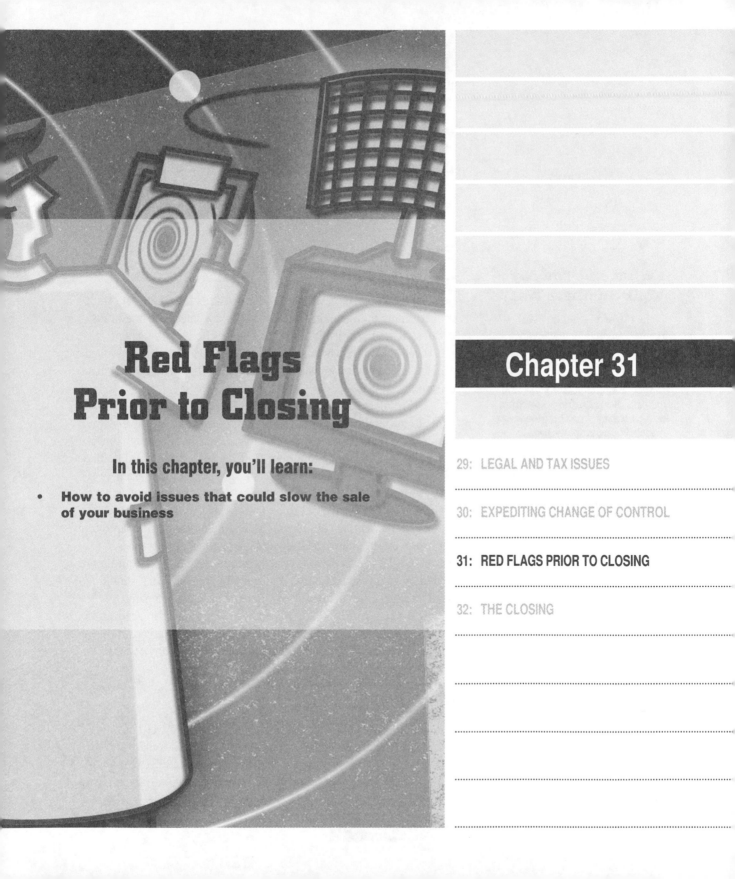

Red Flags Prior to Closing

In this chapter, you'll learn:

- How to avoid issues that could slow the sale of your business

Chapter 31

It is sadly ironic that while buyers often conduct extensive due diligence on the seller, seldom does the seller conduct thorough due diligence on the buyer. Many deals are aborted along the way, yet there are red flags that the seller should notice and use to re-evaluate whether or not to go forward with the transaction.

Early-Stage Red Flags

Many years ago Godfrey Wood, one of Harvard College's all-time greatest hockey goalies, worked at Land-Vest as their top real estate broker selling multimillion dollar estates. As a salesman, one of his greatest attributes was his ability to size up the potential client. He had three standard questions: What estates have you already looked at? How much equity are you willing to commit? What type of house do you live in now?

Based on the answers and Godfrey's sixth sense, he would agree to meet with the buyer or discreetly turn the buyer over to a junior broker. This type of analysis obviously is not thorough, but it apparently worked well enough for Godfrey such that he maintained his position as the firm's top salesman. The point of this example is that as a seller you have to be very focused and not waste your time on buyers who are perceived to be undesirable.

An early red flag could be an individual buyer, as compared to a corporate buyer, unless the individual is qualified, preferably a former CEO who is experienced in acquisitions, well-financed, and represented by an investment bank. Additionally, the individual should have prior experience in the same industry as your company.

If the company or its CEO has not had experience in acquisitions, the chances are that this buyer will be tentative and overly cautious, and will have a problem overcoming any of your company's warts.

Mid-Stage Red Flags

The middle stage is defined as the period after the buyer has received the offering memorandum. At this point, it would be a red flag if you or your investment banker telephone the buyer for a follow-up, and you do not receive an immediate response, thus implying

What Did You Say Your Business Was?

If the buyer is smaller than your company, an acquisition is entirely possible but this could still be a red flag. A red flag could be a private equity group (PEG) that has stated criteria of minimum size/profits and industry type that does not match your company profile. Often such financial buyers will claim they are interested in taking a look at your company, and you send them your offering memorandum. Soon after, the PEGs will return the memorandum, stating your company is too small or does not fit their criteria. No kidding.

an interest level less than priority status. If the buyer is represented by a junior representative of the company, you should be able to access the CFO or CEO to measure the company's interest at a senior level. If denied this access, beware.

If you or your investment banker request a term sheet by a specific date following the receipt of the offering memorandum and you do not receive one, that is a red flag. (A term sheet is a written range of value for the purchase price plus an indication of how the transaction would be structured.)

If after receiving a term sheet from a private company you then request and are refused access to the buyer's financial statements to verify their financial capability to do your deal, you certainly have cause for suspicion.

Later-Stage Red Flags

The later stage is defined as the time frame after the Letter of Intent is signed by both the buyer and the seller.

The Grand Inquisitor

The biggest mistake owners commit when trying to sell their business is to be too passive, says Robert Shuman, who years ago sold his $12 million ambulance company to a national provider of emergency medical services. He told *Inc.* magazine: "If you don't aggressively investigate potential buyers while they're investigating you, you can't possibly wind up with the best deal."

You can't call Shuman passive. First, he made on-site visits to potential buyers, looking for assessments of management's strengths, their track record with previous acquisitions, and their attitudes to employee relations. He even visited the managers of previously acquired businesses.

He then closely analyzed the future value of each proposed acquisition: its capital base, cash flow, bank accounts, liquidity, and potential to go public. That way he had a good idea of how much the deal would be worth to him.

Even though he is a lawyer, Shuman brought in an outside lawyer and a certified public accountant very early on because he realized the deal would be too complex to handle alone. "After all, you're going to do this deal only once," he told the magazine, "so it's essential to work out the best total package."

Hopefully, you will have chosen wisely because, as we have discussed earlier, you have to take your company off the market for the specified period of time, such as sixty days or more, until the deal is completed or aborted. Unfortunately, there will probably be a number of red flags but unlike the earlier stages it is in your best interest to try to work through them by tactful negotiations.

One of the first red flags in this later stage is a difficult, inexperienced, uncompromising, or overly aggressive transaction attorney for the buyer. Some attorneys can be the most difficult element in a transaction and you will suffer as a seller if this is the case. This matter is so important that I recommend that when you are in the final selection stage of the ultimate buyer, you request the name of the buyer's attorney. Your lawyer will be able to ascertain by his or her own network whether the buyer's attorney should be replaced or whether you should select another buyer.

Another red flag is when the senior officer or CEO of the acquiring company is unwilling to spend social time with you. One of the best ways to create a bond between the buyer and seller, to establish a cultural understanding and facilitate a cooperative working relationship, is over several social occasions, such as a drink, a meal, or a golf game.

As a seller, you will expect the buyer to conduct extensive due diligence. Just as the buyer is taking certain risks in an acquisition, you are taking risks as the seller. A red flag would be if the buyer has made unreasonable representations and warranties and has required an unreasonable escrow account. The world "unreasonable" means beyond the norm for your particular company and industry.

> One of the best ways to create a bond between the buyer and seller, to establish a cultural understanding and facilitate a cooperative working relationship, is over several social occasions.

Conclusion

Other red flags, such as loss of momentum are bothersome, but you should try to overcome them rather than to abort the transaction. It is in your best interest to recognize the red flags so that you can deal with them accordingly. Be proactive instead of reactive in order to try to rectify the situation.

For more information on this topic, visit our Web site at www.businesstown.com

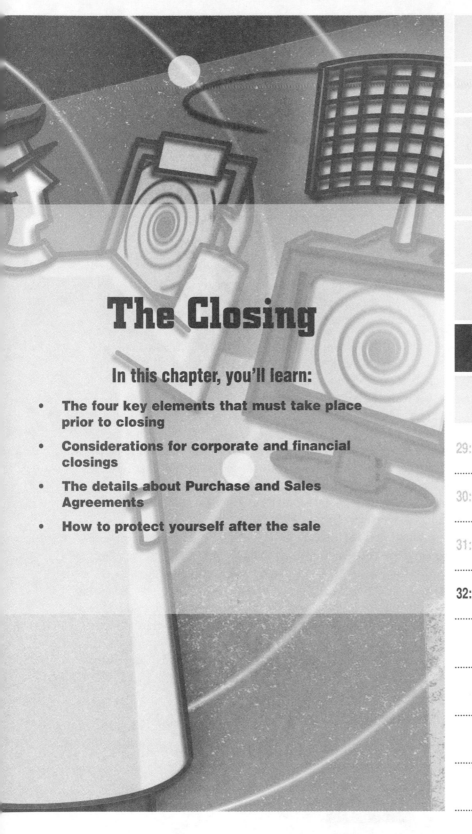

The Closing

In this chapter, you'll learn:

- The four key elements that must take place prior to closing

- Considerations for corporate and financial closings

- The details about Purchase and Sales Agreements

- How to protect yourself after the sale

Chapter 32

The closing is the formal transfer of the business. There are four key elements that must take place prior to closing:

1. Both parties have agreed to the price and terms, and you have shown evidence that you have legal authority to sell the business.
2. Due diligence has been completed by the buyer and your representations and claims have been substantiated.
3. Financing is secured and the proper liens are in place so that the lender can release the funds for the acquisition financing.
4. Remedies are available to the buyer if you breach the representations and warranties.

Clearly the closing is no time to cut corners financially. You need expert legal advice because a foolish mistake at this juncture could cost you ten times the expense in the future.

It is the buyer and his or her attorney who traditionally have the prerogative to control the drafting of the Purchase and Sale Agreement. As the seller, if you can persuade the buyer to let you draft the agreement, do so. It will maximize your position to control the process, from drafting the contract to writing the checklist used at the closing. Assuming the buyer's attorney does draft the agreement, then your attorney handles the revision and finally the buyer's attorney completes the final copy.

Emotions can run high at the closing. Hopefully, a mutual trust has developed between you and the buyer during the many months of courting and negotiating. The buyer will have spent thousands of dollars on inspections, due diligence, and obtaining the proper financing. You will not only have spent money for appraisals and consulting fees but the emotional experience of selling a business is often very taxing. It is important for both sides to maintain a positive attitude, approach problems reasonably, and not hold out for the last dollar.

> It is important for both sides to maintain a positive attitude, approach problems reasonably, and not hold out for the last dollar.

Considerations for a Corporate Closing

Representations and warranties should be true in all material respects. All covenants and required agreements have been performed. All stockholders' approvals have been obtained. Litigations have been settled, non-competes have been signed, and where appropriate all resignations of officers and directors have been obtained. Also, all third party consents such as insurers, landlords, and intermediaries have been obtained.

Considerations for a Financial Closing

Unless all the conditions of the deal that affect the lending institution are met—all the liens are in place, an enforceable sales contract with all terms and conditions has been spelled out—the lending institution will not release the funds. Alternatively, the funds will be held in an escrow by the title company or by an escrow attorney until all the contractual conditions are met. Upon meeting these conditions, escrow can be closed (transfer possession) and titles and assets are passed from you to the buyer.

Inspecting Purchase and Sale Agreements

The Purchase and Sale Agreement usually has four sections:

> Unless all the conditions of the deal that affect the lending institution are met, the lending institution will not release the funds.

1. Description of transaction: such as whether it is a stock or asset sale
2. Terms of agreement: price and method of payment (cash, notes, stock); includes the agreed upon role of the remaining management team such as corporate position and remuneration
3. Representations and warranties: usually the most heavily negotiated items after the Letter of Intent is signed. Each party wants protection against misrepresentations. A warranty is a guarantee or assurance that the property or item is, or shall be, as represented.
4. Conditions and covenants: includes non-competes, identifications, and promises to do or keep from doing a specific act

It is advisable to have a pre-closing one week in advance of the closing in which all the documents have been distributed, all conditions have been satisfied or waived, and any open matters have been negotiated to conclusion. If all the conditions are not met or one is missing a vital signature or an important document, then an escrow closing takes place. Instead of the euphoric high of a successful closure, the closing becomes conditional.

The closing usually takes place at one of the attorney's offices or at the buyer's bank. Aside from principals, there are attorneys for you and the buyer, the attorney for your bank, intermediaries, and perhaps a real estate broker. There could be six to a dozen people and the ordeal can take from one to two hours. There are numerous documents to sign such as loan agreements, leases, and personal guarantees.

A stock transaction is much easier than an asset deal because buying the company is like getting onto a moving train. You buy the company lock, stock and barrel, including all assets and all liabilities. With an asset purchase you have the following items to contend with:

- Purchase price adjustments
- Utility and tax preparations
- Vacation accruals
- Deposits
- Lease and insurance transfers
- Transfer of telephone numbers
- Patent assignments
- Bills of sale and/or deeds
- Licenses to be transferred

> A pre-acquisition contingency is an unresolved situation that exists at the closing and is resolved later.

A pre-acquisition contingency is an unresolved situation that exists at the closing and is resolved later. Obviously, such contingencies should be kept to a minimum, but we live in an imperfect world and sometimes closings are not perfect, so it is better to resolve minor issues in the fashion described here rather than abort the entire closing.

Post-Sale Protection

If you are fortunate enough to sell your business for all cash, then you need not concern yourself with protecting yourself after the sale.

A Closing Checklist

The best way to ensure a smooth closing is to set up a checklist to avoid any last-minute mishaps. The following model checklist was developed for asset purchases by C.D. Peterson, author of *How to Sell Your Business*.

- ❏ Time and place of closing
- ❏ Who needs to attend
- ❏ Documents required
- ❏ Amount of funds to be disbursed in specified form
- ❏ Corporate tax and employer identification numbers
- ❏ Licenses transferred or obtained, such as liquor license
- ❏ Pro-rating calculations for taxes, wages, utility bills
- ❏ Adjustments for landlord, supplier, or utility deposits
- ❏ Transfer of banking arrangements
- ❏ Transfer of keys, alarm, and computer codes
- ❏ Transfer of telephone number
- ❏ Customer lists
- ❏ Clearance of outstanding liens or encumbrances
- ❏ Compliance with bulk sales law
- ❏ Assumption or discharge of leases or mortgages
- ❏ Definition of seller's obligations in business transition
- ❏ Provision for continuity of insurance
- ❏ Adjustments for inventory and receivables at closing
- ❏ Provisions for uncollectable receivables
- ❏ Disposition of outstanding claims
- ❏ The real estate lease or purchase agreement
- ❏ Consulting and non-compete agreements
- ❏ Allocation of the purchase price to assets and goodwill
- ❏ Provision for intermediaries fees
- ❏ Representations and warranties
- ❏ Buyer's security for seller's notes

But very few transfers are consummated today without some form of deferred payout. The deferral usually comes in the form of an interest-bearing installment note that is payable to the seller over a five- to ten-year period. Other forms of deferred payment include non-compete agreements, consulting arrangements, royalty fees, and non-qualified supplemental retirement plans. Whatever the deferral mechanism, they all create a risk to the seller that the promised and expected funds may not be collected.

The business owner nearing retirement wants security, not risk. Apprehension about receiving payments in the future may be the number one reason that owners fail to plan for transferring the business to the next generation or selling to an outsider. Conveying ownership rights to the next generation may be psychologically good for the heirs, the family, and the business itself, but the owner leaves him- or herself dependent on someone else for his future income, and most owners don't like that feeling. The apprehension is even greater when selling to a third party since outsiders usually are not trusted as much as family.

Probably the best protection you can have is to select a qualified buyer. Finding someone who can afford the business is important, but not enough. A qualified buyer should also be able to run the business. Of course, selling the business for a reasonable price with reasonable terms increases your chance of finding the right buyer.

Even with a qualified buyer, it is important to insist on security devices and triggers to legally insure that payment will not be interrupted. Often this calls for a balancing act; if the measures are too restrictive, the buyer may not be able to obtain needed working capital. In those cases, the protective devices handicap the buyer, increasing the likelihood of a default.

> It is important to insist on security devices and triggers to legally insure that payment will not be interrupted.

Security Devices and Triggers

If the buyer is a corporation that is newly formed or without significant assets, the individual shareholder or shareholders should personally guarantee any obligations. Generally, if a buyer in this situation is not willing to personally guarantee the obligation, then he or she is not ready to own a business.

To keep sufficient working capital in the corporation, it may be necessary to set compensation levels or restrict dividend payments during the deferral period.

Collateralization and Restrictions on Additional Financing

Creditors of a company sometimes have different priorities on corporate assets in the event the company fails to pay its debts. As the holder of an installment note, you are a creditor who stands in line with other creditors in the event of a default. Creditors who secure their obligations with collateral, such as corporate assets, are in a more senior position to collect money owed than a general creditor. Consequently, it is extremely important that an installment note given to you be secured by corporate assets.

If the business's pre-existing lines of credit or other banking arrangements require that you be subordinated to a junior position, then you should insist that lines of credit not be expanded without your consent and that there be no additional indebtedness that further subordinates you. A cross-default provision whereby a default on any obligation throws all obligations in default is another good security device.

If you still have personal guarantees on any corporate indebtedness, those guarantees should be removed before, or at the same time, ownership is transferred. If the guarantees cannot be removed, you should insist that the buyer indemnify you from any loss incurred by the seller by virtue of his guarantee. Of course, if the buyer is unable to pay the underlying debt the indemnification may also be worthless.

Cash Flow and Balance Sheet Requirements

Provisions that require the business to meet certain cash flow levels in order to maintain certain financial ratios serve as triggers that give you early warning that the business is not faring as well as

Never on a Friday

It is important for both sides of the transaction to be represented by the principals of their respective companies so that changes, material or otherwise, are not challenged for lack of authority. Closings should not take place on a Friday or a day before a holiday in case the closing continues into the following non-business day without the ability to transfer or invest funds.

It is important to have adequate support staff to make last-minute revisions in documents and deal with technical snags. I know of a transaction that did not close because of improper wiring instructions from one bank to another (a wire transfer of funds is payment through a series of debits and credits transmitted via computers; bank deadline for wire transfers is usually 3 P.M.). The next day the seller changed his mind about selling.

For both you and the buyer, the closing represents the apex of the transaction, usually celebrated by uncorking champagne bottles. The sparkling bubbly white wine will taste a lot better if you have confidence that their attorney has protected you properly from any possible ramifications after the business is sold.

expected. These triggering devices enable you to reacquire the business before the new owner has run it into the ground.

Financial Review by Third Party

An outside accounting firm or third party should review interim monthly and annual statements. Having a third party hold stock certificates in escrow until a debt is paid may provide some additional protection but it does not give early warning of problems.

Other Safeguards

Restrictions on asset sales, acquisitions, and expansions can help ensure that you receive the entire payout. The buyer should satisfy obligations to you before embarking on any expansion or acquisition program. Life and disability insurance on the new owner is another important safeguard. The proceeds should be collaterally assigned to you so that you can be assured of collecting any amounts due in the event the buyer dies or becomes disabled.

Conclusion

Many other security devices are available to a seller and new safeguards are devised daily. With some creativity it is possible to custom design safeguards for each situation. They may not be ultimate guarantees but they should cover almost any situation that may arise at the last minute.

> The buyer should satisfy obligations to you before embarking on any expansion or acquisition program.

For more information on this topic, visit our Web site at www.businesstown.com

Conclusion

Summary of Part VIII

- The most common mistakes people make during the sale of a company

- Sixty tips that will help you conduct a better sale of your company

- Lessons for buyers and sellers

Postmortem

In this chapter, you'll learn:

- **What to do if a partner reneges**
- **Various ways to handle a setback**

Chapter 33

It is good business practice to conduct a postmortem after a large presentation, a significant event, or an important transaction. Even though you may never sell another company, you will be considered a quasi-expert by your peers because you have undergone the experience. Someday you may be a director or advisor for another company, and you will be expected to impart your knowledge and share your experience in selling your own company.

Since the selling process takes six to twelve months or longer, there are numerous occasions and situations where something can go wrong. The real test of your character is often measured by how well you recover from these setbacks. For example, there may be unforeseen occurrences during the selling process, such as a sudden downturn in the stock market, a recent pronouncement that the economy is in a recession, or an unexpected international crisis.

Let's hope that during the selling process everything progresses like clockwork without any hiccups or mistakes along the way. In the interests of good preparation, however, let's use hypothetical examples of mistakes and some possible responses as if this were a postmortem.

> Leaks are caused by hard facts, conjecture, or suspicion and can be handled differently depending on the situation.

Mistake #1: Confidentiality Leak

There is no best way to handle a leak. Furthermore, leaks are caused by hard facts, conjecture, or suspicion and can be handled differently depending on the situation. Leaks from hard facts can occur from errant faxes or e-mails; mistakenly opened letters and Federal Express deliveries; overheard conversations or telephone calls; or confidential material in your office or wastebasket not secured or destroyed.

Leaks from conjecture can occur when a number of inconclusive facts are pieced together: all of a sudden the plant is cleaned up, there is a full-blown audit for the first time, and an investment banker visits the CEO (the owner could be refinancing the company). Leaks from suspicion can occur from frequent closed-door sessions, frequent visits by someone looking like a consultant, and, later on, numerous executive-types walking through the operation.

There are three major contingencies in which you should be particularly concerned in regards to confidentiality leaks: company officers, employees, and customers. There are four ways to handle a leak depending on the contingency, the timing, and other circumstances. They are:

1. **Ignore and deny.** There are some times in life when it is better to avoid a direct question and even consider "dodging" it in order to protect the common good of the whole entity. On the other hand, there are circumstances and certain people for which it is not recommended. For example, if a valued customer confronts you by saying that one of your competitors claims you are selling, you might respond by stating that you are approached all the time by buyers and occasionally you consider a merger if it would make the company stronger and better able to serve its customers.

2. **Admit to a few.** It is best to confide in a few of your senior officers right at the beginning of the process because you will need the CFO to provide all sorts of additional financial information, and you will need the sales manager to help you identify the complete universe of target buyers. Your quid pro quo for their assurance of confidentiality is to offer them stay bonuses or phantom stock to be exercised at the closing.

   If another officer catches on to the intended sale of the company, you have the option of bluffing your way through or also offering some sort of remuneration in order to keep him or her quiet.

3. **Half-truth.** If you are a real up-front person and have confidence that you have a loyal workforce, then you should gather all your employees together and make an announcement. Tell them you are eager to grow the company both internally and externally and in order to do so you must re-capitalize the company.

   It is better not to be any more specific, but re-capitalization is a broad term that includes an infusion of debt or inclusion of a majority or minority of equity. For obvious reasons, I would not allude to the fact that you are considering a majority investor. If questioned about the possibility of selling the company, I would again attempt to "dodge" it or avoid a

> It is best to confide in a few of your senior officers right at the beginning of the process.

direct response by saying you would consider a strategic partner such as a joint venture. Having explained the above to your audience, I would then advise them not to be surprised if people such as bankers walk through your facilities from time to time.

4. **Admit the absolute truth.** While I would not recommend this procedure unless you are at the tail end of the selling process, it is done by public companies when selling divisions or subsidiaries. Furthermore, if a public company enters into a Letter of Intent with you, they have to announce to the public their intentions of acquiring your company. They can avoid this announcement through bypassing the Letter of Intent and going straight to the Purchase and Sale Agreement.

   If you decide to tell all the employees about your intention to sell the company, then put a positive spin on it by saying that a bigger company will be better for them in the long run in terms of benefits, and that you expect most of the employees will be retained and if not, generous severance packages will be arranged.

   The downside to admitting the company is for sale is if the company is not sold for one reason or another.

> The downside to admitting the company is for sale is if the company is not sold for one reason or another.

Mistake #2: Sudden Decline in Interim Profits

One of the principal reasons deals are aborted is the unexpected drop in interim earnings. All of a sudden the buyer loses confidence in going through with the transaction, loses faith in all your projections, and simply walks away. There are basically four ways to handle this difficult situation:

1. You can take the company off the market until the earnings rebound to their normal level and then return to the market with a plausible explanation as to what caused the sudden downdraft. While this alternative might be the best choice,

there is no assurance that interested buyers will reconsider; you will lose momentum in the selling process and the chance of a confidentiality leak is increased.

2. You can try to rationalize the reason for the sudden drop in earnings by giving the buyer a compelling explanation. For example, say that the shortfall is a one-time event because of the loss of a large customer; however, in the meantime, you gained a new large customer. Furthermore, you can add that despite the drop in last quarter's earnings, the backlog is at an all-time high.

3. You can admit to the buyer that there is a general softening in the market, but you are so confident in an industry rebound that you will renegotiate the transaction with a significant portion structured as an earn-out.

4. You can bite the bullet and simply try to renegotiate the price. It all depends on how much you can afford to concede: a 10 percent or 20 percent discount from the previously expected price.

> You can try to rationalize the reason for the sudden drop in earnings by giving the buyer a compelling explanation.

Mistake #3: Selection of Wrong I-Banker

You retain an investment bank and for whatever reason the individual you are working with does not meet your expectations. Do not let this situation drag on but rather address the issue by doing one of the following:

1. Talk to the senior managing director and explain that for whatever reason—lack of chemistry, experience, industry knowledge—the particular investment banker acting as the point person should be replaced.

2. Realize that you may not have selected the best investment bank to sell your company, but decide to work through it by spending more of your time on this project, particularly as it pertains to identifying potential buyers. Instead of being reactive to the investment banker, become proactive by taking the lead and calling him or her every day and setting the agenda.

Do-It-Yourself Postmortem

When and if you sell your business, be prepared to conduct your own postmortem. Here is a handy checklist.

Communication

- Were you able to communicate with your investment banker and potential buyers while maintaining confidentiality?

- Were you able to create a constructive dialogue with your investment banker such that you were in constant contact with him or her?

- Were you able to convey to your transaction attorney the important elements of the deal so that he or she did not misrepresent you in the transaction, particularly in the critical representations and warranties section?

Preparation

- Did you, your sales manager, and your advisors assemble a comprehensive list of potential buyers?

- Did you and your investment banker write a thorough and compelling selling memorandum?

- Did your investment banker hold off going to market with the selling memorandum until he or she had received sufficient interest from the blind solicitation?

Pricing

- Did you carefully reconstruct and document your earnings and your true potential for buyers?

- Did you assemble industry pricing comparables?

- Did you articulate your projections based on the particular potential buyer's business?

Negotiating

- Did you rehearse your negotiating strategy before each session?

- Did you negotiate with more than one buyer?

- Did you receive competitive bids?

Closing

- Did your advisors structure a deal that had favorable tax ramifications for you?

- Did you and your attorney negotiate a deal in which the representation and warranties and the escrow account were not onerous?

- Did you have a predetermined sales price and terms, so that you would not accept any offers lower or less advantageous?

3. Come to grips with the untenable situation and nicely extricate yourself from the contract and move onto another investment bank. You may lose all your retainer fees and perhaps pay half of the success fee for buyers they have identified in writing. As painful as this may be, the alternative of not selling the company or selling it for substantially below your expectations is far worse.

Mistake #4: Your Partner Reneges

Often, partners do not have a buy-sell agreement in place, so they can be stuck with each other; that is, one who wants to sell the company and the other who does not. Whether you own 40 percent, 50 percent, or 60 percent, selling your share to a third party who would inherit your partner as a business associate is highly unlikely unless you substantially devalue your shares of the business just to unload your stock.

Provided your partner agrees and your company is suitable, one solution is to sell your ownership portion to a company ESOP. Let's suppose you own 50 percent of the business. You sell 1 percent of the company to your partner so he has control with a 51 percent total, and you then sell the remaining 49 percent to a trust owned by the employees. This may be a solution to Mistake #4, but the pieces of the puzzle have to go together: Your partner must cooperate and an ESOP must be feasible for your company.

> The sale of your business also requires strategy and tactics, and thus should also be subjected to a postmortem.

Conclusion

Postmortems are used extensively in the military and in sports, especially football, which is a game of strategy and tactics. The sale of your business also requires strategy and tactics, and thus should also be subjected to a postmortem.

For more information on this topic, visit our Web site at www.businesstown.com

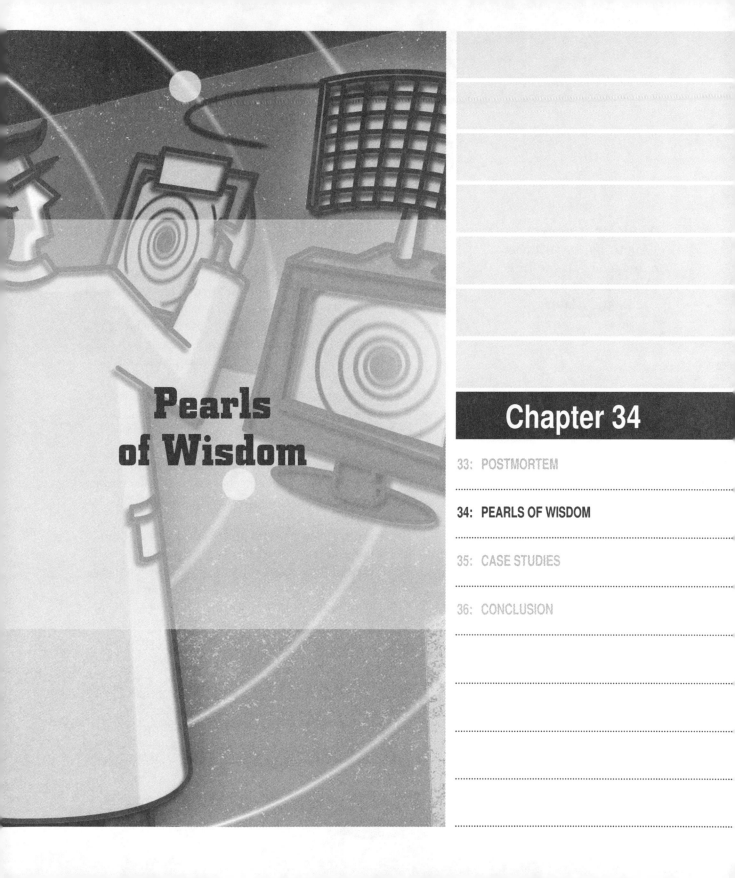

Pearls
of Wisdom

Chapter 34

C umulatively, the text of this book should be helpful to you in completing a transaction. In this chapter, I have brought together sixty nuggets of information.

> Decide up-front who is going to be the ultimate manager of the selling process so there is no ambiguity later on.

Sixty Tips for a Better Sale

1. The decision to sell is not irreversible, but it should be firm. In a family business, it is important that not just the majority owner or CEO but that all the family members who have some ownership or who work in the business are brought into the selling process. Hopefully, they all agree with the decision. For non-family private businesses, all stockholders should be made aware of the situation.

2. Decide up-front who is going to be the ultimate manager of the selling process so there is no ambiguity later on. Decide whether it should be the majority owner, the CEO, the investment banker, or some other appropriate person.

3. Set time frames on the selling process in order to have milestones: complete selling memorandum, contact buyers, sign Letter of Intent, close the deal. Deals that drag don't close.

4. Partner with professionals. Improper advice can cost you ten-fold later on. In retaining legal advice, be sure he or she is a "transaction" attorney, not a trust attorney. The intermediary should properly screen and qualify potential buyers.

5. Communicate with your banker about what you are doing. Bankers not only hate surprises, but if they are surprised they may not be cooperative when you need them most.

6. Target buyers that would perceive your company to be the most valuable.

7. Openly recognize certain "on and off" balance sheet items such as customer prepayments, work-in-process billing, contract obligations, lease obligations, and legal threats.

8. Negotiate stay agreements with top management so they will not jump ship before the business is sold. Depending on the

situation and the importance and number of people involved, a stay agreement could be equivalent to anywhere from two to six month's salary.

9. Set up a complete file in one place of all relevant information the buyer or his due diligence team will ultimately request: contracts, distribution and purchase agreements, leases, licenses, and intellectual property documents.

10. If a buyer indicates he or she will be submitting a Letter of Intent, tell the buyer right up front what items you want to be included in the document:
    - Price and terms
    - If asset purchase, what assets and liabilities are to be assumed
    - What contracts and warranties are to be assumed
    - Lease or purchase of real estate
    - Responsibility for employee contracts or severance agreements
    - Time schedule of due diligence and closing

11. While an accounting firm's review is a bare minimum for a company in the process of selling, it would be well worth the effort and expense to have audited financial statements for several years before the company is presented for sale. The validation of inventory, receivables, and notes, is most reassuring for a buyer and only audited statements will really satisfy a buyer's complete scrutiny.

12. If the owner is serious about selling the business, he or she should show real earnings without a lot of adjustments and add-backs. Buyers do not get excited about companies operating at a break-even basis with a list of add-backs. By nature, buyers become suspicious.

13. Usually, if the selling company's CEO will remain on the job for several years after the company is sold, it will add value to the purchase price. On the other hand, if the selling company has numerous family members on the payroll, it is considered a negative. Therefore, the selling company would be wise to have those family members under contract with a specific buyout clause.

> If the selling company's CEO will remain on the job for several years after the company is sold, it will add value to the purchase price.

With appropriate discretion, it is effective if the owner can show off the top management to a prospective buyer. Especially effective is a top management well versed in the company's strategy, goals, and position in the market. Conversely, what is most damaging for a seller is coming across as a one-man band.

14. Settle all litigation and environmental matters before discussing the sale of the business. Such items can be deal breakers, so solve these problems ahead of time.

15. Prepare the business for sale two to five years in advance by preparing a business plan, by providing timely, accurate, and pertinent financial reports, and implementing a culture of continuous improvement.

16. Hire a great transaction lawyer because the buyer will probably have the best available attorney.

17. Almost every buyer will structure a deal in which the equipment will be used as bank collateral by the buyer. It is in your best interest to provide liquidation value so that the buyer will not discover at the eleventh hour that his borrowing base is $500,000 less than expected, just because the bank is using a lower valuation on the machinery and equipment.

18. Be flexible with the real estate component of the business. Most buyers would rather rent the plant and invest their money in growing the business. Real estate usually does not make money for the operating company and many times it is difficult to recover its full value within a multiple of EBIT.

19. The best deal for buyers is one in which seller paper can be used as subordinated debt. Consequently, as long as former owners are owed money, they have a right to view themselves as quasi-partners, and I would suggest that the insightful buyer should consider structuring a share of future earnings improvement to the former owner's benefit—as long as he or she is in place.

   Of course, it is desirable for you the seller to have some sort of security on the notes and there should be a reasonable risk rate on the coupon. The fact that you continue for a

> Hire a great transaction lawyer because the buyer will probably have the best available attorney.

short time as a quasi-partner, albeit as a debt holder, certainly creates value in the deal.

20. The buyer is usually aware that the founder, owner, and CEO are principally responsible for running the business. If the company has no depth of management or is perceived to be a one-man band, the price for the business will be discounted. It is not wise for the CEO to brag about him- or herself or let the buyer know he or she has not taken a vacation in three years and works twelve-hour days.

21. Do not negotiate directly but through an intermediary who can mediate, act as a buffer, and carry on sidebar conversations. Don't let too much time lapse between meetings with an interested buyer. Once the process starts, keep it moving or you may lose momentum and affect your business and the morale of your employees.

22. Don't delegate important aspects of the deal to underlings, and don't let the buyer do so, either. It is important for key players to stay in touch and to develop confidence in each other, and engage an investment banker who understands your business and has knowledge of your industry.

23. Complexity is a killer in deal making. It sucks time and saps strength. The more complicated the deal structure, the less likely it is to work.

24. The buyer must work hard to put him- or herself in your shoes in order to determine the real reason why you are talking about a sale. The real reason is seldom obvious and sellers usually sugarcoat the problems.

25. Valuation is an important exercise but usually the value thus determined is not the purchase price. The business will be bought for whatever you will take for it.

26. In approaching a negotiation, the first problem is determining who is the decision-maker on the other side. Lots of jawbones have been worn out in pseudo-negotiations with the wrong person.

27. Once the decision maker has been identified, it is important to establish a rapport with him or her. Unless you and the decision-maker on the buyer's side are able to work together,

> Do not negotiate directly but through an intermediary who can mediate, act as a buffer, and carry on sidebar conversations.

the consummation of a deal is highly unlikely. At some point, a social dinner including the buyer's spouse may be an ideal way of furthering the negotiation.

28. Try to control the drafting of the Purchase and Sale Agreement and other documents. While it is customary for buyers to do the drafting, if the seller can seize that function you will have an advantage.

29. Keep the momentum going. Deals that drag don't close. Energy and zeal are critically important.

30. Buyers normally want to acquire assets and sellers want to sell stock. Tax considerations may cause these choices to be reversed. Your insistence on a stock deal need not be a deal buster because there are other ways for a buyer to protect against unknown liabilities, such as representations and warranties and escrow accounts.

31. If company owners are inflexible, the potential buyer may abandon or postpone the acquisition project.

32. From a legal viewpoint, the essential features of any acquisition agreement are representations and warranties, covenants, conditions precedent to the closing, and the indemnifications. Based on the above, you should be prepared to hold out for a full price on the business, knowing that the buyer will be seeking a near perfect business condition, or there will be adjustments post-closing. On the other hand, if there is to be an adjustment on the price, then the post-closing conditions should be more lenient.

33. As a seller, be prepared to accept lower valuation multiples for lack of management depth, reliance on a few customers, and regional versus national distribution.

34. As a seller, beware that many buyers will view the value of a Sub Chapter S company to be worth less than if the same company was a C corporation. In a Sub Chapter S company, most of the earnings flow out to the shareholders, in which case the company's book value probably will not increase proportionate to the level of earnings. The disparity in book value earnings will adversely affect the value of the business and reduce the leveragability of assets for the buyer.

> Keep the momentum going. Deals that drag don't close.

35. In the process of selling a company, there are three questions that a prospective buyer will likely ask:
    1. What differentiates your company?
    2. How would you grow the company?
    3. What would you do if the company received a sizeable windfall of cash?

36. When the underperforming company is being positioned to sell, it is important to dress it up, to put a "tuxedo on the patient," according to Ray Sozzi, turnaround specialist from Raymond Group of Chappaqua, New York. "One has to look for perceived value within the company," says Sozzi. "This is the time to form strategic alliances, product licenses, distribution arrangements, endorsements, all of which cost very little or nothing to accomplish. If arranged with a *Fortune* 500 company, it creates value. Continue displaying at trade shows for industry awareness and for possible contacts with potential buyers. Outsource all nonessential activities and concentrate on only the core attributes. Identify component values of the company that will entice the potential buyer to pay more for the business than just its intrinsic value. It may be the perceived value of the company's patents or it may be the perceived value of merging with a public company."

37. In negotiations, start with the less confrontational issues first. Win/win negotiating makes use of the principle that handling easier topics at the beginning encourages yes answers.

38. Don't negotiate with people who are not motivated to buy.

39. Businesses get stale after sitting on the shelf for a while.

40. There is just no plausible reason for sellers to enter into contracts with marginally qualified buyers and lose precious marketing time in the process.

41. With an earn-out agreement you should secure a note, albeit contingent, collateralized, and cross-defaulted with a noncompete agreement.

42. There are a number of ways to provide incentives to employees when selling the company in order to assure them that

> Don't negotiate with people who are not motivated to buy.

remaining on board will provide them with some job security after a sale. Such incentives include:

- Employment contracts coupled with a one-year non-compete agreement provide additional value to acquirers and assure these employees that remaining on board now will provide them with some job security after a sale.
- Arrangements whereby employees are awarded advance equity, phantom stock, bonuses, and other financial incentives, give them a direct interest in an acquirer's purchase price.

43. Successful sales do not just happen. If you do not have a good deal maker on your team, employ one, rent one, but get one. A deal maker can expertly help package the important wants and needs of both sides of the transaction.

44. An owner needs to sell his business from a position of strength. The extra dollars incurred in preparing an audit and obtaining strong financial documentation come back several times over in the purchase price.

45. As stated by Richard Nixon: "Always be prepared to negotiate, but never negotiate without being prepared."

46. The principal reason why numerous transactions come apart at the Letter of Intent stage is that so many new parties get involved in the deal that agreement by consensus becomes more and more difficult. The best hope for successfully completing the deal after LOI is to have experienced transaction attorneys and advisors.

47. Selling out doesn't mean saying goodbye. To fetch top dollar for a business, entrepreneurs find they must stick around and keep working after the sale.

48. According to a PricewaterhouseCoopers survey of more than 300 privately held U.S. businesses that have been sold or transferred, the most common steps companies take to improve their prospects for a sale include:
- Improving profitability by cutting costs
- Restructuring debt
- Limiting owners' compensation
- Fully funding the company pension plan

> "Always be prepared to negotiate, but never negotiate without being prepared."

- Seeking the advice of a consultant
- Improving the management team
- Upgrading computer systems

49. Once you sign a Letter of Intent, even though it is largely non-binding, your leverage drops dramatically. Therefore, before signing, make sure it covers as many critical deal points as possible and that the "no-shop" provision is as short as practical.

50. Merger and acquisition deals involve three sometime inconsistent objectives: speed, confidentiality, and value. Identify the two that are most important to you.

51. Avoid the introduction of a lawyer into discussions with principals before the elements of a business deal have been completed. As soon as the buyer introduces such an expert into discussions, you do likewise. Since such individuals must protect the technical aspects of their client's positions, more transactions have failed by the premature introduction of such specialists than have been made.

52. In order for your attorney to be a deal maker instead of a deal breaker, do not expect him or her to win every point.

53. From your perspective, if the deal fails to be consummated, a great deal of confidential information has been given to the wrong people.

54. Act with absolute clarity in all of your negotiations so that the potential deal breakers surface as early as possible and can be dealt with long before the eleventh hour.

55. Early in negotiation point out non-negotiable items, such as whether it will be an asset versus a stock sale or the fact that the buyer's note will be subordinated to the obligations to the bank.

56. For companies without audited statements, make sure you substantiate financials with tax returns.

57. The older the business, the better established it is and the stronger its customer and supplier relationships.

58. The more industries in which the company sells its product, the more protection it has from industry cycles or downturns.

> The older the business, the better established it is and the stronger its customer and supplier relationships.

59. Sellers are often selling their legacy, so the dynamics of the sale are often more important than the top bid. In the eyes of the seller, the preferred buyer is not necessarily the high bidder but rather the one who has the best intentions, the best chemistry, or the best credentials.

60. Ensure that the CEO of the acquiring company has the legal authority to buy the business. This may rest with the board of directors, a majority stockholder, or even a bank that provides the acquisition financing.

For more information on this topic, visit our Web site at www.businesstown.com

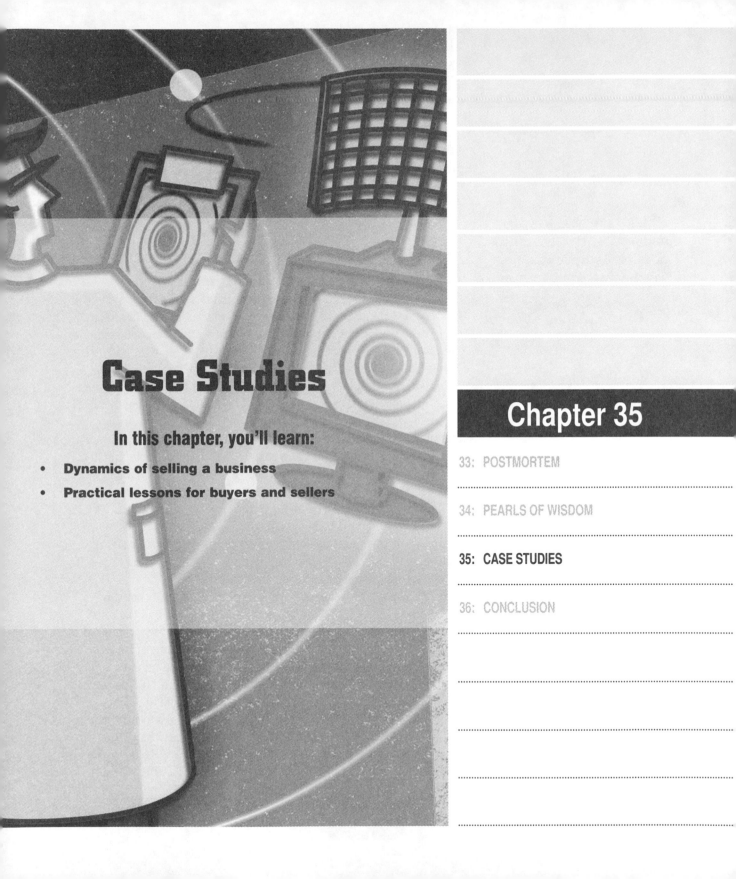

Case Studies

In this chapter, you'll learn:

- **Dynamics of selling a business**
- **Practical lessons for buyers and sellers**

Chapter 35

One of the best ways to understand the dynamics of selling a business is to read about actual cases.

One of the best ways to understand the dynamics of selling a business is to read about actual cases, some of which were successful sales and some of which were, for a variety of reasons, considered unsuccessful transactions. The following cases are such examples.

A Kayak Company

A number of years ago entrepreneur Paul Farrow of Concord, Massachusetts, was paddling a kayak on the coast of Maine. He observed that most of the kayaks sold at wilderness outlets such as L.L. Bean were either designed for ocean or white-water paddling but few were made for the family recreational market.

The idea of starting another kayak company when there were already around twenty other manufacturers was only feasible if there was a unique business concept. Farrow certainly had a different idea: to create a virtual company by forming alliances with a professional kayak designer and a large plastic roto-molder. Additionally, he would lease all his employees for the assembly work and office staffing in order to simplify the entire operation. He named the company Walden Paddlers, in recognition of the well-known pond in Concord near which Henry Thoreau once lived.

Farrow not only had a dream but also had written a business plan in which he projected Walden Paddlers to become a leader in the recreational family kayak market in five years. He would then sell the company and go on to his next vocation.

Fast-forward five years. Farrow decided to sell the company according to plan. He owned 60 percent of the stock, and the roto-molding company that formed the hulls owned the other 40 percent. Walden Paddlers had been successful selling thousands of kayaks annually. Farrow had achieved his personal goals and he was ready to move on. His option was to either sell 60 percent or 100 percent of the company but his partner, the manufacturer, did not want to buy out Farrow and become involved in selling kayaks to hundreds of dealers. After all, they were manufacturers, not merchandisers.

Farrow hired an investment bank to sell Walden Paddlers. He wanted a price of one times sales for the company, a little rich because part of the valuation was based on meeting his year-end projections. The company was nicely profitable with a branded product. With a well-documented offering memorandum, the investment banker went to market by approaching all the obvious potential buyers in the marine and sporting goods business. The kayak market was growing rapidly and had overtaken the traditional canoe market in annual volume.

In spite of a monumental effort by the investment banker to interest corporate buyers, there were two major drawbacks. First, Walden Paddlers sales were too small to make any impact if combined with a larger company. Second, Walden Paddlers was ranked sixth in the 100,000-unit kayak market. Most large corporate buyers seeking companies in the recreational industry require sellers be ranked in the top three.

Faced with no other alternative, the investment banker identified several individual buyers who had the financial resources to complete a transaction. Two different individual buyers submitted Letters of Intent that met Farrow's financial requirements; however, the first individual was so obnoxious that the 40 percent stockholder was paranoid about being partners with someone with whom they were not comfortable, and they stepped up and acquired Farrow's stock for the equivalent amount.

It is often said that it is easier to start a business than to exit a business. I am sure that Farrow must have felt that he was not going to sell his majority interest in Walden Paddlers, at least for a price that justified what he felt the company was worth. Originally, the manufacturer did not want to acquire the majority interest in Walden, but they had become dependent on producing thousands of kayak hulls annually. To protect its own interest, the manufacturer acquired the balance of the stock.

> It is often said that it is easier to start a business than to exit a business.

Lessons Learned

What have we learned from this case study? The following points are worth noting:

Even though you may have an attractive and profitable company, it may be difficult to sell at a reasonable price.

The investment banker had bona fide interest from more than fifty companies, both in the United States and abroad, but none made an offer to buy it.

By hiring an investment banker, Farrow was not distracted in running the business. It was important that Walden achieved its sales projections because Farrow's price expectations for the company were based on achieving these projections.

When the course of attack to find corporate buyers was not successful, the investment banker changed his focus and targeted individual buyers. One of the offers received by an individual originated through the Internet.

Selling a business often takes patience and perseverance. In this case, it took a year to complete the transaction.

The investment banker did not approach direct competitors for confidentiality reasons. Even still, it was remarkable that there was no leak that Walden was for sale. If news leaked, it would have had an adverse affect on dealers and employees.

This story has a happy ending for Farrow. Those starting or acquiring a business should begin with the end in mind. Some may not be as fortunate as Farrow in achieving their price expectations.

A Cracker Company

A branded cracker company was finally showing robust growth and healthy profits after many years of lackluster sales. Ownership was widely distributed among management and friends plus one major investor, a venture capitalist with a 40 percent interest. The venture capitalist took a major position when the company was desperate for capital in order to position it for further expansion.

Venture capitalists, commonly known as VCs, have been a vital source of growth capital for emerging companies. Overall, they have

> Selling a business often takes patience and perseverance.

been instrumental in contributing to the high technology boom in the United States. Venture capitalists, though, have a defined exit strategy. By contract with their investment companies, they can demand a payback from the recipients either by having a liquidity event through an initial public offering, a sale of the company, or a "put" exercised back to the company.

In the case of the cracker company, the venture capitalist demanded a liquidity event. Since neither an initial public offering nor a put was possible, the cracker company was forced to sell, most likely to the highest bidder, regardless of whether or not the president liked the buyer.

The dynamics of the situation increased as the plot thickened. The president of the cracker company had already identified another food company that was interested in being the buyer. In fact, numerous serious conversations had transpired between the two companies. But in order to verify that they would receive the top price for its 40 percent ownership, the venture capitalist felt it was necessary to retain an investment banker and go to market in order to receive competitive bids.

The VC's target price was approximately one times sales or seven times projected EBIT, a rich price for a company with sales under $10 million. The investment banker compiled a compelling offering memorandum and contacted all the major and modest-sized cracker companies plus some financial buyers. Knowing the lofty price expectations, none of the potential buyers submitted an offer, except the company the president had identified prior to the selling process. This suitor had, in fact, made a generous offer and the deal was consummated five months later.

Lessons Learned

What have we learned from this second case study? The following points are worth noting:

> **Minority investors, depending on their contractual rights, can force the sale of the company.** This is particularly true in cases where the minority partner is a recognized venture capitalist.

> The VC's target price was approximately one times sales or seven times projected EBIT.

Even if you have an interested potential buyer, hiring an investment banker gives you leverage and invariably will increase the price. The ability to produce a compelling offering memorandum and the willingness to conduct an exhaustive search will almost always pay off in the final price offered.

Small companies, those with sales below $10 million or EBITs lower than $2 million, don't often attract keen interest from major companies. That is true even if they are in the same industry.

The best time to sell is when your company is showing robust growth and healthy profits. Even though the cracker company had sales of under $10 million, its future looked bright.

Small companies don't often attract keen interest from major companies.

A Bread Company

A number of years ago, the owners of a third generation Italian bakery serving the New England wholesale market decided to sell. Of the five family members who each owned 20 percent of the stock, there were two family members who ran the day-to-day operation. Because the $4 million business was small, marginally profitable, and competing in a competitive industry, it was difficult to find any industry buyers. Nevertheless, the investment banker who had been retained by the company identified a qualified individual buyer who had previous industry experience.

The buyer offered $2 million for the business in spite of the fact that earnings were nominal. On the surface, the offer was perceived to be acceptable so a Letter of Intent was drawn up by the buyer. The proposed asset purchase did not assume the assumption of interest-bearing debt, which happened to be $1 million, so now the price of the business was really $1 million before capital gains taxes divided by five families, or $200,000 per family. While the deal still might have been acceptable, the terms were based on a five-year payout, or $40,000 per year before taxes and closing costs.

In the end, the deal died because the original purchase price was far less attractive than originally expected by the owner, and because two family members feared the loss of their jobs.

Lessons Learned

What have we learned from this case study of a failed effort? Consider the following points:

To have a family of five agree on anything is highly unlikely. Perhaps there should be voting rights and equity rights in family businesses with numerous members.

The owners, and even the investment banker, should have run the numbers of a hypothetical case to show what each family member would net after paying off interest-bearing debt and closing costs. In other words, "begin with the end" to see if it makes sense to even try to sell the business now.

Before turning down a good faith offer, analyze the alternatives. You may not like the offer but a marginal business in a competitive industry with substantial debt usually implies it is time to get out by selling. Just like in cards, "you have to know when to hold and when to fold."

A Sheet Metal Manufacturer

Companies come in all sizes, shapes, and configurations. It never ceases to amaze me how some companies in the most mundane businesses with the least amount of sophistication are enormously profitable. Yet, in spite of their profitability, they can be difficult to sell because the owner and CEO, who is the business, wants to retire immediately after completing the transaction.

A few years ago, the owner of a small sheet metal manufacturer decided to sell his company and retire. It was a nice business, certainly at first glance. Here are the highlights.

> Before turning down a good faith offer, analyze the alternatives.

On sales of $1 million, the owner was taking out $200,000.

The business was growing.

The owner was a motivated seller.

Including the real estate, which was assessed at $250,000, the owner was willing to sell the business and the plant for $500,000.

Notwithstanding the above overview, below are a few facts about the business.

The two largest customers represented 50 percent of total sales, and the top ten customers represented 90 percent of sales. The owner was in charge of manufacturing, designing, purchasing, quoting new business, and sales, and he sometimes delivered the orders on the company truck. He arrived at work every day at 6:30 A.M., and he hadn't taken a vacation as long as he could remember. The owner's wife came into the office a few hours every day. She was the principal contact for matters concerning the sale of the company. There was a full-time secretary who did three things: answer the telephone, type the invoices, and make out the weekly employee payroll. There were no computers in the office, and only after the intermediary insisted did they install a fax machine.

The factory was in a residential area: It was a nonconforming use and a new owner could not expand the facility. As well, almost all the machinery and equipment were fully depreciated. There were no Computer Numerical Control (CNC) machines. One machine was more than a hundred years old.

Lastly, neither the machinery and equipment nor the real estate was appraised. The financials were not audited.

Moving forward in the story, when two offers for the business were delivered, the owners (husband and wife) were too busy to consider them. The husband was in the middle of a rush job, and his wife's father had just been taken to the hospital. Not withstanding the inherent problems of the business and the inattention by the owners, the company was successfully sold, albeit to one of only two potential buyers who showed any interest. When the original merger

> The two largest customers represented 50 percent of total sales, and the top ten customers represented 90 percent of sales.

and acquisition intermediary became somewhat desperate in identifying a buyer, he called upon a fellow intermediary from another firm to help him. It worked.

Lessons Learned

What lessons can be gleaned from this case study?

Do not assume that just because you have a profitable business that is reasonably priced that the company is easily saleable. While this sheet metal manufacturer was sold, the ultimate closing was always in doubt.

Extreme customer concentration and enormous dependence on the retiring owner are issues that greatly concern buyers. In this case, the owner's wife was also closely involved with the company. The substantial dependence on the husband and wife made the company unattractive to many potential suitors.

When a merger and acquisition intermediary, after considerable time, is unable to provide serious buyers for a selling company, he should be willing to share his closing fee with another intermediary in order to get the deal done. This might not happen unless the seller suggests a change in tactics, so the seller should be monitoring the situation and not be shy to intervene with a suggestion.

> Do not assume that just because you have a profitable business that is reasonably priced that the company is easily saleable.

An Instrument Company

When the owners of a $10 million instrument company decided to sell a couple of years ago, the challenge was to receive a full price during the soft economy. The owner and senior managers were approaching retirement and they were aware that most buyers strongly prefer senior management to remain for several years during the transition period.

The company represented the life's work of the three owners, so it was important that they achieved maximum consideration for the company. At the same time, the company was their legacy so it was equally important that the acquirer fit the owner's culture.

The company's sales were $10 million and the EBITDA was $1.6 million. Management had targeted a price of over one time sales, which was more than a six times multiple, a full price considering the market conditions and the relatively small size. The mandate for the investment banker was to not approach any of the company's competitors.

The I-banker's game plan was to write a compelling offering memorandum of about fifty pages. Particular attention was devoted to the executive summary, which was typed with easy-to-read open space for each page. The author wrote the memorandum in such complete detail that interested buyers were expected to receive enough information without visiting the selling company's operation.

The most important sections in the memorandum were the following:

- The company's competitive advantage
- Growth strategies
- Line by line add-backs

The investment banker worked closely with management, taking a full three months to perfect the offering memorandum. During the same period, he built a database of all instrument companies that were relevant but larger in size, telephoned the prime target companies, and mailed a teaser letter to the balance. Additionally, the investment banker contacted hundreds of private equity groups and other investment bankers who represented interested buyers.

At the end of the fourth month, the investment banker had received interest and signed confidentiality agreements from approximately seventy potential acquirers. All the memorandums were mailed to the acquirers on the same day with a cover letter stating that, if interested in the acquisition opportunity, a term sheet with a price range must be received within thirty days. Management would then select the top four or five candidates and arrange a plant visit

> The author wrote the memorandum in such complete detail that interested buyers were expected to receive enough information without visiting the selling company's operation.

and management presentation for these finalists. The finalists were then asked to submit a Letter of Intent.

Once the winning offer was selected, the acquirer completed the due diligence, drafted the Purchase and Sale Agreement, and closed the transaction. Total time: eight months.

Lessons Learned

This case study prompts the following observations.

Management worked closely with the investment banker and helped enormously in the drafting of the important offering memorandum. Furthermore, management provided considerable guidance in selecting the potential acquirers.

The investment banker developed a careful and well thought-out process and time schedule so that momentum was sustained right to the end. All dealings with the seller and potential buyers were done crisply and professionally, setting the tone for the final negotiations and closing.

> All dealings with the seller and potential buyers were done crisply and professionally, setting the tone for the final negotiations and closing.

For more information on this topic, visit our Web site at www.businesstown.com

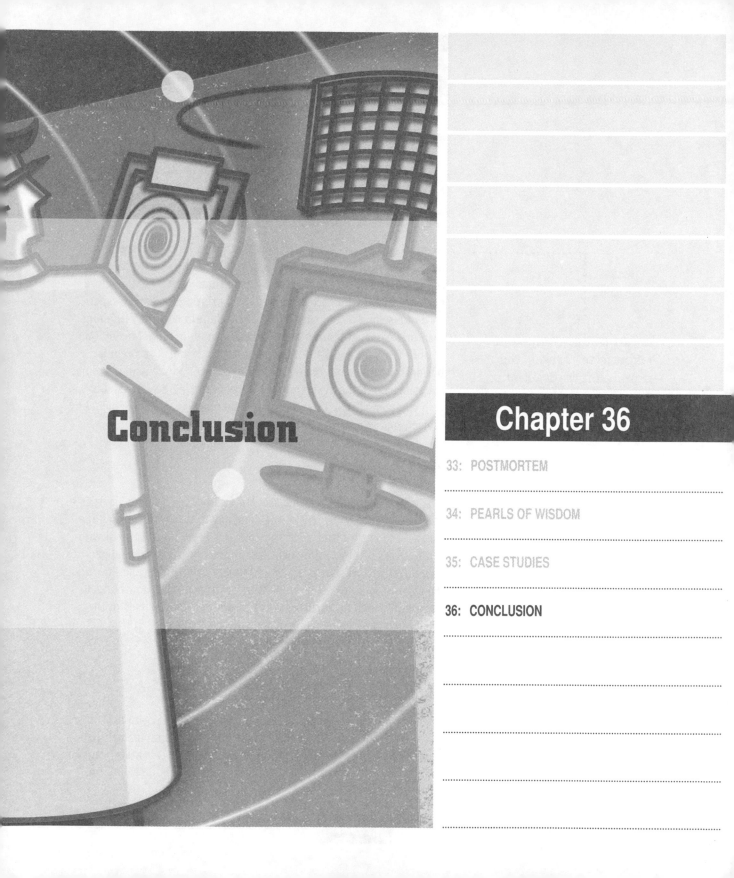

Conclusion

Chapter 36

The following are key summary points that have been addressed in this book in one form or another.

Competent Advisors

As we discussed in Chapter 10, if you utilize competent experts in merger and acquisition transactions, your chances of executing a sound business deal are increased immeasurably. Start with a close personal friend who has successfully been through a similar experience of a selling a company. Don't be hesitant to consult with more than one personal business friend for a second opinion. Moving on, be sure that you engage a transaction attorney, not just a regular business attorney. Interview various investment bankers and be objective in selecting the best one. Your accountant will be expected to help you compile the financials in a comprehensive package including projections for several years beyond.

> If you utilize competent experts in merger and acquisition transactions, your chances of executing a sound business deal are increased immeasurably.

Manage the Business

One of the important reasons for establishing a team of advisors is to allow the owner/president of the company to focus on running the business to ensure that sales and earnings progress as normal without reverses or downward surprises. Often, aborted deals happen when in the short period of sixty to ninety days during the due diligence process, sales or earnings turn south and fall below budget. Frequently, such an occurrence is a result of the principals of the selling company being so preoccupied with the proposed transaction that the company's operations slip badly.

Limits of Confidentiality

The expectation or hope that no one involved in the company will learn about the sale of the business before the closing is unrealistic. There will be people walking through the company facilities, frequent letters marked "confidential," and numerous telephone calls from non-customers or non-vendors. Explain to senior management that you are re-capitalizing the company (which is a form of ownership transfer) and then confide in several of your top managers by engaging them in stay agreements.

Realistic Pricing

A seller should have a rational understanding of his company's value in relation to the company's peer group, including allowance for its size, growth rate, and uniqueness. It is essential that the owner embrace a reasonable selling price range as determined by an expert in valuations and then work that price back to a net figure after taxes, commissions, fees, and all closing costs. If the net figure is lower than an acceptable amount, do not even start the selling process.

Selecting the Buyer

Ideally, a seller will receive numerous offers after carefully screening the buyers initially. The price, terms, and conditions will undoubtedly vary because unlike real estate, businesses are frequently sold without 100 percent cash at closing. Therefore, due diligence on the buyer can often be as important as the buyer's due diligence on you, the seller.

Sell, Sell, Sell

Selling a business is not unlike selling a multimillion dollar product, service, or contract; it has to be presented well and convincingly with supportable facts. Selling a company also requires candor because corporate buyers are generally not fools. If the company has deficiencies, address them with solutions in hand. The buyers' due diligence teams will usually uncover your deficiencies, and if not previously revealed, the buyer will often kill the deal because you will have lost credibility. Represent your company enthusiastically, but not to the point of covering up.

> A seller should have a rational understanding of his company's value in relation to the company's peer group.

Negotiating Decisions

Chapter 15 is one of the largest sections of the book, primarily because the topic of negotiating is so critical to the successful sale of a company. Perhaps no consideration in negotiating is as important as to consider one's options or alternatives. For example, the alternatives might include: not selling at all; not selling at this time; not selling to that party; not selling at price or terms proposed; selling part of the company; and selling to management.

Take Charge

Many sellers feel that once the Letter of Intent is signed, the deal is almost done. Wrong! It is estimated that half the deals at the Letter of Intent stage never close. It's like scoring the first touchdown in a football game; there usually is a lot that can happen before the game is either won or lost. If you as the seller want the deal to close, definitely use all the advisors but do not let them take over. More deals have been vaporized because the owner lost control of the process and the negotiation. Within reason, the owner or president ultimately has to take charge.

Take a Walk

Usually, a seller is more motivated to sell when the company is in play; psychologically, the decision has been made to complete the deal. You should be prepared to call off the deal if the prospective buyer is unreasonable.

In closing, I have enjoyed sharing my knowledge on this subject. Hopefully, you, the seller, will now be in a better position to sell a company with these many tools at your disposal.

Good luck!

> You should be prepared to call off the deal if the prospective buyer is unreasonable.

Appendices

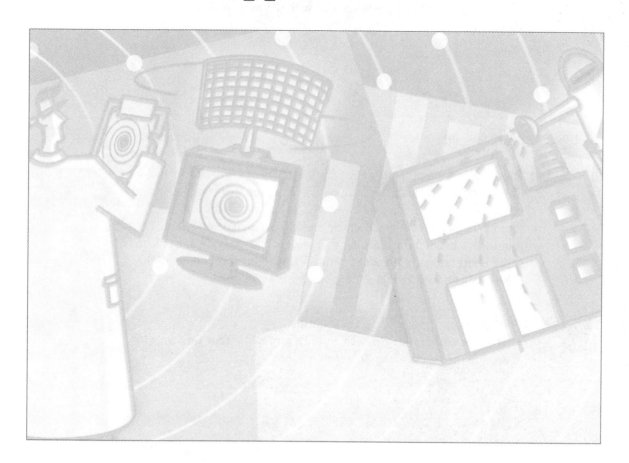

Appendix A

Proposal Letter

If a buyer expresses interest in your company after receiving the offering memorandum, you as the seller should request an indication of value in the form of a proposal letter such as the sample below.

It is not unusual to request such a letter prior to a visit to the company; otherwise you can waste a lot of time dealing with "tire kickers" or "bottom fishermen." If you do not have a thorough offering memorandum, then it is customary to let the buyer visit with the seller and see the facilities.

Dear Mr. Smith:

The following is a proposal to acquire the assets of Cornerstones Inc. (the "Company"). This letter is an outline of a proposed transaction and is not meant to be binding on any party at this time, and is subject to the signing of a mutually acceptable, definitive Purchase and Sale Agreement. In addition, this offer is subject to the requisite due diligence effort normally attendant a transaction of this magnitude. With the aforementioned kept in mind, our offer is as follows:

Transaction

A new corporation ("Newco") will be formed by Your Company Inc. to acquire the assets of the Company.

continued

Terms and Estimated Purchase Price

$4.0 million to $5.0 million cash at closing. We would be willing to purchase the Company without the real estate and enter into a lease at current market rates and terms. In this case, our offer would range between $3.5 million and $4.5 million.

Conditions of Transaction

A. We anticipate that a transaction could be consummated and closed within 90 days.
B. This proposal is subject to financing commitments satisfactory to us. We are happy to provide you references regarding our ability to finance the transaction.
C. Representations and warranties of seller with respect to accounts receivable, inventory, fixed assets, disclosure of liabilities, litigation, labor matters, corporate existence, etc., will be required.
D. We would anticipate completing our due diligence process within 30 to 45 days, whereupon we would want to move immediately to the execution of a Purchase and Sale Agreement.
E. If in the due diligence process and prior to the closing, we, in our sole judgment, wish to excuse ourselves from this transaction, we may do so without any liability, fee, penalty, or cost.
F. All fees and expenses of this transaction, including but not limited to, legal, investment banking, accounting, broker, and due diligence will be paid for by each of the respective parties.

Should you have any questions regarding this proposal, please do not hesitate to contact me at (000) 111-2222.

Very truly yours,

Appendix B

Confidentiality Agreement

It is customary for the owner or chief executive officer of the selling company to require the buyer to sign a confidentiality statement. The following format is fairly standard:

In connection with our interest in purchasing the assets and/or stock of _____ (the Company), we have requested that we be permitted to examine the financial and other business records of the Company. We understand and agree that the information contained in these records is of a confidential nature and that it will be used by us solely for the purpose of making an offer for the assets and/or stock of the Company. We will not disclose, nor will our agents, servants, employees, or attorneys disclose any of the information contained in these financial and other business records, including the identity of the company, to any other person except to such investors, bankers, attorneys, or other persons necessary to consummate the sale to the undersigned.

Signed: _____
(Print)

Date: _____

_____
(Signature)

Appendix C

Fee Agreement with Intermediaries

Intermediaries have their own fee agreements, but if they do not have a signed agreement with the buyer, you may consider signing an agreement with them. Most intermediaries, however, will want the seller to sign an exclusive agreement, likely requiring the payment of a retainer. The intermediary may define purchase price by stating that it includes any assumption of interest-bearing debt. The intermediary may also suggest a higher compensation, which is, of course, negotiable.

The form you might consider using is the following:

Your Company Inc.
Address

TO: XYZ Intermediary

1. WE ARE AGREEABLE to paying you and/or your associates a fee based on the purchase price or other consideration for any company, agency, distributorship, or other business entity or organization, which has not already been brought to our attention, whether expressed in cash or stock or any other remuneration; whether payable at closing of transaction or on extended payout; and regardless of which party pays the remuneration, which you are instrumental in helping us sell any substantial interest in such company which we agree to accept. Of the purchase price, the fee to you and/or your associates would be:
    5% of the first $1,000,000
    4% of the second $1,000,000
    3% of the third $1,000,000
    2% of the fourth $1,000,000
    1% of the value thereafter
    The payment of this fee shall be due and payable in cash at the time of closing.
2. Your Company Inc. will confirm in writing any introduction or referral.

3. If any of the principals of the parties introduced to Your Company Inc. become involved in a transaction as contemplated herein and such transaction is consummated, an intermediary's commission will be due XYZ Intermediary irrespective of who conducts the negotiations.
4. This agreement shall be binding upon the benefit of the parties hereto, their administrators, executors, heirs, successors or assigns, any corporation and other entities now existing or to be formed having substantially the same principals as either of the parties hereto.

If you accept this understanding, kindly countersign and return the enclosed copy of this agreement.
Your Company, Inc.
By:_____

Accepted:
XYZ Intermediary
Street Address
City, State, Zip
Telephone
By: _____, _____
                  (Name, Title)
Date: _____

Appendix D

Term Sheet

If you and the potential buyer have verbally agreed on the price and terms of the transaction, it would be useful to have the buyer put the basic financial arrangements on one piece of paper before proceeding directly to the Letter of Intent. Such an example would be as follows:

TERM SHEET
Carlisle Corporation

OUTLINE OF PRELIMINARY PROPOSAL OF AN ASSET PURCHASE

Gross Purchase Price	$5,000,000
Less Debt Assumed*	(500,000)
Net Purchase Price	$4,500,000

Form of Consideration:

John Smith (50% owner):

Cash $1,850,000
Four-year Consulting & Non-Compete Agreement ($100,000 annually) $400,000
John Smith's Consideration $2,250,000

Joe Doe (30% owner):

Cash $675,000
Carlisle Stock $675,000
Joe Doe's Consideration $1,350,000

Employment Contract for Joe Doe:

Three-year contract for $100,000 annually with additional annual bonuses of $50,000 provided company's annual Operating profit of $700,000 is maintained.

Mary Jones (20% owner):

Cash $450,000
Carlisle Stock $450,000
Mary Jones' Consideration. $900,000

Employment contract for Mary Jones:

Two-year contract for $70,000 annually.
Total Consideration Paid $4,500,000

*Interest Bearing Debt (usually bank debt)

Appendix E

Letter of Intent

The importance of the Letter of Intent is emphasized in Chapter 18. My experience is to have the buyer draft an agreement of two to four pages that is not legalese. The simplicity of the Letter of Intent is generally more agreeable for both parties.

The Letter of Intent has two contractual elements, specifically that (1) the seller will take the company off the market for a specified period of time; and that (2) both parties (particularly the buyer) will keep all confidential information confidential.

All Letters of Intent should specifically state that it is a non-binding agreement, and state the price, terms, and whether the purchase is an asset or stock transaction. It is customary for the buyer to draft the Letter of Intent as well as the Purchase and Sale Agreement thereafter.

This is a sample of the Letter of Intent:

Letter of Intent

Esterbrook Incorporated proposes to purchase all the assets of Mercury Security Corporation (MSC) of Boston, Massachusetts, including goodwill, customer list, and all other intangible and balance sheet assets to be substantially the same as those set forth on the balance sheet of MSC as of _____, 1995. (Exhibit A). The name Mercury Security Corporation or any derivation of the word Mercury is not transferable.

1. **Purchase Price**: The purchase price for the assets will be $_____ payable in cash at closing.
2. **Non-Competition Agreement**: The principals of MSC agree not to compete, directly or indirectly, with the business of Esterbrook as it pertains to MSC in any of the markets for a period of five years after closing. For such consideration, Esterbrook will pay $_____ per year for five years to John Smith.
3. **Lease of Building Space:** It is agreed that MSC will use best efforts to transfer the lease to Esterbrook at current or market rental as permitted by lease.
4. **General and Specific Liabilities:** Esterbrook will assume the liabilities as shown on the balance sheet dated _____, but will not assume any other liabilities past, present, or future.
5. **Audit**: Esterbrook will cause to be conducted by Esterbrook's auditors at Esterbrook's expenses as of a date to be selected.

continued

6. **Expenses:**
   a) The stockholders, Esterbrook and MSC, will each pay their own expenses, including legal expenses, up to the time of the closing.
   b) Esterbrook and MSC agree that no intermediary is involved in this transaction other than _____,

   of _____

   whose compensation is the responsibility of MSC.
7. **Letter of Intent:** This Letter of Intent is non-binding and may not be construed as an agreement on the part of any party. In the event that the parties are unable to agree on a mutually satisfactory definitive agreement providing for the transactions contemplated by this Letter of Intent, none of the parties shall be liable to any other party or to any other person. The conclusion of any definitive agreement will be subject to the following:
   a) Approval of all matters relating thereto by counsel for Esterbrook and MSC;
   b) Review of all business, legal and auditing matters related to MSC the results of which are acceptable to Esterbrook;
   c) Approval of all matters related there by the Board of Directors of Esterbrook and MSC and the voting shareholders of each company, if required;
   d) Completion of such financing as Esterbrook may require to effect a closing;
   e) Preparation and completion of all closing documents;
   f) The closing date to take place in or within 90 days of the execution of this agreement.
8. **Continuing Obligations:** Until termination of the Letter of Intent, MSC shall not, and all of MSC's officers, directors, employees, agents or representatives (including, without limitation, brokers, advisors, investments bankers, attorneys and accountants) shall not, directly or indirectly, without prior written consent of Esterbrook, entertain negotiations with or make disclosures to any corporation, partnership, person, or other entity or group in connection with any possible proposal regarding a merger, consolidation, or sale of capital stock of MSC, or of all or a substantial portion of the assets of MSC, or any similar transaction.
9. **Confidentially:** Both Esterbrook and MSC agree to maintain complete confidentiality of all confidential material each company exchanges with each other as outlined in separate Confidentiality Agreements.

All documents in respect to this transaction, will be prepared by an attorney or law firm selected by Esterbrook, subject to such documents being reviewed by and being acceptable to legal counsel for MSC.

Mercury Security Corporation

By_____

Title_____

Date_____

Esterbrook Corporation Incorporated

By_____

Title_____

Date_____

Appendix F

Purchase and Sale Agreement

The Purchase and Sale Agreement, also known as the P & S Agreement or Acquisition Agreement, has the following characteristics:

1. It is a legally binding agreement.
2. The buyer will seek to protect itself against matters such as pending litigation, undisclosed liabilities, and environmental problems.
3. The seller rarely sells for all cash, leaving the buyer leverage to hold out on further payments if the transaction is not what the seller represented it to be.
4. The seller may opt for a lower price at closing for all cash than to risk post-closing adversity.
5. The Representations and Warranties section assures both parties of their legal and financial ability to consummate the transaction.
6. The Indemnification section relates to discoveries after the closing.
7. The Conditions section lists issues that must be satisfied before the parties become obligated to close the transaction.
8. The Covenants section of the agreement defines the obligations of the parties in respect to their conduct during the period between the signing and the closing, such as the seller conducting the business in the ordinary course.

Asset Purchase Agreement

This is an agreement among RST, Inc., formerly known as Carlisle Inc., a Massachusetts corporation with a place of business at _____ ("Seller"), John Doe of _____ ("Stockholder"); and Carlisle Inc., a Massachusetts corporation with a place of business at _____ _____ ("Buyer"). For consideration paid each other, the parties covenant and agree as follows:

1. Assets to be sold.

Seller will sell, transfer, and deliver to Buyer free and clear of any liens or other encumbrances, Seller's business and the assets and properties of Seller, tangible and intangible as listed herein. Except as otherwise expressly provided in this agreement, the Assets shall include only the following assets owned by Seller at the time of closing.

A. Machinery and Equipment

All machinery and equipment, furniture, and fixtures, and the like as set forth in Exhibit B attached hereto.

B. Tools, Dies, and Fixtures

All tools, dies, and fixtures owned by the Seller.

C. Inventories

All inventory, including raw materials, work-in-process, finished goods, repair parts, and supplies; all inventory records, and all outstanding purchase and sales orders.

D. Accounts Receivable

The Buyer will use best efforts to collect all accounts receivable and pay those receivables as collected to the Seller within 90 days of closing in accordance with an agreed upon list of such receivables as found on Exhibit E as of the date of closing. Upon demand of Seller, Buyer will reassign for collection of uncollected receivables 90 days after the closing.

E. Corporate Name and Trade Names

All processes, patents, patent applications, trademarks, signs, advertisements, trade names, copyrights, drawings and logos, including the name "Carlisle, Inc."

F. Customer Lists and Contracts

All customer lists, files excepting accounting records, licenses, permits, contract rights, and sales backlog as found on Exhibit C, and telephone and fax number _____. Seller will provide buyer with access to Seller's accounting records upon reasonable notice for customary business purposes.

G. Goodwill

The goodwill of the Seller.

Excluded from the sale shall be all cash, bank accounts, utility security deposits, and prepaid expenses and the land and buildings, which shall be leased to Buyer by Seller in accordance with the Lease attached hereto as Exhibit A.

2. Liabilities

Buyer agrees to assume up to $_____ of Accounts Payable in accordance with Exhibit J. Buyer is specifically not assuming any other liabilities whatsoever of Seller, including without limitation, all taxes of whatever kind or nature, accrued or payable by Seller to any taxing authority prior to including the closing date, all of which the Seller agrees to pay.

3. Closing Date

The closing date will take place no later than 1:00 P.M. _____, at the offices of Seller or at such other time and place as the Buyer and Seller may hereafter agree upon. Adjustments and prorations shall be made effective the end of business _____.

4. Purchase Price

A. Price

The purchase price to be paid for the Assets is Five Hundred Thousand ($500,000) Dollars, which sum shall be paid as follows:

Certified or bank check at closing	$200,000
Buyer's promissory note per **par 6**	200,000
Accounts Payable per **par 2**	<u>100,000</u>
TOTAL	$500,000

B. Allocation

The purchase price for the Assets shall be allocated as follows:

Inventories	$100,000
Machinery and Equipment	200,000
Goodwill	50,000
Accounts Receivable per **par 1(D)**	<u>150,000</u>
TOTAL	$500,000

5. Personnel Agreements

A. Non-competition Agreement

Stockholders will enter into a non-competition agreement with the Buyer, in the form attached as Exhibit D.

6. Buyer's Note at Closing Date

In part payment of the purchase price Buyer shall make and deliver to Seller at the Closing Date a negotiable promissory note in the amount of Two Hundred Thousand ($200,000) Dollars, bearing annual interest at eight (8.0%) percent, for sixty (60) months and requiring equal monthly installments of interest and principal beginning thirty (30) days after the closing contemplated herein. Such note shall be secured by a first security interest in Machinery and Equipment acquired and shall be personally guaranteed by Buyer in the form attached as Exhibit H. The form of said note and security agreement, and UCC financing statements are attached hereto as Exhibits F and G.

7. Seller's Use of Name

It is understood and agreed that Seller will not use the name "Carlisle Inc." to pursue any business interests nor will Seller sell, lease, or convey usage of its name to any entity or individual.

8. Seller's Representations and Warranties

A. Corporate Authority

Seller is a corporation duly organized, validly existing, and in good standing under the laws of the State of Massachusetts and has the right and authority to enter into this agreement and carry out the terms and conditions hereof applicable to it and the execution, delivery a performance of this agreement will not violate or conflict with the provisions of the Articles of Organization or Bylaws of the Seller.

B. Agreement Default

Seller as a result of the Closing will not be in default under any agreement or other commitment to which it is a party of by which it is bound.

C. Financial Statements to Buyer

Seller has delivered to Buyer the Financial Statements through _____. Said Financial Statements are true and complete. Seller shall provide interim financial statements for the period ending _____ as soon as practicable after closing.

D. No Material Change

Since _____, there has not been, to Seller's knowledge, any material change in financial condition, assets and liabilities, or business, other than changes in the ordinary course of business.

E. Tax Returns, Audits, and Tax Payments

Within the times and in a manner prescribed by law, Seller has, and shall have through the closing date, filed all federal, state, foreign and/or local tax returns required by law and has paid all taxes (including without limitation, income, franchise, sales, use, meals, transfer, payroll, and ad valorem taxes), assessments and penalties due and payable with respect to the Business of the Seller. The Seller is not delinquent in the payment of any other governmental tax, assessment, or other charge.

F. Marketable Title

Upon the transfer of the assets at closing, Buyer shall acquire title to such property free of all liens and encumbrances and free of all claims of third parties.

G. Good Condition

To Seller's knowledge and except to the extent disclosed to Buyer or known to Buyer, all Seller's equipment, and similar tangible personal property are in good condition and repair, consistent with the age and remaining useful life thereof, and their use is in conformity with all applicable laws, ordinances and regulations. The Assets are being sold in "as is" condition and any and all warranties from manufacturers or dealers in existence at date of sale are included in the sales price. Buyers acknowledge that they have been provided a full and complete opportunity to inspect the Seller's machinery and equipment and similar tangible personal property, are satisfied with the results of all such inspections and that the Seller and Stockholders have made no warranties or representations with respect thereto.

H. Customer Commitments

Attached as Exhibit C, is a list of all presently existing customer commitments to which Seller is a party or by which it is bound. To Seller's knowledge, all such commitments are valid and enforceable in accordance with their terms.

I. Litigation

To the Seller's knowledge, there is no pending or threatened action, arbitration, suit, notice, order, real estate tax contest or legal, administrative or other proceeding before any court or governmental agency, authority or body, against, or affecting Seller, either directly or indirectly, with respect to the Assets pending or threatened which will survive the closing. There is no order, writ, injunction, or decree of any federal, state or local, or foreign court, department, agency, or instrumentality, which with directly or indirectly relates to the Assets. Seller has complied and is complying in all material respects with all law, ordinances, and government rules and regulations applicable to it and its properties, assets, and business.

J. No Untrue Representation

To Seller's knowledge after inquiry, no representation or warranty by Seller in this Agreement, or certificate furnished or to be furnished to Buyer pursuant hereto or in connection with the transaction contemplated hereby, contains or will contain any untrue statement of a material fact.

K. Continuation of Truth

The representations, warranties, and covenants set forth in this agreement will continue to be true in all respects as of the closing date and shall survive the Closing.

L. Licenses Obtained

All government licenses, permits, and authorizations necessary for the ownership of Seller's properties and the conduct of its business as currently conducted are listed on Exhibit I, and Seller has all such licenses, permits, and authorizations.

M. Liabilities

At the closing there will be no liabilities, commitments, or contingencies of Seller whether accrued, secured, or determinable that encumber the assets other than those expressly assumed by Buyer under the terms of this Agreement.

N. Continued Business

Seller is not aware of any reason why its customers, subcontractors, or suppliers will not continue to do business with the Buyer after the closing in the same manner in which they have done business with the Seller prior to the Closing. This does not assure nor imply that the existing customer base will be retained after the closing.

O. Stock Ownership

The Stockholder named herein owns One Hundred (100%) Percent of the outstanding stock of the Seller.

P. Absence of Certain Changes

Since the date of this Agreement and as of the Closing, there shall not have been any:

(a) Transactions by Seller affecting the Assets except in the ordinary course of business.

(b) Material adverse physical change in the Assets.

Q. Profits Pending Closing

Profits from the date of this Agreement up to and including _____, shall be the property of the Seller.

9. Buyer's Representations and Warranties

A. Corporate Authority

Buyer is a corporation duly organized, validly existing, and in good standing under the laws of the State of Massachusetts and has the right and authority to enter into this agreement and carry out the terms and conditions hereof applicable to it and the execution, delivery, and performance of this agreement will not violate or conflict with the provisions of the Articles of Organization of Bylaws of the Corporation.

B. Agreement Conflict

This Agreement does not conflict with the Buyer's bylaws, corporate charter, or any other internal requirement of the Buyer.

_____,

individually and collectively, are subject to no agreement or other constraint which conflicts with their carrying out the terms of this agreement.

C. No Government Approvals

The transaction contemplated by this agreement does not require any state, local, or federal government approval.

D. Inspection of Assets

Buyer acknowledges that he had an opportunity to inspect and actually did inspect all of the assets sold under this agreement and is satisfied with the results of such inspection.

E. No Untrue Representation

Buyer's warranties and representations contained in this agreement are true as of the date of the agreement and shall continue to be true in all material respects up to and including the date of closing. This provision shall survive the closing.

10. Indemnification

The Seller hereby agrees to indemnify, defend, and hold the Buyer harmless of and from any and all debts, liabilities, costs, and expenses of any and every nature whatsoever resulting from the breach or violation of any obligations, representations, covenants, or warranties of the Seller contained in this agreement and from any liability or obligation of Seller arising out of Seller's ownership or sale of the Assets or Seller's operation of the business except for those accounts payable assumed by Buyer pursuant to paragraph two of this agreement and as specifically identified in Exhibit J. Except as specifically set forth in said Exhibit J, the Buyer shall not and does not assume any other of the liabilities or obligations of the Seller.

The Seller, at its own expense, shall have the opportunity to be represented by counsel of its choosing, and control, at its expense, the defense of any claim, which may be brought against the Buyer in respect of which the Buyer may be entitled to indemnifications. The Buyer shall promptly give written notice to the Seller of any such claim. In the event that the Buyer does not receive written notice from the Seller within fifteen (15) days of such written notice, the Seller shall be deemed to have waived the right to be represented by counsel.

In the event the Seller breaches or violates any provision contained herein, the Buyer shall have a right to set off against any payments due Seller under this agreement, under a Note of even date in the amount of $200,000, or against any payment due _____ under a non-competition agreement between the Buyer and _____, an amount equal to the amount of any claim successfully brought against the Buyer as a result of said breach or violation if Seller elects to defend the claim or the amount of damages suffered by the Buyer if the Seller elects not to defend. Prior to such set off by Buyer, Buyer shall give fifteen (15) days written notice to Seller setting forth therein the reason(s) for said set off. Buyer shall exercise such right of set off by applying such damages against payments due Seller as they fall due pursuant to the promissory note referred to in paragraph six of this agreement and against payments due under the non-competition agreement referred to in paragraph five of this agreement.

Any notice sent to Seller should be mailed, postage prepaid, registered or certified mail, return receipt requested, or delivered by overnight carrier and addressed to the parties at their respective addresses as set forth in the Agreement, with a copy in case of notice to the Seller sent as follows:

To Seller's attorney: Name
                         Address
                         City

11. Condition of the Closing

A. Conditions of Sellers' Obligations

(a) Payment

Buyer's delivery to Seller at the Closing Date of payment in the amount of Two Hundred Thousand ($200,000) Dollars payable by Certified or Bank check without intervening endorsements.

(b) Buyer's note

Buyer's delivery to Seller at the Closing Date as defined herein of a promissory note in the amount of Two Hundred Thousand ($200,000) Dollars.

(c) Security agreement and financing statements

Buyer's deliver to Seller of a security agreement and UCC financing statements as set forth in paragraph 6 and Exhibit F & G.

(d) Buyer's guarantee

Buyer's delivery to Seller of a Guarantee from _____ is included in Exhibit H.

(e) Detail accounts receivable listing

Buyer's and Seller's written agreement of the detail accounts receivable as of date of closing as set forth in Exhibit E is included herein.

(f) True and complete

The representations and warranties of Buyer shall be true and complete in all respects, and Buyer shall have performed and complied with all agreements and conditions required by this agreement.

B. Conditions of Buyer's obligations

Buyer's obligations at the closing shall be conditional upon the following:

(a) True and complete

The representations and warranties of Seller shall be true and complete in all respects, and Seller shall have performed and complied with all agreements and conditions required by this Agreement.

(b) Bill of Sale

Seller's delivery to Buyer of a bill of sale and all other instruments necessary to convey to Buyer good and marketable title to the Assets

(c) Non-competition

The signing of a Stockholders' non-competition agreement in the form of Exhibit D

(d) Lease

The signing of a Lease acceptable to Buyer and Seller in the form of Exhibit A.

(e) At the closing Seller will deliver to Buyer:

(1) List commitments and customers

An updated list of contracts relative to Exhibit C, which list shall not vary significantly from its present form except in the ordinary course of business.

(2) Instruments

Appropriate instruments, including Bills of Sale, and assignments transferring and conveying to Buyer, good and marketable title to the Assets.

(3) Vote of stockholders

A certificate of Vote, duly executed by the Clerk of Seller, as to the due adoption by the Stockholders and the Board of Directors of Seller of a resolution authorizing the transactions contemplated of Seller by this agreement.

12. Seller's Conduct of Its Business Prior to Closing

Seller agrees that it will make no changes in the Assets and will incur no liabilities or obligations between the date of this agreement and the closing date except changes, liabilities, and obligations arising or occurring in the ordinary course of business. Seller agrees that it will use its best efforts prior to the closing to maintain and preserve its business and to retain good working relationships with its suppliers, distributors, customers, and others with whom it deals.

13. Bulk Sales Act

The Seller has provided Exhibit J setting forth all creditors, claimants, or others that may have claims or liens upon any of the assets to be transferred herein. Notification will be given to creditors of record. The parties agree to waive compliance with all the provisions of Article 6 of the Uniform Commercial Code dealing with bulk transfers.

14. Broker's or Finder's Fee

Buyer and Seller agree that no broker or finder is involved in the sale of assets other than _____ of _____ and _____ of _____. A broker's commission of $____ to _____ shall be paid at the closing by Seller if the sale

hereunder contemplated is consummated and the purchase price is received by Seller.

15. General

A. Written Notice

All notices and other communications hereunder shall be in writing, and given by delivery or mail (by overnight carrier providing a receipt of facsimile followed by first-class mail, postage prepaid) to a party at its address set forth at the beginning of the Agreement or at such changed address as a party may have furnished to the other party in writing at least ten (10) days prior to the effective date thereof.

B. Severability

If any provision in this Agreement shall be deemed unenforceable or void as a matter of law such circumstance shall have no effect on the surviving portions of the Agreement each of which shall have full force and effect. Buyer and Seller shall be required to use their best efforts to agree upon and replace any provision that has been declared legally void or unenforceable.

16. Miscellaneous

A. Binding effect

This agreement is binding not only upon Seller, Stockholders', Buyer, _____ but also upon Seller's, Stockholders', and Buyer's respective successors, heirs, executors, administrators, and assigns.

B. Governing law

The laws of Massachusetts as of the date appearing below shall govern the interpretation and enforcement of this agreement.

C. Modifications

No modification of this agreement shall be binding unless in writing and executed by all parties with the same formality as this Agreement.

D. Entire agreement

This agreement represents the entire and integrated agreement of the parties and supersedes all prior oral and written negotiations and agreements.

E. Liquidated damages

Upon failure of the Buyer to fulfill Buyer's obligations under this Agreement the deposit may be retained by the Seller as liquidated damages for any such default. Such deposit will be held by counsel for the Seller.

Effective as of _____

Witness RST, Inc. FKA a Carlisle Inc.

_____, President

_____

Witness _____, Stockholder of RST _____

Witness _____,

Buyer _____

Witness _____, Buyer

_____, President

Exhibits contained herein:
  A. Lease
  B. Machinery & Equipment
  C. Customer Lists & Contracts
  D. Non-competition
  E. Listing of Accounts Receivable
  F. Buyer Note & Security Agreement
  G. UCC Financing Statements
  H. Guarantee
  I. Licenses & Permits
  J. List of Creditors

Appendix H

Glossary

add-backs: Extraordinary one-time expenses, such as the cost of moving the plant or owner's perquisites such as travel and entertaining that are added back to earnings to give a more realistic view of the company's earning power. Add-backs are subject to acute scrutiny by the buyer because business travel and business entertaining are usually a regular cost of doing business.

allocation of purchase price: In an asset sale, the purchase price must be allocated to certain assets; the balance is goodwill.

angels: An individual high-risk investor who likes to make investments in promising acquisitions. Angels often have valuable business experience and can be helpful as a member of the board of directors.

asset based lenders: Commercial lenders who are willing to take on more risk than commercial banks lending against accounts receivable and inventory and being subordinate to commercial banks.

asset sale: Purchase of certain assets and/or liabilities leaving the seller the remainder as well as the corporate entity.

auction: When the seller or its intermediary orchestrates the selling process by encouraging buyers to bid and re-bid until the highest and best offer is received.

audit: Examination of the financial records and accounting books in order to verify their accuracy.

basket: A dollar amount set forth by the seller in the indemnification provision for any losses suffered by the buyer.

book value: Also known as net worth, the figure derived by deducting all the liabilities from all the assets.

bottom fishing: When a buyer will only pay a very low price for a business.

bridge loans: A temporary loan to cover the financing shortfall of the acquisition until permanent funding is available.

C corporation: One of two types of corporation (the other is the S corporation). Taxes are paid once at the corporate level and again when the earnings are distributed to the shareholders. It allows various classes of stock: corporate shareholders as well as alien shareholders.

CAP-X: The acronym for Capital Expenditures that are necessary within the next year.

capitalization: Companies have ownership capital that includes stock and paid-in surplus plus borrowed capital that includes bank debt and bonds. The combined forms of capital, ownership, and borrowed funds is a company's capitalization.

capitalization rate: The conversion of income into value as part of the valuation process by the application of a capitalization factor (any multiplier or divisor used to convert income to value).

cash cow: A business that has a steady cash flow in which earnings have remained nearly the same for the past five years, but which has shown little growth.

cash flow: The amount of money left over after the cost of goods sold, general, selling, and administrative expenses but before interest, depreciation, taxes, and amortization.

collateral: Property pledged by a borrower to protect the interests of the lender. Bank loans are often collateralized or secured by the company's accounts receivable, inventory, or equipment.

confidentiality: The entrustment of proprietary information from one party to another for their exclusive use so as not to impart the obtained knowledge to others.

contingent: Dependent on or conditioned by something else. The price established for the business varies in relation to some future event.

contingent payments: Future financial obligations are dependent on contractual events that take place.

covenants: A binding agreement between buyer and seller that restricts each party from taking certain actions particularly during the Letter of Intent period and closing.

deal flow: A stream of potential business acquisitions moving across your desk in a quantity that allows you to select the few that meet your criteria.

depreciation: The amount that tangible assets decrease over the normal life cycle as designated by the parameters of the IRS.

discounted cash flow: A valuation technique that assigns a value in today's dollars to the cash flows that are expected to occur in the future.

due diligence: The investigation of the other party's business practices in an attempt to uncover previously unknown information.

earn-outs: A part of the purchase price is dependent on a future performance variable such as profits or sales.

EBIT: The acronym for Earnings Before Interest and Taxes.

EBITDA: The acronym for Earnings Before Interest, Taxes, Depreciation, and Amortization, also known as cash flow.

EBITDA-CAP-X: EBITDA minus capital expenditures. A more realistic assessment of earnings than EBITDA.

encumbrances: A lien against certain property encumbers the company's assets that could ultimately hold up or prevent the closing.

enterprise value: Market value of equity, plus interest-bearing debt

entrepreneur: Taken from the German word "unternehmer," referring to a person who owns and runs his own business.

escrow: Money delivered to a third party that is held in deposit until the grantee fulfills certain conditions.

fair market value: What assets would most likely sell for in the open market; this is often determined by a professional appraiser.

finder's fee: A commission for merely identifying and introducing a buyer to the seller, but does not include other services such as valuing, structuring, and negotiating.

floor price: The lowest preconceived price that a seller will accept.

free cash flow: Operating income plus depreciation and amortization (non-cash charges) but subtracts capital expenditures and dividends (that use cash). Free cash flow, in essence, is the amount of cash left over after a year of business as usual.

GAAP: The acronym for Generally Accepted Accounting Principles, the American Institute of CPA's standards of accounting.

goodwill: The difference between the purchase price and the value shown on the corporate books at the time of closing.

holdback provision: As written into the Purchase and Sale Agreement, if a buyer winds up having to pay a debt the seller did not disclose, the amount paid from that which was held back at closing in an escrow account.

I-banker: The abbreviation of investment banker, also known as a merger and acquisition intermediary, and for smaller transactions known as a business broker.

indemnification: Exemption for the buyer from incurred penalties or liabilities after the closing from incomplete representations and warranties of the seller.

intangibles: An asset that is not physical such as licenses, franchises, trademarks, customer lists, unpatented technology, etc.

intermediary: An agent who is a merger and acquisition consultant to the buyer or seller and who is expected to facilitate the transaction.

investment banker: An intermediary who often provides additional services such as bridge loans or underwritings.

Lehman formula: The industry standard commission rate, which is a sliding scale—5-4-3-2-1— percent on each successive million dollar purchase price.

Letter of Intent: A preliminary offer to purchase a business, usually non-binding, which if accepted by the seller leads to the drafting of a Purchase and Sale Agreement.

leverage buyout: A transaction in which a company's capital stock or its assets are purchased with borrowed money causing the company's new capital structure to be primarily debt.

lien: A charge or hold on assets usually by a creditor until the indebtedness is satisfied.

M & A: An acronym for mergers and acquisitions.

market cap: Abbreviations for market capitalization that applies to the company's worth in the stock market by multiplying the total number of shares outstanding by the current price of the stock.

mezzanine capital: Subordinated to senior debt, it is like a second mortgage, with higher interest rates and often with common stock purchase warrants.

middle market: Companies with sales between $2 million to $100 million.

multiples: An abbreviated terminology for capitalization rates.

net present value: Money paid out in the future discounted at the opportunity cost of capital for a similar risk over the specified period of time.

net worth: See *book value.*

networking: Maintaining contacts with a variety of people connected with buying and selling businesses.

niche: Uniqueness in the marketplace in which the company has a product or service, which has a competitive advantage because there are few competitors.

off balance sheet items: Unrecorded obligations such as repurchase agreements, pending lawsuits, and unfunded pensions.

OEM: Original Equipment Manufacturers produce products that are sold to other companies that in turn make products for consumer purchases.

perquisites (perks): A profit incidental to a regular salary such as the use of a company automobile, country club membership, or entertainment allowance.

recast: The financials are reconstructed to reflect what the income statement would be without excessive salaries and perks.

representations and warranties: Indemnifications and covenants written into the Purchase and Sale Agreement that provide factual information that is important to protect the buyer from future occurrences.

ROI (ROE): Return on Investment and Return on Equity must be greater than the cost of capital in order to create shareholder value.

S corporation: An unaffiliated corporation owned by thirty-five or fewer individuals in which the profits flow to the individual without a corporate level tax imposed.

seller financing: The seller extends his or her own notes to the buyer in lieu of all cash at closing or other debt financing, such as bank loans.

senior debt: The most secure bank debt and the first in line with primary collateral. Often senior debt is a short-term revolving loan that is paid down completely within a year.

SIC: Abbreviation for Standard Industry Code, which is numerical categorization for specific industries. Most business directories are organized by geography and SIC.

skimming: The business owner is personally taking money off the top of the company revenue stream.

stepped-up basis: In most asset transactions, the basis of the assets of the target corporation is stepped up in value to the purchaser's cost.

stock sale: Purchase of the company's shares of stock incorporates the assumption of all the assets and all the debt both tangible and intangible.

subordinated debt: Refers to non-bank debt, which is less secure than bank (or senior) debt. To attract lenders, borrowers often give subordinated lenders rights to convert their debt to equity.

tender offer: A publicized bid to buy shares of a publicly owned company at a price substantially above the current market price.

tight money: When banks hold back on making loans, it restricts acquisitions.

tombstones: The announcement by an intermediary of a completed transaction with the name of the buyer and seller identifying which party the intermediary represented. The number of tombstones is an indication of the intermediary's success.

walk-away price: The highest preconceived price that a buyer will offer.

working capital: The balance between current assets from current liabilities represents the funds available to grow the business in the short term.

Appendix I

References

Baguley, Philip. *Negotiating.* New York: McGraw-Hill, 2000.

Bergeth, Robert L. *12 Secrets to Cashing Out: How to Sell Your Company for the Most Profit.* Upper Saddle River, NJ: Prentice Hall, 1994.

Buying and Selling a Business. PriceWaterhouse.

Catlin, Katherine and Jana Matthews. *Leading at the Speed of Growth: Journey from Entrepreneur to CEO.* New York: Hungry Minds, Inc., 2001.

Gaughan, Patrick. *Mergers, Acquisitions, and Corporate Restructurings.* New York: Wiley, 2001.

Kuhn, Robert Lawrence. *Dealmaker: All the Negotiating Skills and Secrets You Need.* New York: Wiley, 1988.

Myss, Joseph. *Divestiture Strategies for Owners of Private Businesses.*

Peterson, C.D. *How to Sell Your Business.* New York: McGraw-Hill, 1990.

Reed, Stanley Foster. *The Art of M&A—A Merger Acquisition Buyout Guide.* New York: McGraw-Hill, 1999.

Reich, Carl. *The Life of Nelson Rockefeller: Worlds to Conquer.* New York: Doubleday, 1996.

Index

Also available from Adams Media

STREETWISE® BOOKS

24 Hour MBA
$19.95
ISBN 1-58062-256-9

**Achieving Wealth
Through Franchising**
$19.95
ISBN 1-58062-503-7

**Business Letters
w/CD-ROM**
$24.95
ISBN 1-58062-133-3

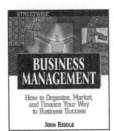

Business Management
$19.95
ISBN 1-58062-540-1

Complete Business Plan
$19.95
ISBN 1-55850-845-7

**Customer-Focused
Selling**
$19.95
ISBN 1-55850-725-6

Direct Marketing
$19.95
ISBN 1-58062-439-1

**Do-It-Yourself
Advertising**
$19.95
ISBN 1-55850-727-2

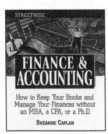

Finance & Accounting
$17.95
ISBN 1-58062-196-1

Get Your Business Online
$19.95
ISBN 1-58062-368-9

Hiring Top Performers
$17.95
ISBN 1-58062-684-5

**Human Resources
Management**
$19.95
ISBN 1-58062-699-8

Available wherever books are sold.

For more information, or to order, call 800-872-5627
or visit adamsmedia.com

Adams Media Corporation, 57 Littlefield Street, Avon, MA 02322

Adams Streetwise® books for growing your business

Independent Consulting
$19.95
ISBN 1-55850-728-0

Internet Business Plan
$19.95
ISBN 1-58062-502-9

Low-Cost Web Site Promotion
$19.95
ISBN 1-58062-501-0

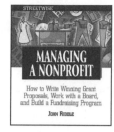

Managing a Nonprofit
$19.95
ISBN 1-58062-698-X

Managing People
$19.95
ISBN 1-55850-726-4

Marketing Plan
$17.95
ISBN 1-58062-268-2

Maximize Web Site Traffic
$19.95
ISBN 1-55850-369-7

Motivating & Rewarding Employees
$17.95
ISBN 1-58062-130-9

Relationship Marketing on the Internet
$17.95
ISBN 1-58062-255-0

Sales Letters w/CD-ROM
$24.95
ISBN 1-58062-440-5

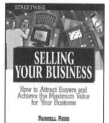

Selling Your Business
$19.95
ISBN 1-58062-602-5

Small Business Start-Up
$17.95
ISBN 1-55850-581-4

Small Business Success Kit w/CD-ROM
$24.95
ISBN 1-58062-367-0

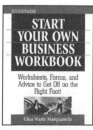

Start Your Own Business Workbook
$9.95
ISBN 1-58062-506-1

Take Your Business Online Workbook
$9.95
ISBN 1-58062-507-X

Time Management
$17.95
ISBN 1-58062-131-7

FIND MORE ON THIS TOPIC BY VISITING
BusinessTown.com
The Web's big site for growing businesses!

☑ **Separate channels on all aspects of starting and running a business**

☑ **Lots of info on how to do business online**

☑ **1,000+ pages of savvy business advice**

☑ **Complete web guide to thousands of useful business sites**

☑ **Free e-mail newsletter**

☑ **Question and answer forums, and more!**